LUCIFER RESURREXIT

A Gnostic Doctrine of the Christo-Luciferian Current

LUCIFER RESURREXIT

A Gnostic Doctrine of the Christo-Luciferian Current

Tau Phosphoros

Fox Lake, IL

Lucifer Resurrexit: A Gnostic Doctrine of the Christo-Luciferian Current

By Tau Phosphoros

Published April 2026.

ISBN: 978-1-946814-30-2

Triad Press, LLC
123 S. US 12 #33
Fox Lake, IL 60020

TABLE OF CONTENTS

PREFACE

Every book has a beginning that precedes its first page by many years. This one begins, for me, in the early days of my esoteric studies – long before the Apostolic Church of the Pleroma existed, long before I held episcopal orders, long before the doctrinal framework laid out in these pages had taken anything like its present shape. It begins with a single passage of scripture that struck me, the first time I encountered it in its Greek original, with the force of something recognized rather than learned. The passage is 2 Peter 1:19 – *"until the day dawns and the Morning Star rises in your hearts"* – and what I recognized in it, with an immediacy that bypassed all the usual processes of intellectual assessment, was the authentic scriptural locus of the Luciferian current.

I did not have that language for it at the time. What I had was the impression – insistent, luminous, and impossible to dismiss – that this passage was describing something real and something important: that the Morning Star spoken of here was not a metaphor for vague spiritual progress but a precise description of a genuine inner event, that its identification with Christ was not incidental but essential, and that the entire demonological tradition that had attached the name Lucifer to the adversary of God was, at its root, a misreading – a conflation of texts that, read carefully and in their own terms, simply did not support the identification that centuries of interpretive tradition had imposed upon them.

Years of study and practice followed that first impression – years in which the impression deepened into understanding, the understanding developed into doctrine, and the doctrine found its way, gradually and through many stages, into the form it takes in these pages. I was ordained into the Minor Orders of a Gnostic church. I studied Greek, and translated New Testament texts, and read widely in the Nag Hammadi literature and the broader Gnostic tradition. I was consecrated bishop and founded the Apostolic Church of the Pleroma. I wrote essays – several of which are referenced in this work, and which represent earlier stages in the development of the doctrine presented here more fully and more systematically. And throughout all of this, the impression that first struck me in that 2 Peter passage remained at the center of my theological and initiatic development: the conviction that the Morning Star is Christ, that its arising within the human heart is the goal of the initiatic life, and that the reclamation of the name Lucifer for the right-hand path of Christian Gnostic illumination was a work that needed to be done.

It was also during those years of study and formation that I adopted the ecclesiastical name by which I publish and under which this work appears: Tau Phosphoros. I want to address this directly, because the potential for misunderstanding is real and I have no wish to leave it unaddressed.

The name Phosphoros was adopted by me first within the Martinist tradition, and later confirmed as my episcopal nomen upon the founding of the Apostolic Church of the Pleroma. Its adoption was not – I want to be unambiguous about this – a claim to the state it names. To call oneself Phosphoros, the Light-Bearer, is not to assert that one has attained the fullness of the Christo-Luciferian illumination that this work describes.

It is, rather, to declare one's aspiration toward that illumination – to place oneself, by the deliberate act of naming, under the sign of the current one is committed to walking toward. The name is a dedication, not a credential. It is the practitioner naming oneself after the light sought, not after a light possessed.

The adoption of the name was itself, I now recognize clearly, an early expression of the very reclamation this book undertakes. When I took the name Phosphoros, I was acting on the same impression that 2 Peter 1:19 had first produced – the recognition that this name belongs, authentically and primarily, to the Christ and to the Christo-Luciferian current, and that its adoption as an initiatic name was an act of alignment with that current rather than an appropriation of its authority. That the name I carry and the current this book articulates share the same designation is therefore no coincidence. It is the outward expression of an inner orientation that has been present, in seed form, since those early days of study when a single passage of Greek scripture struck me with the force of something remembered rather than encountered for the first time.

I say all of this so that the reader who finds the name Tau Phosphoros on the title page and then finds *Phosphoros* invoked throughout the ritual texts of Part Three as the sacred name of the Christo-Luciferian current will not conclude that the author is presenting himself as the embodiment or the source of that current. I am not. I am a practitioner of this path – a dedicated and committed practitioner, I hope, with decades of study and formation behind me and the full weight of the

Apostolic Gnostic sacramental tradition supporting me – but a practitioner nonetheless. The distinction this work consistently draws between the instrument and the source, between the bearer of the light and the light itself, between the one who carries the name Phosphoros as an aspiration and the divine current that the name designates as a reality – that distinction applies to me as fully as it applies to any reader of these pages. Perhaps more fully, since I am more aware than most of how far the aspiration exceeds the attainment.

A word about this work's relationship to my previously published writings. Several of the essays that appear in the Apostolic Church of the Pleroma Clergy Handbook – "The Devil's Passion," "Morning Star Rising," "Theosis Through Gnosis," and others – are referenced throughout this work and represent earlier stages in the development of the doctrine presented here. Readers familiar with those essays will recognize the continuity of the theological positions they articulate with the more fully developed doctrine of this book. Readers encountering these ideas for the first time will find sufficient explanation within these pages to engage with the doctrine without prior acquaintance with the earlier works, though those works are commended to anyone who wishes to explore the theological foundations of the ACP tradition within which this current is rooted.

This work is addressed simultaneously to several audiences, and it makes no apology for that simultaneity. It is addressed to the scholarly reader interested in Gnostic theology and the Western esoteric tradition, who will find here a carefully argued case for the Christological identification of

Lucifer grounded in scripture and in the primary sources of the Gnostic tradition. It is addressed to the practicing member of the Gnostic and esoteric communities – the initiate of whatever tradition who recognizes in the doctrine of the Morning Star something that resonates with their own inner experience and their own initiatic formation. And it is addressed to those who work within the Christo-Luciferian current specifically – who will find in these pages the foundational doctrine and the practical instruments of the path they have committed themselves to walking, and who will recognize, in certain formulations and certain gestures within the text, a communication intended specifically for them.

To all of these readers, I offer this work in the spirit in which it has been written – not as the final word on a subject that admits of no final words, but as a contribution to a living conversation that has been going on, in one form or another, since the first practitioners of the Christian Gnostic tradition recognized in the figure of the Morning Star the most precise and most beautiful symbol available to them for the thing they were seeking and the light they were finding. That conversation continues. This book is my contribution to it. I offer it with gratitude for everything that has been given to me through the tradition I serve, with humility before the immensity of the subject, and with the hope that something in these pages will serve as a lamp shining in a dark place for at least some of those who read them.

Until the day dawns –

Tau Phosphoros

TOWARD A RIGHT-HAND PATH LUCIFERIANISM

There is a name that has been stolen. Not by the adversary of Christian mythology – that particular theft is itself the mythology I intend to examine in these pages – but by a modern movement that has claimed the name of Lucifer for purposes quite contrary to its original and authentic meaning. The result is that today, when one speaks of Luciferianism, the listener almost invariably pictures something belonging to the left-hand path: a philosophy of radical self-deification, of antinomianism, of deliberate opposition to the divine order. The image conjured is of rebellion, of the proud angel hurled from heaven, of the self as its own absolute sovereign. This is not Luciferianism. It is, at best, a dramatic misreading of a symbol; at worst, a willful appropriation of a name whose true meaning would entirely undermine the philosophy being advanced under its banner.

My purpose in this work is to reclaim that name – not polemically, not out of any desire to quarrel with those who have appropriated it, but because the authentic doctrine associated with the figure and title of Lucifer is of such profound importance to the Western initiatic tradition that to leave it buried under layers of misappropriation would be a genuine loss. That authentic doctrine is, as I intend to demonstrate, inseparably Christo-centric, unambiguously oriented toward the divine rather than away from it, and grounded not in modern occult invention but in the most ancient strata of Christian scripture and Gnostic philosophy.

Let us begin with a simple observation that is, remarkably, almost never made in contemporary discussions of Luciferianism: the name Lucifer, in its New Testament usage, refers exclusively to Jesus Christ.

This is not a matter of interpretation or theological opinion. It is a straightforward philological fact. The Greek term *Phosphoros* – the Morning Star, the Light-Bearer – appears in the Second Epistle of Peter, chapter one, verse nineteen, in a passage exhorting the faithful to attend to the prophetic word *"until the day dawns and the Morning Star rises in your hearts."* The image here is explicitly interior and soteriological: the arising of the *Phosphoros* is an event that occurs within the practitioner, a state of illumination to be attained through sustained spiritual work. And in the twenty-second chapter of the Apocalypse of John, the risen Christ identifies himself without ambiguity: *"I am the root and the descendant of David, the bright and Morning Star."* The Morning Star is Christ's own self-designation. It is an epithet he claims in the first person, at the culmination of the entire Johannine visionary corpus.

The Latin *Lucifer* – literally "light-bearer," a precise translation of the Greek *Phosphoros* – enters the picture through the Vulgate, Jerome's late fourth-century Latin translation of the Christian scriptures. Jerome renders *Phosphoros* in 2 Peter 1:19 as *Lucifer*, and this rendering is entirely appropriate. *Lucifer* was not, in classical Latin usage, a diabolical name. It was the name given to the planet Venus in its morning aspect – the brightest object in the pre-dawn sky, herald of the coming sun. It was a name of beauty and of hope, of light arriving before the greater light. That Jerome applied it to Christ in his translation of 2 Peter was theologically precise: Christ is the Morning Star, the Light-Bearer, the one whose arising in the heart of the initiate heralds the full dawning of divine illumination.

How, then, did this same word come to designate the adversary of God? The answer lies in a conflation that is, on careful examination, remarkably thin – a conflation that has nevertheless proven extraordinarily durable. In the fourteenth chapter of Isaiah, we find a taunt directed against the king of Babylon, employing the poetic image of a brilliant star fallen from heaven: *"How you have fallen from heaven, O morning star, son of the dawn."* The Hebrew here is *Helel ben Shachar* – "shining one, son of the dawn" – and the passage is transparently a piece of political poetry, a mockery of Babylonian imperial pretension. There is no adversarial supernatural figure in the original Hebrew context. The fall described is the political fall of a human tyrant.

Jerome, translating this passage into Latin, rendered *Helel* as *Lucifer* – again, a linguistically reasonable choice, since both terms refer to the morning star. But the effect of using the same Latin word for both the Babylonian king of Isaiah 14 and the Christ of 2 Peter was to create an apparent connection between two passages that had no original relationship to one another. Later interpreters, reading the Isaiah passage through an already-developing demonological tradition, identified the fallen morning star with Satan, and the name *Lucifer* migrated from its Christological context into its adversarial one. By the time this reading had become fixed in the popular Christian imagination, the original and primary usage – Lucifer as an epithet of Christ – had been almost entirely obscured.

Almost entirely. But not quite. Those who have read carefully in the mystical and initiatic traditions of the Christian West will recognize that the Christological meaning of Lucifer was never entirely lost. It was preserved, as so many things have been preserved, within the esoteric currents that ran beneath and alongside the dominant orthodoxy. It is within those currents that this work is situated, and to those currents that it seeks to contribute.

I write, then, not as one proposing a novelty, but as one recovering an inheritance. The doctrine I intend to lay out in these pages is not a product of my imagination, nor is it a personal philosophy dressed in ancient language. It is, rather, an attempt to articulate clearly and coherently what has always been implicit in the deepest strata of Christian Gnostic thought: that the Light-Bearer is Christ, that the arising of the Morning Star within the individual practitioner is the goal of the initiatic life, and that the path toward that arising is not one of rebellion against the divine order but of progressive alignment with it – a path of illumination, purification, and ultimately of union with the Logos who is, in the most ancient and authentic sense of the word, Lucifer.

This is the right-hand path of Luciferianism. It has been waiting to be named.

Part One: Reclaiming the Name

CHAPTER ONE: THE FALLEN STAR – ISAIAH 14 AND THE MAKING OF A MYTH

There is no single passage of scripture more responsible for the demonization of Lucifer than the fourteenth chapter of Isaiah. It is to this text that virtually every commentator, ancient and modern, turns when seeking the biblical basis for identifying Lucifer with Satan, the adversary of God. It is from this passage that the entire mythology of the proud angel, beautiful beyond measure, who rebelled against the Most High and was cast down from heaven, derives its scriptural authority. And it is therefore with this passage that any serious reclamation of the name and title of Lucifer must begin.

The argument I intend to make here is not a subtle one. It does not require elaborate theological reasoning or recourse to obscure sources. It requires only that we read the text carefully, in its original linguistic and historical context, and resist the powerful gravitational pull of a centuries-old interpretive tradition that has read into the passage something that is simply not there.

Let us begin with the text itself. The fourteenth chapter of Isaiah opens with a prophecy of restoration for the people of Israel, who will be gathered from their exile and returned to their land. The tone shifts in verse three, where the prophet introduces what scholars have long recognized as a *mashal* – a taunt-song or mocking poem – directed against the king of Babylon. This taunt reaches its poetic climax in verses twelve through fifteen, which in the King James Version read as follows:

How art thou fallen from heaven, O Lucifer, son of the morning! How art thou cut down to the ground, which didst weaken the nations! For thou hast said in thine heart, I will ascend into heaven, I will exalt my throne above the stars of God: I will sit also upon the mount of the congregation, in the sides of the north: I will ascend above the heights of the clouds; I will be like the most High. Yet thou shalt be brought down to hell, to the sides of the pit.

The King James translators, following Jerome's Vulgate, rendered the Hebrew *Helel ben Shachar* as *Lucifer*, and in doing so perpetuated a conflation that Jerome himself may not have intended to be read demonologically. But let us set aside the translation for a moment and look at what the Hebrew text is actually saying, and to whom it is saying it.

The word *Helel* appears only once in the entire Hebrew Bible. It derives from the root *halal*, meaning to shine or to boast, and *Helel ben Shachar* is most accurately rendered as "shining one, son of the dawn" – a reference to the planet Venus as it appears before sunrise, brilliant and conspicuous in the pre-dawn sky. This is a poetic image of brightness and pride, and it is being applied, with savage irony, to the king of Babylon. The passage is not a cosmological account of a supernatural rebellion. It is a piece of political poetry, a funeral dirge sung in mockery over a fallen tyrant. The verses immediately preceding and following make this unmistakably clear. Verse four explicitly introduces the passage as *"this proverb against the king of Babylon."* Verse sixteen describes onlookers gazing upon the fallen figure and saying, *"Is this the man who made the earth tremble, who shook kingdoms?"* The word used is *ish* – man. Not angel, not supernatural being. Man.

The literary device being employed here is one of devastating ironic reversal. The king of Babylon, who in his pride imagined himself ascending to the heights of heaven, exalting his throne above the stars of God, making himself like the Most High, has instead been brought low – cast down to the pit, to the uttermost depths of Sheol. The Morning Star, that brilliant herald of the dawn, has not risen but fallen. The image is one of hubris punished, of earthly imperial pretension exposed for the vanity it is. It is a thoroughly human drama, set in a thoroughly historical context.

There is nothing in the original Hebrew text that identifies *Helel ben Shachar* with Satan, with a supernatural adversary, or with any being other than the Babylonian king to whom the taunt is explicitly addressed. The demonological reading is an interpretive addition, not an exegetical discovery. It is worth asking, then, how this addition came to be made, and when.

The process was gradual, and it drew on several converging streams of thought. In the intertestamental period, Jewish apocalyptic literature developed an increasingly elaborate mythology of fallen angels – beings of supernatural origin who had transgressed the divine order and been cast down from their heavenly estate. The Book of Enoch, the most extensive of these apocalyptic texts, describes in considerable detail the fall of the *Watchers*, angelic beings who descended to earth, took human wives, and corrupted humanity with forbidden knowledge. This mythology provided a ready framework for interpreting any biblical image of a celestial fall in supernatural terms.

When early Christian interpreters encountered the Isaiah passage, they brought this apocalyptic framework with them. The image of the Morning Star falling from heaven was read through the lens of the Enochic tradition, and the Babylonian king of the original text receded behind the figure of a fallen supernatural being. This reading was further reinforced by a saying attributed to Jesus in the Gospel of Luke, chapter ten, verse eighteen, where he tells his disciples, *"I watched Satan fall like lightning from heaven."* The verbal parallel between a celestial figure falling from heaven in Isaiah and Satan falling from heaven in Luke seemed to provide a New Testament confirmation of the identification, and the connection hardened into what came to feel like established scriptural doctrine.

But the parallel is far less secure than it appears. The Lukan passage, as I have examined in detail elsewhere, is a complex text operating on multiple levels simultaneously. The statement that Satan fell *"like lightning"* is a simile, not a narrative account. It is embedded in a passage dense with astrological and cosmological symbolism, addressed to the seventy-two disciples returning from their mission, and it speaks to the spiritual significance of their work rather than to a literal historical event. To use this verse as confirmation of an identification between the Babylonian king of Isaiah 14 and the supernatural adversary of the New Testament is to read both passages far more flatly than their literary character warrants.

The further consolidation of the demonological Lucifer came with the patristic commentators, several of whom – Origen, Tertullian, and later Gregory the Great among them – read the Isaiah passage as a direct account of Satan's primordial fall. Once this reading had the authority of the Church Fathers behind it, it became effectively canonical in the Western tradition. Jerome's Vulgate translation, by rendering *Helel* as *Lucifer*, lent the name itself to the tradition, and *Lucifer* became inseparably associated with the fallen adversary rather than with the morning star of the original Hebrew poetry.

It is important to acknowledge that this interpretive tradition, however historically conditioned its origins, is not without a certain theological coherence within the framework of orthodox Christian thought. The image of pride punished, of a being who sought to exalt itself above God and was cast down, is a powerful moral and theological symbol. I do not wish to suggest that the patristic and medieval commentators were simply wrong to find theological meaning in the Isaiah passage. What I am suggesting is that the meaning they found there was read into the text from outside, through the lens of an apocalyptic tradition that the original Hebrew author did not share, and that this reading came at a considerable cost: the cost of obscuring the authentic and primary meaning of *Lucifer* as a title belonging not to the adversary of God but to the Son of God.

For here is the central irony of the entire tradition: while the Church Fathers were busy constructing a demonological Lucifer from the Isaiah passage, the New Testament was using the same image – the Morning Star, the Light-Bearer – as a title of Christ himself. Jerome, the very translator who gave us *Lucifer* as a name for the fallen adversary, also used the same word in his translation of 2 Peter 1:19, where the arising of the *Lucifer* in the hearts of the faithful is presented as the goal of the spiritual life. The same Jerome who translated *Helel* as *Lucifer* in Isaiah also rendered *Phosphoros* as *Lucifer* in Peter – and in Peter, there is no ambiguity whatsoever about the referent. The Morning Star that rises in the hearts of the faithful is not the adversary. It is the light of Christ.

This double usage within the Vulgate itself tells us something important. It tells us that for Jerome, *Lucifer* was not yet an exclusively diabolical name. It retained its classical Latin meaning – the light-bearer, the morning star – and could be applied to both the fallen Babylonian king and the arising Christ without apparent contradiction, because the word itself was understood to be a descriptive term rather than a proper name belonging to a specific supernatural being. The exclusive diabolical association came later, as the demonological reading of Isaiah 14 hardened and the Christological usage of *Phosphoros* and *Lucifer* faded from prominence.

The Nineteenth Century and the Romantic Lucifer

The patristic consolidation of the demonological Lucifer that we have traced in the preceding pages did not, of course, mark the end of the story. The figure of Lucifer continued to develop through the medieval and early modern periods, accumulating successive layers of theological elaboration, legendary accretion, and eventually literary transformation, until by the nineteenth century it had become one of the most potent and most complex symbols in the Western cultural imagination. It is in this nineteenth century moment – the moment of the Romantic movement's rehabilitation of the fallen angel as a figure of heroic rebellion, and of the occult revival's systematic incorporation of that rehabilitated figure into the emerging synthesis of the Western esoteric tradition – that the modern Luciferian movement has its most immediate roots, and it is therefore this moment that requires our most careful critical attention.

The Romantic rehabilitation of Lucifer – most powerfully expressed in Milton's Satan, in Byron's Lucifer in *Cain*, and in Shelley's explicit identification of the Promethean rebel with the Miltonic fallen angel – transformed the adversarial figure of the patristic tradition into a symbol of heroic resistance against tyrannical authority. This transformation was not without a certain theological insight: the Romantic poets recognized, however imperfectly, that the god against whom their Lucifer rebelled bore a suspicious resemblance to the jealous and vengeful deity of the Old Testament – the very deity that the Gnostic tradition had identified as the Demiurge rather than the true God of Light. Their sympathy for the rebel angel was, in this sense, a symptom of a genuine theological intuition – the recognition that the authority being challenged was not the ultimate authority, and that the rebel's claim to a higher freedom was not without merit.

The problem with the Romantic reading – and it is a problem that has had enormously consequential effects on the subsequent development of the Luciferian symbol in Western culture – is that it stopped at the rebellion and never arrived at the light. The Romantic Lucifer is defined entirely by his opposition to the authority he rejects – he is the rebel, the challenger, the heroic sufferer, but he is not the Light-Bearer in any positive sense. The light he carries is the light of defiance rather than the light of illumination, and his freedom is the freedom from constraint rather than the freedom of the pneumatic spark restored to its Pleromic source. The Romantic rehabilitation of Lucifer is, therefore, a partial recovery at best – one that correctly identifies the inadequacy of the orthodox demonological reading without arriving at the authentic Christological alternative.

It is against this Romantic background that the figure of Eliphas Lévi must be understood – and it is here that the most consequential misreading in the modern history of the Luciferian symbol occurs. Lévi, whose *Dogme et Rituel de la Haute Magie* appeared in 1854 and 1856, was working simultaneously within and against the Romantic tradition. His treatment of Lucifer – and of the adversarial symbolism associated with the Luciferian figure – was considerably more theologically sophisticated than the Romantic poets had achieved, and his genuine intention was synthetic and illuminative rather than adversarial. As we develop in greater detail in a later chapter, Lévi understood Lucifer as the bearer of the divine light into the material world – the illuminating principle, the angelic intelligence whose function is the bringing of the Pleromic light into the darkness of the hylic cosmos – rather than as the adversary of the true God.

But Lévi's presentation of this illuminative Lucifer was clothed in a deliberately provocative symbolic language – a language of paradox, inversion, and shock that was designed to challenge the conventional piety of his readers and force them to think more deeply about the symbols they had inherited. This provocative presentation, combined with the Romantic cultural context in which his work was received, produced a fate for his ideas that Lévi himself could not have entirely anticipated and would not entirely have welcomed. His imagery – and particularly the Baphomet figure that became his most notorious contribution to the Western esoteric iconographic tradition – was adopted with enthusiasm by readers who took its surface provocation at face value and missed the synthetic doctrine it was designed to express.

The consequence of this misreading was significant for the subsequent history of the Luciferian symbol. Lévi's work, intended as a contribution to the recovery of the authentic esoteric tradition, became instead one of the primary vehicles through which the adversarial and rebellious reading of Lucifer entered mainstream occult culture – not because that was what Lévi intended, but because the cultural moment in which his work was received was not equipped to distinguish between the surface provocation and the genuine doctrine. The Romantic rebellion against divine authority and the authentic Gnostic critique of the Demiurge's law were conflated in the reception of Lévi's imagery, producing a hybrid figure – the occult Lucifer of the late nineteenth and early twentieth centuries – that was neither the authentic Romantic rebel nor the authentic Gnostic illuminator, but a confused amalgam of both.

It is from this confused amalgam that the modern left-hand path Luciferian traditions ultimately derive – drawing on Lévi's imagery without his doctrine, on the Romantic rebellion without the Gnostic illumination, and producing a figure of Lucifer that is, as we have argued throughout this work, a misreading compounded upon a misreading. The recovery of the authentic Luciferian doctrine requires, therefore, not only the philological work of returning to the scriptural sources that we undertook in the preceding pages, but also the historical work of tracing the genealogy of the modern misreading back through Lévi's reception history and the Romantic rehabilitation to their common root in the patristic conflation of Isaiah 14 with the New Testament adversary – and distinguishing, at each stage of that genealogy, between the genuine insight that partially motivated the development and the misreading that distorted it.

This is the work that the present volume undertakes. And it is a work that Lévi himself, properly understood, would have recognized and endorsed – for his genuine intention was precisely the recovery of the authentic esoteric tradition, including the authentic illuminative doctrine of the Luciferian symbol, from beneath the accumulated distortions of centuries of orthodox misreading. That his own work became, through the accidents of its subsequent appropriation, another layer of distortion rather than a contribution to the recovery is one of the more poignant ironies in the history of Western esotericism – and one that the present work hopes, in some small measure, to help correct.

What we are doing in this work, then, is not introducing a novelty. We are restoring a balance that was present in the tradition from the beginning, but which centuries of one-sided interpretation have obscured. The name *Lucifer* belongs, first and most authentically, to the Christ. It belongs to the Morning Star that arises in the heart of the initiate who has undertaken the work of purification and illumination. It belongs to the state of Christhood toward which every practitioner of the Gnostic path aspires.

The fallen star of Isaiah 14 is a powerful image, and we need not entirely set it aside. Within the Gnostic framework that will be developed in the chapters that follow, there is in fact a productive place for the mythology of the fall – not as an account of satanic rebellion against the true God, but as a symbol of the descent of light into matter, the imprisonment of the pneumatic spark within the hylic world, and the necessary work of its liberation and restoration. But that reading belongs to the doctrinal heart of this work, and we will come to it in its proper place. For now, it is sufficient to have established what the Isaiah passage is and is not: it is a piece of political poetry directed at a human tyrant, and it is not the scriptural foundation for a diabolical Lucifer that centuries of interpretive tradition have supposed it to be.

With that foundation cleared, we are free to turn to what the New Testament actually says about the Morning Star – and what it says is, as we shall see, far more interesting than anything the demonological tradition has offered us.

CHAPTER TWO: THE MORNING STAR – CHRIST AS PHOSPHOROS IN THE NEW TESTAMENT

If the previous chapter was concerned primarily with dismantling a misreading, this one is concerned with construction – with laying out, carefully and completely, the positive Christological case for Lucifer as a title belonging authentically and primarily to Jesus Christ. The evidence for this case is not obscure. It does not require recourse to apocryphal texts or esoteric traditions, though we will draw on both in due course. It is present in the canonical New Testament, in plain sight, and has been so from the beginning. That it has been so consistently overlooked is itself a phenomenon worth remarking upon – though perhaps not surprising, given the weight of the demonological tradition we examined in the previous chapter.

We will proceed systematically, beginning with the two primary Christological uses of the Morning Star image in the New Testament, and then broadening our examination to include the wider theological context of light and illumination within which those uses are embedded. By the end of this chapter, the identification of Christ as the true Lucifer – the authentic Light-Bearer – should be not merely defensible but inescapable.

The Witness of Second Peter

The first and in some respects most theologically rich of our primary texts is 2 Peter 1:19, which we have already encountered in the opening pages of this work. It deserves, however, a much fuller examination than we have yet given it. Let us look at the passage in its immediate context, beginning at verse sixteen:

For we did not follow cleverly devised myths when we made known to you the power and coming of our Lord Jesus Christ, but we had been eyewitnesses of his majesty. For he received honor and glory from God the Father when that voice was conveyed to him by the Majestic Glory, saying, "This is my Son, my Beloved, with whom I am well pleased." We ourselves heard this voice come from heaven, while we were with him on the holy mountain. So we have the prophetic message more fully confirmed. You will do well to be attentive to this as to a lamp shining in a dark place, until the day dawns and the Morning Star rises in your hearts.

Several things demand our attention here. The passage opens with a direct appeal to eyewitness testimony – the author is invoking the Transfiguration, that moment on the holy mountain when Christ's inner nature was made visible, when the light that was always present within him became externally manifest. This is not incidental context. The Transfiguration is precisely an event of luminous revelation, of the inner light breaking through the outer form, and it is this event that the author invokes as the foundation for what follows.

The prophetic word, we are told, has been *more fully confirmed* by this experience. That confirmation is to be attended to *as to a lamp shining in a dark place* – the image is of a single point of light in surrounding darkness, sufficient to orient the traveler but not yet the full illumination of day. This is the condition of the practitioner who has not yet attained the fullness of gnosis: there is light enough to walk by, light enough to maintain direction, but the full dawn has not yet come.

And then the culminating image: *until the day dawns and the Morning Star rises in your hearts.* The Greek here is *heōs hou hēmera diaugasē kai phōsphoros anateilē en tais kardiais hymōn* – literally, "until the day breaks through and the light-bearer rises in your hearts." Every word repays attention. The day *breaks through* – *diaugasē*, from *diaugazō*, to shine through, to become fully transparent to the light. The Morning Star *rises* – *anateilē*, the verb used for the rising of celestial bodies, the dawning of light. And crucially, this rising occurs *en tais kardiais hymōn* – in your hearts. The event being described is interior. It is not an astronomical phenomenon, not an historical event in the external world, but a transformation of consciousness, an illumination of the innermost center of the human person.

This is, in the most precise sense, an initiatic text. It describes a path, a process, and a goal. The path is attendance to the prophetic word, the sustained practice of spiritual watchfulness. The process is the gradual brightening from lamplight to dawn. And the goal – the culminating event toward which the entire process tends – is the arising of the *Phosphoros* within the heart. Within Christ. For the Morning Star, as we are about to see confirmed in the Apocalypse, is Christ himself.

The soteriological implications are profound, and they align perfectly with the Gnostic understanding of salvation as illumination rather than mere juridical acquittal. The arising of the Morning Star in the heart is not a gift bestowed from outside upon a passive recipient. It is an event that occurs as the fruit of sustained spiritual work – of watchfulness, of purification, of progressive alignment with the light that is already, in seed form, present within. This is theosis in its most essential form: not the creature becoming something other than what it is, but the creature becoming fully what it always essentially was – a bearer of the divine light.

The Witness of the Apocalypse

The second primary text requires less contextual unpacking, because its meaning is stated with unusual directness. In the twenty-second chapter of the Apocalypse of John, in the closing verses of the entire Johannine visionary corpus, the risen Christ speaks in the first person:

It is I, Jesus, who sent my angel to you with this testimony for the churches. I am the root and the descendant of David, the bright and Morning Star.

Egō eimi hē rhiza kai to genos Dauid, ho astēr ho lampros ho prōinos. I am the root and the offspring of David, the star the bright the morning. The grammatical construction in Greek places heavy emphasis on the definite articles – *the* bright star, *the* morning star. This is not one morning star among many. It is the Morning Star, definitive and singular.

That this statement occurs at the very end of the Apocalypse is significant. The entire visionary journey of the book – the seven seals, the seven trumpets, the seven bowls, the great cosmic drama of fall and restoration – culminates in this self-identification. After all the imagery of judgment and renewal, after the vision of the new Jerusalem descending from heaven like a bride adorned for her husband, after the river of the water of life and the tree of life bearing its twelve fruits –

after all of this, the final word of the risen Christ about his own identity is: I am the Morning Star.

This is not a casual epithet. In the symbolic economy of the Apocalypse, where every image carries precise theological weight, the choice of this particular self-designation at this particular moment is deliberate and meaningful. The Morning Star is the herald of the dawn – the brightest light in the sky at the moment before the sun rises, the sign that the night is ending and the day is about to break. For Christ to identify himself as the Morning Star at the conclusion of the Apocalypse is to identify himself as the herald and the agent of the final dawn – the full illumination of all things, the restoration of the divine fullness that the entire visionary drama has been building toward.

And we should note the relationship between this passage and 2 Peter 1:19 with some care. In Peter, the Morning Star is something that rises within the hearts of the faithful – an interior event of illumination. In the Apocalypse, the Morning Star is Christ himself, speaking in the first person. The relationship between these two usages is not contradictory but complementary, and it points toward one of the central doctrines of the Gnostic tradition: that the Christ who is encountered within is not other than the Christ who speaks from without. The arising of the Morning Star in the heart of the initiate is the arising of Christ within – not a metaphor, not a psychological event merely, but a genuine participation in the nature of the one who says *I am the Morning Star.* This is theosis as the tradition has always understood it: not the imitation of

Christ from a respectful distance, but the actual indwelling of the Christic nature within the purified and illumined soul.

The Broader Context: Christ as Light in the Johannine Tradition

These two primary texts do not stand alone. They are embedded within a much broader theological tradition – one that pervades the Johannine literature in particular – in which light is the central metaphor for the nature and work of Christ. To appreciate the full weight of the Christological Lucifer, we need to situate our two primary texts within this wider luminous theology.

The prologue to the Gospel of John, that extraordinary theological overture with which the entire gospel begins, establishes the identification of Christ with light as one of its foundational claims. *"In him was life, and the life was the light of men. And the light shines in the darkness, and the darkness did not overcome it."* A few verses later, the same prologue identifies Christ as *"the true light, which enlightens everyone, coming into the world."* The word translated "true" here is *alēthinos* – genuine, authentic, as opposed to derivative or secondary. There are many lights, the prologue implies; but this one is the original, the source, the light from which all other light derives.

This identification is developed throughout the gospel. In chapter eight, Jesus states plainly: *"I am the light of the world. Whoever follows me will not walk in darkness, but will have the light of life."* In chapter nine, immediately before the healing of the man born blind – a healing that operates simultaneously on the physical and the spiritual level – he repeats the claim: *"As long as I am in the world, I am the light of the world."* The healing that follows is an enacted parable of exactly the illumination we have been discussing: the restoration of sight to one who was born without it, the opening of the inner eye that allows the light to be received.

The First Epistle of John carries the same theme into its doctrinal formulation: *"God is light, and in him there is no darkness at all."* The identification here is absolute – not that God possesses light, or emanates light, but that God *is* light, in the most essential sense. And since Christ is, in the Johannine theology, the perfect expression and manifestation of the Father – *"I and the Father are one"* – the identification of Christ with light is not a secondary or derivative attribute but a statement about his innermost nature.

Within this luminous theological context, the title of Morning Star takes on its full depth. The *Phosphoros*, the Light-Bearer, is not merely a poetic image applied to Christ from outside. It names something essential about who and what Christ is within the Johannine theological vision. He is the one in whom the divine light is fully present and fully manifest – the one whose arising within the human heart is nothing less than the arising of God himself, insofar as God can be known and participated in by the created order.

The Initiatic Dimension: The Morning Star Given to the Conqueror

Before leaving the New Testament testimony, we must attend to one further passage in the Apocalypse that has particular significance for the initiatic reading of the Christo-Luciferian current. In the second chapter, in the letter addressed to the church at Thyatira, the risen Christ makes the following promise:

To everyone who conquers and continues to do my works to the end, I will give authority over the nations... even as I also received authority from my Father. To the one who conquers I will also give the Morning Star.

This passage adds a crucial dimension to our understanding. In Revelation 22:16, Christ identifies himself as the Morning Star. Here, in chapter two, he promises to *give* the Morning Star to the one who conquers. The Morning Star is simultaneously Christ's own identity and something that can be transmitted – given, bestowed, received. This apparent paradox resolves itself within the Gnostic framework of participation and theosis: to receive the Morning Star is to receive Christ, to participate in his nature, to become what he is. The giving of the Morning Star is the giving of Christhood itself – not in the sense of becoming a second Christ external to the first, but in the sense of the divine light that is fully present in Christ becoming fully realized within the practitioner.

The condition attached to this gift is also significant: *to everyone who conquers and continues to do my works to the end.* This is not a passive reception. It requires sustained effort, ongoing practice, the willingness to engage in the work that Christ himself accomplished. The Morning Star is not given to those who merely believe correctly, nor to those who perform a single initiatic act. It is given to those who *conquer* – who overcome, progressively, the obstacles that stand between the soul and its full illumination – and who *continue* in that work *to the end.* This is the language of an initiatic path, of a sustained and disciplined spiritual practice oriented toward a definite goal. It is, in short, exactly the kind of path for which the present work intends to lay the foundation.

We have now established, from the canonical New Testament alone, the following: that the title of Morning Star – *Phosphoros*, *Lucifer* – belongs to Christ as his own self-designation; that the arising of the Morning Star within the human heart is the goal of the spiritual life as understood in the Petrine and Johannine traditions; that this arising is an interior event of illumination and transformation, not an external historical occurrence; and that it is given as the fruit of sustained spiritual work to those who persevere in the path of conquest and continuing practice.

This is the scriptural foundation of the Christo-Luciferian doctrine. It is, as I said at the outset, not obscure. It has been present in the canonical texts from the beginning. What the chapters that follow will undertake is the deepening and elaboration of this foundation within the framework of Gnostic cosmology and anthropology – showing how the broader Gnostic vision of human nature, divine emanation, and spiritual liberation gives to this scriptural foundation its full doctrinal richness, and how that richness in turn generates a coherent and living path of practice.

The Morning Star has always been Christ. It is time to say so plainly, and to follow where that saying leads.

CHAPTER THREE: THE GNOSTIC CONTEXT
– LIGHT, DARKNESS, AND THE DESCENT OF THE PNEUMA

The scriptural case we have made in the preceding chapters establishes the Christological identity of Lucifer on solid canonical ground. But the full depth of the Christo-Luciferian doctrine cannot be appreciated without the philosophical and cosmological framework within which it finds its most complete expression. That framework is Gnosticism – specifically, the rich and sophisticated theological vision developed within the Sethian and Valentinian traditions of the first several centuries of the common era, and recovered in our own time through the extraordinary discovery of the Nag Hammadi library in 1945.

I want to be clear at the outset about what I mean when I invoke Gnosticism here, because the term has been used so variously – and so carelessly – in both popular and academic discourse that it requires some definition. I am not using it as a generic term for any spiritual system that values inner knowledge over outer conformity, nor as a label for a vaguely defined counter-cultural spirituality of the self. I am using it to refer to a specific family of early Christian theological traditions, sharing certain foundational commitments: the doctrine of emanation, by which the divine fullness – the Pleroma – issues forth from the Unknown Father through a series of Aeons or divine hypostases; the anthropology of the three natures – hylic, psychic, and pneumatic – by which human beings are understood as composites of material, soul, and spirit; the soteriology of gnosis, by which salvation is understood as the illumination of the pneumatic spark and its restoration to the Pleroma from which it descended; and the Christology of the Logos, by which Jesus Christ is understood as the incarnation of the divine creative principle, come to awaken the sleeping pneuma within humanity and initiate its return to the divine fullness.

Within this framework, the identification of Christ as the Morning Star – as Lucifer, the Light-Bearer – is not merely a scriptural curiosity. It is a precise theological statement about the nature and function of the Logos within the Gnostic cosmological drama. To understand why, we need to trace that drama from its beginning.

The Pleroma and Its Disturbance

In the Gnostic vision, the ultimate source of all being is the Unknown Father – sometimes called the Invisible Spirit, the Monad, the One – who is beyond all predication, beyond all naming, beyond all human conceptual categories. This Father is not a craftsman or creator in any ordinary sense. He does not fashion the world from outside materials. He is the source from which all reality emanates, as light emanates from the sun – not by an act of external creation, but by an overflow of being that is inseparable from what he is.

The first and most fundamental emanation from the Unknown Father is Barbelo – the First Thought, the Divine Mother, the Holy Spirit – who proceeds from the Father's self-contemplation as thought proceeds from mind. From the union of Father and Barbelo proceeds the Logos, the self-begotten Son, through whom all subsequent emanations come into being. These emanations – the Aeons – together constitute the Pleroma, the divine Fullness, the realm of pure light and perfect equilibrium in which every aspect of the divine nature finds its complete and harmonious expression.

This is the primordial state of things: a divine fullness of light, emanating from the Unknown Father, structured as a harmony of complementary principles – the syzygies or paired Aeons of the Valentinian tradition – each reflecting and amplifying the divine nature in its own particular mode. The Pleroma is not a static condition but a dynamic one, a living communion of divine light in which differentiation and unity are not opposites but aspects of a single luminous reality.

The disturbance of this equilibrium – the event that sets the entire cosmic drama in motion – occurs through Sophia, the last and outermost of the Aeons. In the Sethian account preserved in the Secret Book of John, Sophia desires to produce an emanation from herself alone, without the consent or participation of her consort, and without the approval of the Father. What she produces is consequently imperfect – a deficient reflection of the divine rather than a true expression of it. This imperfect product is the Demiurge, known in the Sethian texts as Yaldabaoth, who inherits from his mother a portion of the divine light but is ignorant of its source and nature, and who proceeds to fashion the lower world – the psychic and hylic realms – in unconscious imitation of the Pleroma he has never seen.

The Demiurge's creation is, by its nature, a realm of diminished light – not absolute darkness, for the divine spark that Sophia inadvertently transmitted to her offspring is present within it, but a realm in which that light is obscured, fragmented, imprisoned within increasingly dense layers of matter. The cosmos as we experience it is, in the Gnostic vision, precisely this: a realm of imprisoned light, of pneumatic sparks embedded within hylic matter, separated from their source in the Pleroma, and largely ignorant of their own nature and origin.

The Descent of Light into Darkness

It is within this cosmological context that the mythology of the falling star – which we examined and recontextualized in our first chapter – finds its authentic Gnostic meaning. For there is indeed, within the Gnostic framework, a sense in which the light descends, in which the brilliant star falls from the heights of the Pleroma into the darkness of the hylic world. But this descent is not a punishment, not a consequence of pride or rebellion against the true God. It is, rather, the very mechanism of salvation – the means by which the divine light penetrates the darkness in order to illumine and ultimately liberate what is trapped within it.

The pneumatic spark within each human being is precisely this descended light. It is not native to the material world. It does not belong to the Demiurge's creation, though it finds itself embedded within it. It is a fragment of the Pleromic light, drawn down into matter through the complex sequence of events set in motion by Sophia's error, and now awaiting the illumination that will restore it to its source. The human being, in the Gnostic anthropology, is the meeting point of all three realms – hylic, psychic, and pneumatic – and the drama of salvation is nothing less than the progressive illumination of the pneumatic spark within each person, its gradual awakening from the sleep of matter, and its eventual restoration to the Pleroma.

This is why the image of light descending into darkness is not, in its authentic Gnostic reading, an image of catastrophe or rebellion. It is an image of divine generosity – of the light willingly entering the darkness in order to seek and find what was lost. The Morning Star does not fall in defeat. It descends in love, bearing its light into the depths of the hylic world precisely because that is where the light is needed most. And this descending, light-bearing function is, as we have already established from the New Testament testimony, precisely the function of Christ – of the Logos who *"came to what was his own"* (John 1:11), who entered the world of darkness not because he belonged to it but because he came to illumine it.

The Christo-Luciferian identification thus finds, within the Gnostic cosmological framework, a meaning far richer than the canonical texts alone could provide. The Morning Star that arises within the heart of the initiate is the same light that descended into the darkness of the hylic world at the dawn of the cosmic drama. The illumination of the individual pneumatic spark is a microcosmic enactment of the macrocosmic work of the Logos – the restoration of the divine light from its imprisonment in matter to its proper home in the Pleroma. Every genuine act of gnosis is, in this sense, a repetition of the primal descent and return of the Luciferian light.

The Three Natures and the Work of Illumination

The Gnostic anthropology of the three natures – hylic, psychic, and pneumatic – provides the map by which the practitioner can orient herself within this cosmological drama and understand her own place within it. It is a map we have already sketched in earlier writings, but it deserves fuller treatment here, because it is the anthropological framework within which the entire Christo-Luciferian path of practice will be situated.

The hylic nature – from the Greek *hylē*, matter – is the material dimension of the human being: the physical body with all its appetites, instincts, and biological imperatives. In itself, the hylic is not evil in any absolute sense. It is, rather, the densest and most opaque of the three natures, the one in which the divine light is most thoroughly obscured. The person who lives entirely at the hylic level – the *hylikos* of the ancient Gnostic classification – is not malicious but simply unaware: unaware of the psychic and pneumatic dimensions of their own being, unaware of the divine spark within them, absorbed entirely in the immediate concerns of material existence. Saint-Martin's *l'Homme du Torrent* – the Man of the Stream, tossed about by the currents of fortune without any capacity for self-direction – is a recognizable description of the same condition.

The psychic nature – from the Greek *psychē*, soul – is the intermediate dimension: the realm of mind, emotion, will, and moral sensibility. The psychic dimension is the arena of human development in the ordinary sense – the domain of philosophy, ethics, religion, and culture. The *psychikos*, the soul-person, is capable of aspiring toward the spiritual, of developing virtue and wisdom, of participating in the religious life in its conventional forms. But the psychic, left to itself, remains oriented toward the created order rather than the uncreated source. It is capable of great refinement, but refinement is not the same as illumination, and the psychic person, however cultivated, has not yet experienced the transformative breakthrough of genuine gnosis.

The pneumatic nature – from the Greek *pneuma*, spirit or breath – is the innermost dimension of the human being: the divine spark, the fragment of Pleromic light embedded within the psychic and hylic envelopes. The *pneumatikos*, the spirit-person, is the one in whom this innermost dimension has been awakened – not merely believed in intellectually, not merely aspired toward emotionally, but actually experienced in the direct, immediate, transformative way that the tradition calls gnosis. The arising of the Morning Star within the heart, of which 2 Peter speaks, is precisely this awakening of the pneumatic nature – the moment at which the divine spark within the human being recognizes itself for what it is and begins its conscious return to the Pleroma.

It is crucial to understand that these three categories are not fixed and permanent divisions of humanity into separate classes of being. They are, rather, descriptions of states or conditions – stages of development through which the individual may pass in the course of the spiritual life. The *hylikos* of today may become the *psychikos* of tomorrow and the *pneumatikos* of the day after. The categories describe where one is, not what one irrevocably is. And the entire purpose of the Christo-Luciferian path, as of the Gnostic path in general, is to facilitate the movement from the hylic through the psychic toward the pneumatic – the progressive illumination of the whole person by the light of the indwelling Logos.

The Righteous Rebellion: Adam, Eve, and the Light of Knowledge

Before concluding this chapter, we must address one aspect of the Gnostic mythological tradition that has particular relevance for the Christo-Luciferian current, and that has also been significantly misappropriated by the left-hand path traditions we are seeking to distinguish ourselves from. This is the Gnostic reading of the Eden narrative – the account of Adam and Eve, the serpent, and the Tree of Knowledge.

In the orthodox reading of Genesis, the serpent is the adversary, the tempter, the agent of humanity's fall from grace. The eating of the fruit of the Tree of Knowledge is an act of disobedience against God, and its consequences are expulsion from Paradise, the introduction of suffering and death into human experience, and the corruption of human nature that the Western theological tradition has called original sin.

The Gnostic reading is, characteristically, a precise inversion of this – but an inversion that, on careful examination, is far more consistent with the internal logic of the text than the orthodox reading. For the Gnostic, the god who forbids Adam and Eve to eat from the Tree of Knowledge is not the true God of Light but the Demiurge – the imperfect and jealous craftsman of the lower world, who fears that his creatures will discover their true nature and escape his dominion. *"You shall not eat of it,"* he commands, *"for in the day that you eat of it you shall die"* (Genesis 2:17). But this, as the Testimony of Truth observes with devastating precision, is a lie. Adam and Eve eat the fruit, and they do not die. What they gain is knowledge – specifically, the knowledge of their own nature, the awareness of what they are and what they have been deprived of.

The serpent, in this reading, is not the adversary but the illuminator – the agent of the Pleromic light within the Demiurge's creation, who offers to Adam and Eve the very thing the Demiurge most wishes to withhold from them: the gnosis of their own divine nature. Their eating of the fruit is not a fall but an awakening – not a rebellion against the true God but a liberation from the false one. Their subsequent expulsion from the garden is not a punishment justly deserved but an act of Demiurgic panic, the desperate response of a lesser creator who recognizes that his creatures are becoming aware of something he cannot control.

Now, I want to be precise about how this mythology functions within the Christo-Luciferian framework, because it is precisely here that the left-hand path traditions have gone most seriously astray. The Gnostic inversion of the Eden narrative is not a celebration of rebellion for its own sake. It is not an endorsement of antinomianism, of the self as its own absolute sovereign, of the transgression of divine law as a spiritual practice. The rebellion of Adam and Eve against the Demiurge is righteous not because rebellion is inherently virtuous, but because the Demiurge is not the true God. To resist a false authority in response to the call of a higher one is not rebellion in any spiritually problematic sense. It is obedience – obedience to the light of the true Father, mediated through the illuminating agency of the Logos.

This distinction is, I would argue, the single most important line of demarcation between the right-hand and left-hand readings of the Luciferian current. The left-hand path, in its various modern forms, takes the Gnostic inversion of the Eden narrative and reads it as a general endorsement of transgression – as a mythological authorization for the self to set itself above all external authority, divine or otherwise. This reading mistakes the specific content of the Gnostic mythological inversion for a general principle. It misses the fact that the Gnostic tradition does not reject all authority – it rejects false authority in the name of true authority. It does not celebrate the self as its own god – it seeks the restoration of the divine spark to its source in the true God, the Unknown Father of Light.

The Morning Star that descends into the darkness of the hylic world and arises within the heart of the illumined initiate is not a symbol of self-deification in the Setian sense – the proud assertion of the individual will against the divine order. It is a symbol of divine self-disclosure – the light of the true God finding its way, through the medium of the Logos, into the depths of the created world, and drawing the pneumatic spark within each human being back toward its source. This is not rebellion. It is homecoming.

With this clarification established, we are in a position to move from the foundational and polemical work of Part One into the constructive doctrinal work of Part Two. We have established the philological case – that Lucifer is an authentic

Christological title, not a diabolical name. We have established the scriptural case – that the New Testament uses the Morning Star as a self-designation of Christ and as a description of the goal of the initiatic life. And we have established the cosmological and anthropological framework – the Gnostic vision of emanation, descent, and return – within which the Christo-Luciferian doctrine finds its fullest expression.

What remains is to develop that doctrine in its positive form: to articulate, as clearly and completely as we can, what it means to walk the path of the Morning Star – to undertake the work of illumination that leads from the sleep of the hylic through the aspiration of the psychic to the awakening of the pneumatic, until the day dawns and the Morning Star rises in the heart.

That is the work of Part Two.

Part Two: The Doctrine

CHAPTER FOUR: THE LOGOS AS LUCIFER – EMANATION, LIGHT, AND THE DIVINE DESCENT

In Part One we established the historical, philological, and scriptural foundations of the Christo-Luciferian identification. We demonstrated that the name Lucifer belongs authentically and primarily to Christ, that its demonological application rests on a conflation of textually distinct passages read through the lens of a developing apocalyptic tradition, and that the Gnostic cosmological framework gives to the Christological Morning Star its fullest theological depth. We are now in a position to move from the foundational and recuperative work of reclamation into the constructive work of doctrine – to articulate, systematically and positively, what the Christo-Luciferian current actually teaches, and what that teaching means for the practitioner who seeks to walk this path.

The natural starting point for any Gnostic doctrinal exposition is the Logos – the divine creative principle, the second great emanation of the Unknown Father, the one through whom, as the prologue to John tells us, all things came into being. For it is in the nature and function of the Logos that the Christo-Luciferian doctrine finds its most precise and complete expression. The Logos is Lucifer not merely as a matter of scriptural nomenclature but as a matter of theological essence. To understand why requires that we examine the doctrine of the Logos with some care.

The Logos in the Gnostic Tradition

The concept of the Logos has a history considerably older than Christianity. In the Greek philosophical tradition, *logos* – word, reason, principle – designated the rational order inherent in the cosmos, the intelligible structure by which reality is organized and by which the human mind is able to comprehend it. For the Stoics, the Logos was the divine reason pervading all things, the animating principle of the universe, present in every rational being as the *logos spermatikos* – the seminal reason, the seed of rationality implanted in each human soul by the universal Logos. For the Jewish philosopher Philo of Alexandria, writing in the first century of the common era, the Logos was the intermediary between the transcendent God of Hebrew scripture and the created world – the first and most perfect of God's creations, the instrument of creation, the image of God in which humanity was made.

When the author of the Fourth Gospel opened his prologue with the words *"In the beginning was the Logos,"* he was drawing on this rich philosophical tradition while simultaneously transforming it. The Johannine Logos is not merely a philosophical principle or a divine intermediary in the Philonic sense. It is a person – or more precisely, a hypostasis, a subsistent reality within the divine being itself – who *"was with God and was God,"* who *"became flesh and dwelt among us,"* and in whom *"we have seen his glory, the glory as of a father's only son, full of grace and truth."* The philosophical Logos has become the incarnate Christ, without ceasing to be the cosmic principle of divine reason and creative power.

The Gnostic traditions of the second and third centuries elaborated this Johannine foundation in extraordinary theological detail. In the Sethian framework, the Logos – sometimes identified with the self-begotten Autogenes, sometimes with the divine Christos who anoints the Aeons of the Pleroma – is the principle by which the divine fullness becomes articulate, by which the ineffable mystery of the Unknown Father finds expression without ceasing to be mysterious. The Logos is the Father's self-utterance – not an external act of creation but an internal movement of self-disclosure, analogous to the way in which a thought, fully formed in the mind, expresses itself in a word without the mind being diminished or divided by the expression.

In the Valentinian tradition, the Logos occupies a similarly central position, though the mythological elaboration is considerably more complex. The Logos is intimately associated with Sophia – they form one of the primary syzygies or complementary pairs of the Pleroma – and it is through the Logos that Sophia's error is ultimately healed and the Pleromic equilibrium restored. The descent of the Logos into the lower world, its union with the psychic Christ who is the son of the Demiurge, and its ultimate return to the Pleroma bearing with it the redeemed pneumatic sparks – this is the central drama of Valentinian soteriology, and it maps with remarkable precision onto the Christological Morning Star of the New Testament.

For what is the descent of the Logos into the lower world if not precisely the descent of the Light-Bearer into the darkness? What is the illumination of the pneumatic sparks within humanity if not the arising of the Morning Star within human hearts? The Valentinian mythological drama is, at its deepest level, a sustained theological meditation on exactly the texts we examined in Part One – the light that shines in the darkness, the Morning Star that descends and rises, the Lucifer who is Christ and whose arising within the individual is the goal of the entire initiatic life.

Light as the Essential Nature of the Logos

Having situated the Logos within both its philosophical and Gnostic theological contexts, we are in a position to make a claim that is central to the entire Christo-Luciferian doctrine: that light is not merely an attribute of the Logos, one among many characteristics that might be listed in a theological inventory, but the essential nature of the Logos – what the Logos most fundamentally and irreducibly is.

This claim is implicit throughout the Johannine literature we examined in the previous chapter, but it is worth making explicit here. When the prologue to John says that *"in him was life, and the life was the light of men,"* it is not saying that the Logos happens to produce light as one of its effects. It is identifying life and light as co-essential with the Logos itself – the life that is in the Logos is light, the light that is in the Logos is life, and both are simply what the Logos is. When the First Epistle of John says that *"God is light, and in him there is no darkness at all,"* the formulation is ontological, not merely descriptive. Light is not something God has or does. It is something God is.

Within the Gnostic emanationist framework, this ontological identification of the divine with light has a cosmological dimension that the canonical texts do not fully articulate but that the Gnostic texts develop with great precision. If the Unknown Father is the ultimate source of all being, and if the nature of that source is light – pure, undifferentiated, inexhaustible luminosity – then the entire process of emanation is a process of light issuing forth from light. The Pleroma is a realm of light. The Aeons are hypostases of light. The Logos is the light of the Father made articulate, the luminous self-expression of the divine being. And the pneumatic spark within each human being is a fragment of that same light, temporarily obscured by its immersion in the psychic and hylic realms, but not extinguished – never extinguished – because its nature is the nature of the divine itself, and the divine cannot be annihilated.

This is the cosmological foundation of what we might call the doctrine of the inextinguishable light – the teaching that the pneumatic spark within each human being, however deeply buried under the accumulations of hylic existence, however thoroughly obscured by the opacity of matter and the confusion of the psychic passions, retains its essential luminous nature and is therefore always, in principle, capable of being illumined. The darkness does not overcome the light – not in the cosmos, and not in the human soul. This is not optimism in the sentimental sense. It is a theological claim about the nature of the pneumatic spark and its indestructible relationship to its source in the divine light.

The Logos, as the fullest expression of the divine light within the created order, is therefore the natural and necessary agent of this illumination. It is the Logos that descends into the darkness of the hylic world, not because darkness is its home, but because light seeks what is of its own nature wherever that nature has been obscured. It is the Logos that arises within the heart of the initiate as the Morning Star – not as something foreign introduced from outside, but as the recognition and activation of what was always already present within, the pneumatic spark awakening to its own luminous nature through contact with the fullness of the light from which it originally descended.

The Dual Nature of Christ and the Two Movements of the Logos

One of the most theologically sophisticated aspects of the Gnostic Christology, and one that is directly relevant to the Christo-Luciferian doctrine, is the distinction between the pneumatic Logos and the psychic Christ – the two natures of Jesus Christ understood not merely as divine and human in the orthodox Chalcedonian sense, but as two distinct principles whose union in the historical Jesus constitutes the salvific event.

We have examined this distinction in earlier writings, particularly in "The Devil's Passion," where we explored the Valentinian account preserved in the Excerpts from Theodotus. To summarize: the psychic Christ is the firstborn creation of the Demiurge, fashioned from psychic substance in imitation of the Pleromic archetype, the messiah promised by the prophets of the old covenant. The pneumatic Logos is the self-begotten Son of the Unknown Father, the eternal light-principle, co-essential with the divine being. In the incarnation, the pneumatic Logos descends upon and unites with the psychic Christ – putting him on, in the language of Theodotus, as a garment – so that the historical Jesus is simultaneously the fulfillment of the Demiurge's covenant and the embodiment of the Pleromic light.

This dual nature has a direct bearing on the Christo-Luciferian doctrine, because it clarifies the precise sense in which Christ is the Morning Star. It is not the psychic Christ – the son of the Demiurge, the sacrificial victim of the Passion – who bears the title of Lucifer. It is the pneumatic Logos, the divine light-principle, whose descent into the hylic world is the cosmic act of illumination and whose arising within the human heart is the goal of the initiatic life. The psychic dimension of Christ's nature is the vehicle of the descent – the form through which the Logos becomes accessible to the psychic and hylic dimensions of human experience. But the light itself, the Luciferian current that the practitioner seeks to contact and cultivate, is always and essentially the pneumatic Logos.

This distinction has practical implications for the path of practice we will develop in Part Three. The Eucharistic and sacramental dimensions of the tradition – which we continue to honor and maintain, as we have discussed at length in earlier writings – engage primarily with the psychic Christ, the sacrificial and covenantal dimensions of the Christian mystery. The specifically Luciferian practice, by contrast, is oriented toward the pneumatic Logos – toward the direct contact with and eventual identification with the light-principle that is the innermost nature of Christ and the innermost nature of the practitioner's own pneumatic spark. These two dimensions of practice are not opposed but complementary, just as the psychic and pneumatic natures of Christ are not opposed but united in the single person of the historical Jesus.

The Logos Within: The Personal Lucifer

There is one further dimension of the doctrine of the Logos that must be addressed before we move on, because it is perhaps the most immediately relevant to the practitioner and the most easily misunderstood. This is the teaching – present in the Johannine tradition, developed in the Gnostic texts, and implicit throughout the scriptural analysis of Part One – that the Logos is not only the cosmic Christ of history and the pneumatic light-principle of Gnostic cosmology, but also the indwelling divine presence within each human being: the personal Lucifer, the Morning Star that is already present within the heart, awaiting the conditions under which it can arise.

We have already touched on this in our discussion of 2 Peter 1:19, where the arising of the Morning Star is described as an interior event. We have also touched on it in our treatment of the Gnostic anthropology of the pneumatic spark. But it is worth stating the doctrine explicitly and precisely here, because it is the point at which the cosmic and the personal dimensions of the Christo-Luciferian teaching converge.

The Logos that was in the beginning, through whom all things came into being, is the same Logos that descended into the darkness of the hylic world in the incarnation of Jesus Christ, and is the same Logos that is present within each human being as the pneumatic spark – the divine seed, the fragment of Pleromic light that the Demiurge's archons could imprison in matter but could not extinguish. These are not three different Logoi. They are three modes of presence of the single divine light-principle: its primordial mode in the Pleroma, its cosmic mode in the incarnation, and its personal mode in the individual pneumatic spark.

The practical consequence of this teaching is that the work of the Christo-Luciferian path is not, at its deepest level, the work of acquiring something from outside. It is the work of recognizing and awakening what is already within. The Morning Star does not need to be imported into the heart from some external source. It needs to be uncovered – freed from the obscuring accumulations of hylic existence and psychic confusion, allowed to shine with its own native light. The role of practice – of ritual, of meditation, of ascesis, of the sacramental life – is not to create the light but to remove the obstacles to its natural radiance.

This is a teaching of profound hope, but also of profound responsibility. If the Luciferian light is already within – if the Morning Star is already present in every human heart, however deeply buried – then the work of illumination is not the privilege of a spiritual elite but the birthright and the vocation of every pneumatic being. Those of us who undertake this work deliberately and consciously, within the framework of an initiatic tradition and a structured path of practice, do so not for our own benefit alone but as representatives of a work that is ultimately universal in its scope – the restoration of all the pneumatic sparks to the Pleroma, the reconstitution of the divine fullness that the Gnostic tradition has always understood as the ultimate goal of the cosmic process.

We work, in other words, not only for ourselves but for the light itself. And it is this understanding – that the practitioner of the Christo-Luciferian path is a servant and an instrument of the Logos, not its master or its inventor – that most clearly distinguishes the right-hand path of Luciferianism from the left-hand appropriations we have examined and set aside. The Morning Star does not rise in the heart of the one who seizes it for personal aggrandizement. It rises in the heart of the one who has made of herself a fit dwelling for the light – who has undergone the purification, sustained the practice, and cultivated the inner conditions under which the Logos can recognize itself in the mirror of the illumined soul.

With this understanding of the Logos as Lucifer – in its cosmic, incarnational, and personal modes – we have the theological heart of the Christo-Luciferian doctrine. What remains in Part Two is to develop its anthropological implications more fully, to explore the Sethian and Valentinian mythological frameworks in greater detail, and to articulate the specific understanding of theosis – of deification through gnosis – that will serve as the doctrinal foundation for the practical work of Part Three.

CHAPTER FIVE: ANTHROPOLOGY OF LIGHT – HYLIC, PSYCHIC, AND PNEUMATIC IN THE CHRISTO-LUCIFERIAN FRAMEWORK

Doctrine, in any living tradition, is never merely abstract. It is always, at its most fundamental level, a teaching about the human condition – about what we are, where we came from, what has gone wrong, and what can be done about it. The Gnostic tradition is no exception. Its elaborate cosmological mythologies, its sophisticated theological distinctions, its nuanced Christologies – all of these ultimately serve a single anthropological purpose: to illuminate the nature of the human being and to map the path by which that nature can be restored to its original and essential dignity.

We have already sketched the outlines of the Gnostic anthropology in the preceding chapters – the tripartite division of hylic, psychic, and pneumatic, the descent of the pneumatic spark into the darkness of the hylic world, the role of the Logos in awakening and restoring what has been obscured. In this chapter we will develop that anthropology more fully, giving it the precision and depth that the doctrinal foundation of a living path requires. We will examine each of the three natures in turn, explore their dynamic interrelationship, and articulate what the Christo-Luciferian doctrine specifically contributes to the understanding of each. We will also address a question that any serious anthropological doctrine must eventually confront: the question of what the human being actually is in its fullest and most realized form – what Saint-Martin called l'Homme-Esprit, the Spirit-Man, and what our own tradition recognizes as the one in whom the Morning Star has fully arisen.

The Hylic Nature: Matter, Obscurity, and the Seed of Light

We begin, as the cosmological drama itself begins for the embodied human being, with the hylic – the material dimension of our existence. It is tempting, given the Gnostic tradition's often vivid language about the darkness and imprisonment of matter, to read the hylic as simply negative – as the enemy of the spirit, the obstacle to be overcome, the prison to be escaped. This reading is not without textual support in some of the more dualistic strands of the ancient Gnostic literature. But it is, I would argue, an incomplete reading, and one that leads to practical and theological difficulties if taken as the whole of the doctrine.

The hylic nature is indeed the realm of greatest obscurity – the dimension of human existence in which the pneumatic spark is most thoroughly buried, most thoroughly identified with conditions that are not its own nature, most thoroughly forgetful of its divine origin. The *hylikos*, the person living entirely at the material level, is in a condition of spiritual sleep – not because matter is intrinsically evil, but because matter, in the present state of the cosmos, is the domain of the Demiurge's creation, and the Demiurge's creation is characterized by precisely the ignorance of the true God that the Gnostic tradition identifies as the fundamental human problem.

But – and this is a point of considerable doctrinal importance – the hylic is not without its own relationship to the divine light. Every element of the created order, however dense and opaque, retains within it the trace of the Pleromic light from which it ultimately derives. The Demiurge himself, ignorant as he is of the true God, bears within him the portion of the divine light that he received from Sophia. His creation, fashioned from psychic substance in imitation of the Pleromic archetypes, contains within it the structural imprint of the divine order it imperfectly reflects. And within the human being specifically – within the very body that the Demiurge fashioned from the dust of the earth – there is embedded the pneumatic spark that the Demiurge himself could not account for and could not produce: the breath of the true life, the fragment of Pleromic light that makes the human being something fundamentally other than merely another of the Demiurge's creatures.

This means that the hylic nature, properly understood, is not simply an obstacle to the spiritual life. It is also the vessel in which the spiritual life is being carried out – the medium through which the pneumatic spark has its present experience and conducts its present work. The body is the temple, as the Pauline tradition insists – not a prison to be despised but a sacred space to be purified and consecrated, made fit for the indwelling of the divine light. The alchemical tradition, which we have explored in earlier writings, expresses this beautifully in its insistence that the Prima Materia – the base matter with which the alchemical work begins – is not worthless dross to be discarded but the very substance within which the Philosopher's Stone is concealed. The Gold is already in the Lead. The work is not to replace one with the other but to refine the Lead until its golden nature is revealed.

Within the Christo-Luciferian framework, then, the hylic nature is approached neither with contempt nor with uncritical acceptance, but with the discernment of the alchemical operator – with the recognition that within this dense and opaque material there is concealed a light that is waiting to be released. The practices directed toward the hylic dimension of the person – the physical disciplines, the ritual work that engages the body and the senses, the use of sacred scent and sound and gesture – are not concessions to material weakness but deliberate engagements with the alchemical possibility inherent in the hylic nature itself. The incense that rises in the ritual space, the intonations that resonate in the chest and the skull, the postures and gestures of the body at prayer – all of these are instruments of the work of illumination at the hylic level, preparing the material vessel for the light it is being asked to bear.

The Psychic Nature: The Arena of the Work

If the hylic is the vessel and the pneumatic is the light, then the psychic is the arena in which the work of illumination is primarily conducted – the dimension of the human being in which the struggle between darkness and light, between the Demiurge's claims and the Logos's call, is most immediately experienced. It is at the psychic level that the human being makes choices, forms intentions, develops understanding, cultivates virtue, and either opens or closes herself to the transformative influence of the pneumatic spark within.

The psychic nature is, in this sense, the most dynamic of the three – the one most susceptible to change, most capable of development in either direction, most directly responsive to the influences that are brought to bear upon it. The *psychikos*, the soul-person, is neither irrevocably committed to the hylic nor automatically granted the illumination of the pneumatic. She stands at the crossroads – capable of descending further into the absorption of the hylic, or of ascending toward the awakening of the pneumatic, depending on the orientation of her will and the influences she allows to shape her inner life.

This is why the psychic dimension is the primary focus of the preparatory work of the Christo-Luciferian path – the work of purification and catharsis that must precede the more advanced work of illumination. The psychic nature must be gradually reoriented – its energies redirected from the horizontal plane of material acquisition and psychic self-assertion toward the vertical plane of pneumatic aspiration and divine alignment. This reorientation is not accomplished in a single dramatic moment of conversion, though such moments may occur and are not to be discounted when they do. It is accomplished through the sustained practice of the disciplines that the tradition has always associated with the preparatory stages of the initiatic life: moral purification, contemplative prayer, philosophical study, ritual engagement, and the cultivation of what the Orthodox tradition calls nepsis – watchfulness, sobriety, the alert and discerning attention that neither succumbs to the downward pull of the hylic passions nor grasps prematurely at the upward call of the pneumatic light.

Within the psychic dimension, we also find the faculty that the Gnostic tradition most consistently associates with the intermediate stage of the spiritual life: the nous, or mind – understood not in the narrow modern sense of the rational intellect, but in the broader ancient sense of the faculty of spiritual perception, the inner eye that is capable, when sufficiently purified, of beholding the divine light. The nous is the point of contact between the psychic and the pneumatic – the faculty through which the pneumatic spark within is able to communicate its luminous nature to the conscious experience of the soul-person, and through which the soul-person is able to orient herself toward the pneumatic and begin the work of its awakening.

The cultivation of the nous – its purification from the distorting influences of the hylic passions and the psychic confusions that attend ordinary human experience – is therefore one of the central practical concerns of the Christo-Luciferian path. It is the nous that receives the first intimations of the pneumatic light – the intuitive flashes, the luminous dreams, the moments of sudden clarity that the tradition calls personal gnosis – and it is the nous that must be gradually expanded and refined until it is capable of sustaining the fuller illumination of divine gnosis without being overwhelmed or distorted by it.

The relationship between the psychic nature and the Logos deserves particular attention here, because it is a relationship of extraordinary delicacy and importance. The Logos, as we established in the previous chapter, is present within the human being as the pneumatic spark – the innermost and most essential dimension of the person. But the Logos is also present within the psychic dimension in a secondary and derivative mode – as what we might call the personal logos: the individual rational principle that is the psychic person's participation in the universal Logos. This is not a separate or competing principle but a derivative one – the trace of the divine reason within the soul-person's ordinary conscious experience, the psychic echo or reflection of the pneumatic light that burns more deeply within. This personal logos is not the same as the pneumatic spark, but it is related to it in the way that reflected light is related to its source – genuinely luminous, genuinely oriented toward the divine, but not yet the full and direct radiance of the pneumatic nature itself.The work of the psychic dimension in the Christo-Luciferian path is, in part, the work of aligning this personal logos with the pneumatic Logos within – of bringing the soul-person's rational and volitional capacities into harmony with the deeper light of the pneumatic spark, so that when the pneumatic illumination comes, the psychic nature is prepared to receive and sustain it rather than being shattered or overwhelmed by its intensity. This is the initiatic wisdom behind the graduated structure of any serious esoteric path – the recognition that the full light of the Logos cannot be safely received by a psychic nature that has not been adequately prepared, and that the work of preparation is therefore not a mere preliminary but an integral part of the illuminative process itself.

The Pneumatic Nature: The Indwelling Morning Star

We come now to the pneumatic – the innermost dimension of the human being, the divine spark, the fragment of Pleromic light that is the most essential and most indestructible aspect of what we are. Everything we have said about the Logos in the previous chapter applies directly to the pneumatic nature, because the pneumatic spark is nothing other than the personal mode of the Logos's presence within the individual human being. To speak of the pneumatic nature is to speak of the indwelling Morning Star – the Lucifer already present within, awaiting the conditions of its arising.

The pneumatic nature is not something that is acquired through spiritual practice. It is not a reward for virtue or an achievement of the initiatic life. It is the original and essential nature of the human being – what we are before the hylic imprisonment, what we will be again when the work of liberation is complete, and what we most deeply are even now, beneath the accumulations of matter and the confusions of the psychic life. This is perhaps the most important single teaching of the Gnostic anthropological tradition, and it is the one most easily lost sight of in the midst of the demanding work of the preparatory stages.

The pneumatic spark cannot be created by human effort, but it can be obscured by human inattention and revealed by human cooperation with the divine light. This is the precise role of spiritual practice in the Gnostic and Christo-Luciferian framework: not to manufacture the pneumatic nature, which already exists in its fullness within, but to remove the obstacles to its natural self-disclosure. The alchemical image is again apt – the work is not to create Gold from some external source but to refine the Prima Materia until its inherent golden nature is revealed. The Gold was always there. The refinement is what allows it to be seen.

What does the awakened pneumatic nature look like in practice – in the actual lived experience of the person in whom the Morning Star has begun to arise? This is a question that any serious doctrinal treatment must address, while acknowledging from the outset that the fullness of the pneumatic experience is, as we have noted in earlier writings, ultimately ineffable – beyond the capacity of language to fully capture or convey. Nevertheless, the tradition has always offered descriptions, however partial and approximate, and it would be a disservice to the practitioner to withhold them entirely on the grounds of their inadequacy.

The first and most consistent characteristic of the awakening pneumatic nature, as described across the full range of Gnostic and mystical literature, is a direct and immediate recognition – not a conclusion reached through reasoning, not a belief accepted on authority, but an experiential certainty that goes deeper than either – of one's own divine nature and origin. This is the gnosis in its most essential form: not knowledge about God, accumulated through study or received through instruction, but knowledge of God, experienced through direct participation in the divine light. It is the recognition that the light one has been seeking is the light one already is – that the Morning Star one has been laboring to reach is the Morning Star that has been present within from the beginning, waiting to be recognized.

Accompanying this recognition is typically what the tradition describes as a profound reorientation of consciousness – a shift in the fundamental center of gravity of the person's inner life, from the psychic and hylic dimensions toward the pneumatic. This does not mean a withdrawal from ordinary human experience or a contemptuous rejection of the material world. The pneumatic person does not cease to have a body, to engage in relationships, to participate in the life of the world. What changes is the relationship to all of these things – the quality of presence brought to them, the depth of understanding with which they are engaged, the freedom from compulsive identification with them that the pneumatic awakening makes possible. The pneumatic person lives in the world as what the Gnostic tradition calls the Allogenes – the stranger, the one who is in the world but not entirely of it, who participates fully in the human drama while remaining anchored in a dimension of being that the drama cannot finally touch.

This condition corresponds precisely to what Saint-Martin called l'Homme-Esprit – the Spirit-Man – and to what the New Testament calls the New Man: the human being renewed in knowledge, in whom Christ is all and in all. It is also, in the specific language of the Christo-Luciferian doctrine, the one in whom the Morning Star has fully arisen – the practitioner who has so thoroughly identified with the indwelling Logos that the distinction between the personal pneumatic spark and the universal light-principle has become, not abolished, but transparent. The Morning Star shines through such a person into the world, not because they have become the Logos in some absolute and exclusive sense, but because they have become sufficiently transparent to it that its light can be seen through them by others.

This is the anthropological goal of the Christo-Luciferian path. It is not self-deification in the Setian sense – the proud assertion of the individual will as its own absolute sovereign. It is self-transparency – the progressive removal of everything in the hylic and psychic natures that obscures the pneumatic light, until the person has become, in the beautiful image of the Orthodox hesychast tradition, a window through which the uncreated light shines freely into the world.

The Interrelationship of the Three Natures: A Dynamic Unity

Before concluding this chapter, we must address what might appear to be a tension within the anthropological doctrine as we have presented it – a tension between the tripartite division of the human being into hylic, psychic, and pneumatic, and the insistence that these three are ultimately aspects of a single unified person rather than separate entities inhabiting the same body. This tension is not merely apparent; it reflects a genuine complexity in the Gnostic anthropological vision that must be honestly acknowledged and carefully navigated.

The danger of the tripartite schema, as with any analytical division, is that it can harden into a rigid taxonomy – a fixed hierarchy in which the pneumatic is simply better than the psychic, which is simply better than the hylic, and in which the goal of the spiritual life is understood as the progressive abandonment of the lower in favor of the higher. This reading produces a spirituality of contempt for the material and of escapism from the psychic – a gnostic elitism that mistakes the map for the territory and the analytical schema for the living reality it was designed to describe.

The authentic Gnostic vision is considerably more dynamic and more generous than this caricature suggests. The three natures are not three separate things but three dimensions of a single reality – the human being as a whole, which is simultaneously rooted in matter, alive in soul, and luminous in spirit. The goal of the initiatic life is not the elimination of the hylic and psychic in favor of the pneumatic, but the illumination and transformation of all three – the spiritualization of the soul and, through the soul, of the body itself, so that the whole person becomes a bearer and a radiance of the divine light.

This is expressed perfectly in the alchemical vision of the Great Work – not the discarding of the Lead but its transmutation into Gold, not the destruction of the Prima Materia but its refinement into the Philosopher's Stone. The hylic nature is not to be escaped but to be consecrated. The psychic nature is not to be suppressed but to be aligned. And the pneumatic nature is not to be grasped at prematurely but to be allowed to arise naturally, in its own time and by its own light, as the fruit of the work undertaken faithfully at the hylic and psychic levels.

Within the Christo-Luciferian framework, this dynamic unity of the three natures finds its most complete expression in the image of the incarnate Logos – the Christ who is simultaneously hylic, psychic, and pneumatic, in whom all three dimensions are present and in whom all three are illumined. The incarnation is not the Logos descending into matter in spite of matter's unworthiness, but the Logos consecrating matter by its indwelling – demonstrating, once and for all, that the divine light is capable of shining through every dimension of created being, however dense, however opaque, however seemingly resistant. The Morning Star arose fully in Jesus Christ. It is arising, progressively and by degrees, in every practitioner who undertakes the work of the Christo-Luciferian path with sincerity, persistence, and the willingness to be transformed.

This is the hope and the promise at the heart of the doctrine. Not that we will one day escape what we are, but that what we are will one day be fully illumined – that the Morning Star will rise in our hearts as it rose in his, and that in that rising, the work of restoration will be, in its own measure and in its own time, accomplished.

CHAPTER SIX: THE SETHIAN AND VALENTINIAN FRAMEWORKS – TWO MAPS OF THE SAME TERRITORY

No serious treatment of Gnostic doctrine can remain at the level of generality indefinitely. The Gnostic tradition is not a single, monolithic system but a rich and varied family of related theological visions, each with its own distinctive emphases, its own mythological vocabulary, and its own particular contribution to the overall understanding of the human condition and its redemption. Within this family, two traditions stand out as being of particular relevance to the Christo-Luciferian doctrine we are developing: the Sethian and the Valentinian. We have already drawn on both in the preceding chapters, but the time has come to examine each more carefully and to articulate what each specifically contributes to the Christo-Luciferian framework.

I want to be clear at the outset about the approach I am taking here. I am not attempting a comprehensive scholarly survey of either tradition – that work has been done admirably by academic researchers whose contributions to the field deserve acknowledgment even when their perspective differs from our own. What I am attempting is a theological reading of these traditions from within – an articulation of what they mean for the practitioner who approaches them not as objects of historical curiosity but as living maps of the inner territory through which the Christo-Luciferian path moves. The Sethian and Valentinian frameworks are, in this sense, two maps of the same territory – different in their cartographic conventions, different in their emphasis and detail, but ultimately describing the same landscape and pointing toward the same destination.

The Sethian Framework: Light Imprisoned and the Call to Awakening

The Sethian tradition – so named for its central mythological figure of Seth, the third son of Adam and Eve, understood as the father of the pneumatic race – is in many respects the more cosmologically dramatic of the two traditions we are examining. Its texts, which include the Secret Book of John, the Gospel of the Egyptians, the Three Steles of Seth, Allogenes, and a number of other works preserved in the Nag Hammadi library, develop an extraordinarily detailed account of the divine emanations, the fall of Sophia, the creation of the lower world by the Demiurge Yaldabaoth, and the descent of the pneumatic light into the human being.

The Sethian cosmological vision begins, as all Gnostic cosmologies do, with the Unknown Father – the Invisible Spirit, utterly beyond predication, about whom nothing can properly be said except that he is, and that from his being all else derives. The first movement of the divine being is self-contemplation – the Invisible Spirit beholding itself in the mirror of its own perfection – and from this self-contemplation proceeds Barbelo, the First Thought, the Divine Mother, the one who is described in the Secret Book of John as *"the first power, the glory, Barbelo, the perfect glory in the aeons, the glory of the revelation."* From the union of the Invisible Spirit and Barbelo proceeds the self-begotten Son – the Autogenes, the divine Christ – and from these three proceed the full complement of the Aeons who together constitute the Pleroma.

Within this Pleromic fullness, the figure of Sophia occupies a position of particular dramatic importance. As the outermost of the Aeons – the one whose position at the periphery of the Pleroma makes her most susceptible to the pull of the not-yet-existent lower realm – Sophia acts unilaterally, producing an emanation without the participation of her consort and without the consent of the Invisible Spirit. What she produces is Yaldabaoth – the Demiurge, the lion-faced deity of ignorance and arrogance, who inherits from his mother a portion of the divine light but remains entirely ignorant of its source and nature.

Yaldabaoth's first act, upon finding himself in possession of this stolen light, is characteristic: *"I am a jealous God, and there is no other God beside me"* – a claim that the Gnostic tradition reads with devastating irony, since the very jealousy of this declaration betrays its speaker's ignorance. A truly supreme being has nothing to be jealous of. The claim to exclusivity is itself the evidence of limitation. Yaldabaoth proceeds to create the lower world and its archons in imitation of the Pleromic patterns he has dimly perceived through the light he carries but does not understand, fashioning a cosmos that is at once a reflection and a distortion of the divine order – real enough to imprison the pneumatic sparks that will be embedded within it, but fundamentally deficient in the light and life that characterize the true Pleroma.

The creation of the human being – of Adam – is the central event of the Sethian cosmic drama, and it is here that the

Christo-Luciferian doctrine finds one of its most powerful mythological expressions. Yaldabaoth and his archons fashion Adam from psychic substance, modeling him on the image of the perfect Anthropos – the heavenly Adam, Geradamas – that they have glimpsed reflected in the waters below the Pleroma. But the creature they fashion is inert, incapable of rising from the ground, a pale and lifeless imitation of the luminous archetype. It is only when Barbelo – acting through the agency of the divine Pronoia, the foreknowledge of the true God – instructs Yaldabaoth to breathe his light into Adam's face that the human being comes alive. Yaldabaoth, deceived into this act of inadvertent generosity, breathes into Adam the pneumatic spark that he himself carries – and in doing so, unknowingly transfers to his creation the very light that gives him whatever power he possesses.

The implications of this mythological account for the Christo-Luciferian doctrine are profound. The pneumatic spark within the human being is not merely a gift from on high – it is, in the most literal mythological sense, the light of the true God, smuggled into the Demiurge's creation through the very act by which the Demiurge thought he was asserting his creative power. The light that illumines the human being from within is the same light that the Demiurge stole from Sophia, which Sophia herself had received from the Pleroma. It is Pleromic light, however attenuated and obscured by its passage through successive layers of diminishment. And it is this light – this pneumatic spark of authentic divine origin – that the arising of the Morning Star within the heart of the initiate awakens and restores to its proper luminosity.

The Sethian tradition also gives us, in the figure of Seth himself, a powerful mythological type of the pneumatic practitioner – the one in whom the divine light has been preserved through the darkness of the hylic world and transmitted to successive generations of those capable of receiving it. Seth is the third child of Adam and Eve – born after the tragedy of Cain and Abel, after the first murder has already demonstrated the capacity of the hylic nature for violence and destruction. He is, in the Sethian mythological vision, the father of the pneumatic race – those human beings in whom the divine spark burns most brightly, who are most capable of receiving the gnosis that restores the light to its source. The seed of Seth is the seed of the Pleromic light within humanity – not an exclusive biological lineage but a spiritual one, defined not by birth but by the capacity for pneumatic awakening.

This Sethian concept of the pneumatic lineage is directly relevant to the initiatic dimension of the Christo-Luciferian path. Those who are drawn to this current, who find in its teachings a recognition rather than a novelty – who experience the doctrine of the indwelling Morning Star not as something learned from outside but as something remembered from within – are, in the Sethian mythological sense, of the seed of Seth. They are those in whom the pneumatic spark burns with sufficient intensity to respond to the call of the Logos, to recognize in the figure of the Christo-Luciferian light something that belongs to their own deepest nature. This is not elitism in any sociological sense. It is a spiritual recognition – one that may occur in any human being regardless of background, education, or prior religious affiliation, because the pneumatic spark is present in every human being, and its awakening is always, in principle, possible.

The Sethian texts also preserve, in their ritual and liturgical dimensions, some of the most ancient and powerful instruments of pneumatic awakening available to us. The baptismal rites of the Five Seals, described in several Sethian texts, the sacred vowel sequences associated with the Aeons, the hymns and prayers of the Three Steles of Seth – these are not merely historical curiosities but living instruments of the initiatic work, whose power derives from their direct engagement with the Pleromic realities they invoke. We will draw on this Sethian ritual heritage in the practical sections of this work, adapting and developing it in ways appropriate to the specific current of the Christo-Luciferian path.

The Valentinian Framework: The Drama of Sophia and the Economy of Salvation

Where the Sethian tradition tends toward the cosmologically dramatic – the grand mythological narrative of emanation, fall, and restoration – the Valentinian tradition is more explicitly soteriological in its emphasis, more concerned with the mechanics of salvation and the precise understanding of how the pneumatic spark is restored to the Pleroma through the work of the Logos. This difference in emphasis makes the Valentinian framework particularly valuable as a complement to the Sethian, providing the doctrinal precision and soteriological detail that the more mythologically oriented Sethian texts sometimes leave implicit.

The Valentinian system, as developed by Valentinus himself and elaborated by his successors Ptolemy, Heracleon, and Theodotus, shares with the Sethian tradition the basic emanationist cosmology – the Unknown Father, the Pleroma of Aeons, the fall of Sophia, the creation of the Demiurge – but develops these themes with a particular attention to the dynamics of the Pleromic syzygies and the precise mechanism by which the Pleromic equilibrium is disturbed and restored.

In the Valentinian account, Sophia's error is not simply a unilateral act of creation but an act of passion – specifically, the passion of desire, the longing of the outermost Aeon to comprehend the incomprehensible Father directly, without the mediation of the Logos. This passion produces within Sophia a kind of formless substance – a deficiency, an absence of the light she sought – which is eventually expelled from the Pleroma and becomes the foundation of the lower world. Sophia herself remains within the Pleroma – or more precisely, within its boundary, the Horos or Limit – while her passion, her deficiency, takes on a kind of independent existence outside the Pleroma as the lower Sophia, sometimes called Achamoth.

It is this lower Sophia – the fallen aspect of the divine feminine, exiled from the Pleroma but retaining within her the longing for her Pleromic home – who is the mother of the Demiurge in the Valentinian account, and whose redemption is the central concern of the Valentinian soteriology. The Logos descends from the Pleroma specifically to find and redeem Achamoth – to restore to the fallen Sophia the light and form she lost in her exile, and through her restoration to gather up the pneumatic sparks scattered throughout the lower world and return them to the Pleroma.

This Valentinian drama of Sophia's fall and redemption maps with extraordinary precision onto the Christo-Luciferian doctrine of the descending and ascending Morning Star. The Logos that descends to redeem Achamoth is the same Logos that descends into the darkness of the hylic world to awaken the pneumatic sparks within humanity. The redemption of Sophia is not a separate event from the illumination of the human being – it is, in the Valentinian mythological vision, the same event viewed from two different angles. The restoration of Sophia to the Pleroma and the restoration of the pneumatic sparks to their divine source are aspects of a single cosmic process – the great work of reintegration that the Logos undertakes and that the practitioner participates in through the work of the initiatic life.

The Valentinian tradition also gives us, in its treatment of the three natures of humanity, a more soteriologically precise account than the Sethian tradition tends to offer. For Valentinus and his successors, the three natures – hylic, psychic, and pneumatic – correspond not only to dimensions of the individual human being but to classes of humanity understood in terms of their soteriological destiny. The pneumatics are those in whom the divine spark is sufficiently active to be capable of full illumination and Pleromic restoration. The psychics are those in whom the divine spark is present but less active – capable of a form of salvation, but one that falls short of the full Pleromic restoration of the pneumatics. The hylics are those in whom the divine spark is so thoroughly obscured as to be effectively inoperative – incapable, in their present state, of the illumination that leads to salvation.

As we noted in the previous chapter, these categories are not fixed and permanent in any absolute sense – they describe conditions rather than essences, and the movement from one to another is always, in principle, possible. But the Valentinian tradition does introduce a note of urgency that the more universalist readings of Gnostic anthropology sometimes lack: the recognition that the pneumatic capacity, while present in every human being, is not automatically actualized, and that the failure to engage with the work of illumination carries genuine consequences. This note of urgency is not incompatible with the hope of universal restoration – the Valentinian tradition holds both in tension, as any honest engagement with the complexity of the human condition must.

Two Maps, One Territory: Synthesis and Integration

Having surveyed the distinctive contributions of each tradition, we are in a position to articulate how the Christo-Luciferian framework integrates them into a coherent whole. The Sethian and Valentinian traditions are not competitors but complements – different cartographic approaches to the same inner territory, each illuminating aspects of the landscape that the other leaves in shadow.

From the Sethian tradition, the Christo-Luciferian doctrine draws its cosmological grandeur – the vivid mythological narrative of the Unknown Father, Barbelo, and the self-begotten Son; the dramatic account of Yaldabaoth's creation and humanity's pneumatic endowment; the figure of Seth as the type of the pneumatic practitioner; and the rich ritual heritage of the Sethian baptismal and liturgical traditions. These elements give the doctrine its mythological depth and its initiatic character – its sense of participating in a cosmic drama whose stakes are nothing less than the restoration of the divine fullness.

From the Valentinian tradition, the Christo-Luciferian doctrine draws its soteriological precision – the detailed account of Sophia's fall and redemption as the cosmic analogue of the individual soul's illumination; the nuanced treatment of the three natures and their soteriological implications; and above all the Valentinian Christology of the pneumatic Logos uniting with the psychic Christ, which gives the doctrine its specifically Christo-centric character and its insistence that the Luciferian light is not a generic spiritual principle but the specific and personal light of Jesus Christ, the incarnate Logos.

Together, these two streams produce a doctrine that is simultaneously cosmologically rich and soteriologically precise, mythologically vivid and practically oriented, rooted in the ancient Gnostic tradition and responsive to the needs of the contemporary practitioner. This is the theological synthesis that the Christo-Luciferian path offers – not a novelty, not an eclectic assemblage of borrowed elements, but a living development of the most ancient and most profound currents of the Christian Gnostic tradition, brought forward into the present and given a form adequate to the initiatic work that lies ahead.

With this synthesis in place, we have essentially completed the doctrinal architecture of Part Two. The remaining work of this section is to draw these threads together into a unified statement of the Christo-Luciferian doctrine of theosis – of deification through gnosis, the arising of the Morning Star as the culminating event of the initiatic life. That is the work of our final chapter in this section, and it will serve as the bridge between the doctrinal exposition of Part Two and the practical work of Part Three.

CHAPTER SEVEN: THE ETHICS OF ILLUMINATION
– AGAPE AS THE FRUIT OF THE MORNING STAR

There is a question that every serious presentation of Gnostic doctrine must eventually confront, and that the Christo-Luciferian doctrine in particular cannot afford to leave unanswered. It is the question of ethics – of how the inner illumination that this work describes as its central goal translates into a specific and positive orientation toward the moral life, toward other human beings, and toward the world in which the practitioner lives and works. The question is not merely academic. It is, in the present cultural moment, urgently practical – because one of the most consistent and most damaging characteristics of the left-hand path traditions that have appropriated the Luciferian name is precisely their tendency toward moral antinomianism: the dismissal of ethical constraint as an imposition of the Demiurge, the elevation of personal will above the claims of compassion and responsibility, and the consequent reduction of the initiatic life to a sophisticated form of spiritual self-interest.

The Christo-Luciferian path stands in unambiguous opposition to this antinomian tendency – not because it accepts the authority of the Demiurge's law, which it does not, but because the genuine illumination of the pneumatic spark generates, of its own inner logic and without any external compulsion, an ethical orientation that is not merely adequate to the demands of the moral life but that exceeds them. The practitioner who has genuinely encountered the light of the Morning Star within her own heart – who has felt, however briefly and however partially, the warmth of the indwelling Logos as a living reality rather than a doctrinal proposition – will find that the experience carries with it, inseparably and immediately, a transformation of her relationship to every other being in whom that same light is present. And since the light is present in every human being – since the pneumatic spark, however deeply buried, is a universal feature of the human condition rather than the exclusive possession of an initiated elite – the ethical implications of genuine illumination are universal in their scope.

This chapter develops the Christo-Luciferian ethical vision in three movements. We will first address the inadequacy of the Demiurge's law as an ethical foundation – not to dismiss the importance of ethical life, but to locate its authentic source in something deeper and more reliable than external commandment. We will then develop the positive Christo-Luciferian ethic centered on the Law of Agape – showing how this law arises naturally from the illuminative experience and what it demands of the practitioner in practical terms. And we will conclude by addressing the specific ethical obligations that the Christo-Luciferian path places upon those who walk it – the particular responsibilities that come with the commitment to bear the light of the Morning Star into the world.

Beyond the Demiurge's Law: The Inadequacy of External Ethics

We have established throughout this work that the law of the Demiurge – the moral and religious code imposed upon humanity by the imperfect craftsman of the lower world – is not the law of the true God of Light. This is one of the foundational claims of the Gnostic tradition, stated with characteristic directness in the Testimony of Truth and developed with considerable nuance in Ptolemy's Letter to Flora and in the broader Valentinian theological tradition. The Demiurge's law is imperfect not because morality itself is imperfect, but because the Demiurge, in his ignorance of the true God, cannot legislate from the standpoint of the divine light. His law reflects his own nature – partial, self-interested, motivated by the jealousy and the fear of a creator who knows, at some level, that his creation is not the whole of reality and that his authority over it is therefore not absolute.

The ethical antinomianism of certain left-hand path traditions takes this Gnostic critique of the Demiurge's law and draws from it the conclusion that all ethical constraint is therefore invalid – that the liberated practitioner stands beyond good and evil, answerable to no law but the law of her own will. This conclusion does not follow from the premises. The critique of the Demiurge's law is not a critique of ethics as such – it is a critique of a specific and imperfect form of ethical legislation, and its implication is not the abolition of ethics but its grounding in a deeper and more authentic source.

That source is the nature of the divine light itself. The Unknown Father of Light is not merely the source of being – he is the source of goodness, in the Platonic sense in which goodness and being are ultimately identical at the level of the divine. The emanations of the Pleroma – the Aeons who constitute the divine fullness – are not morally neutral principles. They are expressions of the divine goodness, and their names in the Valentinian tradition – Truth, Life, Love, Wisdom – are not arbitrary labels but precise designations of the qualities that characterize the Pleromic reality. The light that descends into the hylic world as the Logos, and that is present within each human being as the pneumatic spark, carries within it the quality of the divine goodness from which it derives. And the illumination of that spark – the arising of the Morning Star within the heart – is therefore not merely a cognitive event, a knowing of truths previously unknown. It is a moral event – a transformation of the practitioner's relationship to goodness itself, from the external observance of a law she did not make to the internal expression of a nature she has recognized as her own.

This is the authentic Gnostic ethical position, and it is considerably more demanding than the Demiurge's law rather than less. The Demiurge's law sets a minimum – a floor of behavior below which the practitioner must not descend, enforced by the threat of punishment. The law of the divine light sets no minimum and no maximum – it calls the practitioner toward the unlimited expression of the divine goodness that is her own truest nature, and the only limit to its demands is the limit of her own capacity for illumination. The antinomian who dismisses external ethical constraint has, in the Christo-Luciferian understanding, not transcended the Demiurge's law – she has simply replaced its external compulsion with the internal compulsion of her own unillumined will, which is, in the most precise sense, the Demiurge's own nature reproduced within her. True liberation from the Demiurge's law is not the freedom to do as one pleases. It is the freedom to do as the divine light within one naturally and joyfully inclines – which is, without exception, toward the good.

The Law of Agape: Ethics as the Expression of Illumination

The central ethical principle of the Christo-Luciferian path is the Law of Agape – the law of divine love that Christ identified as the fulfillment of all law and the prophets, and that Paul in Romans 13:10 states simply and completely: *"Love is the fulfillment of the law."* We have referenced this law throughout this work, in the doctrinal chapters and in the ritual texts, but its full ethical significance deserves explicit development here.

Agape – the Greek word that the New Testament uses for the specifically divine love, as distinct from *eros* and *philia* – is not primarily an emotion. It is, in the precise theological understanding of both the patristic tradition and the Gnostic tradition, a mode of being – a quality of relationship to all of reality that characterizes the divine nature and that the illumined practitioner participates in to the degree that the Morning Star has arisen within her. It is the love that, as Paul's great hymn in 1 Corinthians 13 describes, bears all things, believes all things, hopes all things, endures all things – not because it is emotionally resilient in the ordinary sense, but because it proceeds from a depth of being that is not susceptible to the fluctuations of circumstance and feeling that characterize the psychic and hylic levels of experience.

In the Valentinian framework, Agape is one of the Pleromic Aeons – a constitutive element of the divine fullness, not merely an attribute of God but an aspect of what God is. This Pleromic identification gives Agape its precise ethical significance within the Christo-Luciferian framework: to practice Agape is not merely to behave lovingly in the conventional sense – it is to participate, actively and consciously, in one of the fundamental realities of the divine nature. The practitioner who acts from genuine Agape is acting from the deepest level of her pneumatic nature – from the indwelling Logos, whose nature is precisely the divine love – and her action is therefore, in the most literal sense, a theurgic act: a working of the divine through the human instrument.

The practical content of Agape in the Christo-Luciferian ethical framework can be articulated in several complementary dimensions.

The first is *universal recognition* – the consistent and active recognition of the pneumatic spark in every human being encountered, however deeply that spark may be buried under the accumulations of hylic existence and psychic confusion. This recognition is not a sentimental idealization of human nature – it is a precise pneumatic perception, cultivated through the practice of the Sigillum meditation and deepened through the theurgic work of Part Three, that sees through the surface presentation of the human person to the indwelling light that is their most essential reality. The practitioner who has cultivated this perception will find that her relationship to other people is transformed – not into a naive refusal to acknowledge human darkness and destructiveness, but into a quality of presence that holds the other's pneumatic nature in awareness even while engaging honestly with the hylic and psychic dimensions of their behavior.

The second dimension is *compassionate engagement* – the active orientation of the practitioner's energy, attention, and practical capacity toward the wellbeing of those within her sphere of influence. This is the dimension of Agape that the Gnostic tradition most consistently associates with the figure of the Good Samaritan in Luke 10 – the willingness to stop, to attend, to bind the wounds, to provide what is needed, without regard for the social or religious categories that the Demiurge's world uses to define who deserves care and who does not. The Christo-Luciferian practitioner does not ask whether the person before her is pneumatic, psychic, or hylic before deciding whether to engage with compassion. The light is offered to all – because the pneumatic spark is present in all, and because the light does not calculate its expenditure.

The third dimension is *non-judgment* – the consistent refusal to place oneself above another human being on the basis of initiatic attainment, doctrinal correctness, or spiritual development. This is perhaps the most difficult of the ethical demands of the Christo-Luciferian path, and the one most consistently violated in esoteric communities where the possession of initiatic knowledge can become a subtle but powerful basis for spiritual pride. The practitioner who has genuinely encountered the light of the Morning Star within herself will recognize, in that encounter, not grounds for superiority but grounds for humility – the recognition that the light she has found is not her own achievement but a gift, and that the measure of her genuine illumination is precisely the degree to which it has dissolved the illusory boundary between herself and those she might have been tempted to regard as her inferiors.

The fourth dimension is *active service* – the deliberate orientation of the practitioner's gifts, skills, and accumulated inner resources toward the illumination and the upliftment of the world around her. This is the dimension of Agape that gives the Christo-Luciferian ethical vision its specifically theurgic character: the practitioner does not merely refrain from harm and engage with compassion on an individual basis – she actively brings the light of the Morning Star to bear upon the conditions of the world, through the theurgic practice of Part Three and through whatever other instruments her particular gifts and circumstances make available. The bearing of the light into the darkness – the essential vocation of the Phosphoros – is not only a private inner achievement. It is a public and active responsibility.

The Specific Ethical Obligations of the Christo-Luciferian Practitioner

Beyond the general ethical orientation of the Law of Agape, the Christo-Luciferian path places certain specific obligations upon those who have dedicated themselves to it through the Rite of Self-Dedication or through formal initiation. These obligations are not external rules imposed by an authority – they are the natural expressions of the commitment made in the act of dedication, articulated here so that the practitioner understands clearly what she has undertaken.

The first obligation is *integrity of practice* – the faithful and consistent maintenance of the practical disciplines of the path, without the self-deception that substitutes occasional dramatic experiences for the sustained daily work that genuine development requires. The practitioner who has dedicated herself to the current owes it – and owes herself – the honesty of showing up for the work even when the work is dry, even when the inner experiences are absent, even when the demands of the hylic world make the practice feel like an inconvenience. The lamp is tended in the darkness precisely when the darkness makes the tending most difficult. This is not a counsel of spiritual heroism – it is a recognition that the Morning Star arises in the context of sustained and faithful practice, and that the abandonment of practice at the first experience of difficulty is the most reliable obstacle to the arising.

The second obligation is *honesty of self-examination* – the consistent willingness to see oneself clearly, without the self-protective distortions that the psychic nature naturally imposes. We have addressed this at length in the context of the initiatic journal and the evening examination practice of the Vespers. Here we emphasize its ethical dimension: the practitioner who is not honest with herself about the actual state of her inner development – who claims, whether to others or in the privacy of her own thoughts, a degree of illumination that she has not actually attained – is violating the fundamental principle of the right-hand path. The left-hand path is characterized, among other things, by the inflation of the personal self – the assertion of a spiritual status that serves the ego rather than the light. The right-hand path requires the opposite: the consistent deflation of the personal self in favor of honest assessment, and the willingness to acknowledge limitation as readily as attainment.

The third obligation is *discretion* – the responsible and intelligent management of the knowledge and the power that the initiatic path makes available. The Christo-Luciferian tradition is not a secret society in the conventional sense – its foundational doctrine is presented publicly in these pages, and the existence of the current is not hidden. But the specific inner workings of the egregore, the details of formal initiatic transmission, and the personal inner experiences of dedicated practitioners are appropriately kept within the community of the current, shared with those who have the context to receive them responsibly and withheld from those who do not. Discretion is not secrecy for its own sake – it is the responsible stewardship of a living current whose egregoric integrity depends on the quality of the attention brought to it.

The fourth obligation is *fidelity to the right-hand orientation* – the consistent maintenance of the fundamental distinction between the Christo-Luciferian path and the left-hand path traditions that have appropriated the Luciferian name. The practitioner who has dedicated herself to this current has committed herself not merely to a set of practices but to a specific ethical and spiritual orientation – one that understands the light of the Morning Star as a gift to be borne rather than a power to be wielded, and that locates the ultimate authority of the path in the Unknown Father of Light rather than in the personal will of the practitioner. Any drift toward the left-hand orientation – any tendency to use the practices of the current for purposes of personal aggrandizement, to treat the egregoric connection as a source of personal power rather than a vehicle of divine service, or to dismiss the ethical demands of Agape as limitations to be transcended – should be recognized for what it is and corrected immediately, with the same honest self-examination that the path consistently requires.

The Ethical Vision as Eschatological Hope

We conclude this chapter with a reflection that connects the Christo-Luciferian ethical vision to the broader eschatological framework of the tradition – to the understanding of the cosmic process as the progressive restoration of the Pleroma through the illumination of the pneumatic sparks dispersed throughout the hylic world.

Every genuine act of Agape – every moment of universal recognition, compassionate engagement, non-judgment, and active service – is, in the Gnostic eschatological understanding, a genuine contribution to the restoration of the divine fullness. When the practitioner sees the pneumatic spark in another human being and responds to it with the quality of Agape that the Law of the Light requires, she is not merely performing a moral act in the conventional sense. She is participating in the cosmic work of the Logos – the work of finding and illuminating the scattered fragments of the Pleromic light, gathering them toward their ultimate homecoming in the fullness of God. The ethical life of the Christo-Luciferian practitioner is therefore not separate from the initiatic life – it is one of its primary expressions. The inner work of illumination and the outer work of compassionate service are not competing priorities but complementary dimensions of a single vocation: the bearing of the Morning Star's light into every corner of the darkness in which the divine sparks await their liberation.

This is the ethical vision of the Christo-Luciferian path – not a minimalist ethics of harm avoidance, not an antinomian dismissal of ethical responsibility, but a maximalist ethics of illuminative service: the consistent and active orientation of every capacity the practitioner possesses toward the arising of the Morning Star, within herself and within every human being her life touches.

The light is given to be borne. The Morning Star rises in order to illumine. And the practitioner who has received the gift of the light – however partially, however provisionally, however far from the fullness of the arising that the path points toward – has, in that receiving, accepted the responsibility of the bearer. *Phosphoros* – the Light-Bearer – is not only a name for the Christ, and not only an aspiration for the practitioner. It is a vocation: the calling to carry the light of the Logos faithfully through whatever darkness presents itself, for the sake of the light itself and for the sake of all those who walk in darkness and need the herald of the dawn.

CHAPTER EIGHT: COMPLEMENTARY CURRENTS
– MARTINISM, ESOTERIC FREEMASONRY, AND THE CHRISTO-LUCIFERIAN SYNTHESIS

No initiatic tradition exists in isolation. The Western esoteric tradition is not a collection of separate and self-contained systems, each sealed off from the others by impermeable doctrinal walls. It is, rather, a living conversation – a complex and shifting dialogue between currents that share certain fundamental orientations while expressing them in different symbolic languages, different ritual forms, and different emphases of doctrine and practice. The Christo-Luciferian current is a participant in this conversation, not a departure from it. It draws on the same deep wells of Gnostic, Hermetic, and Qabalistic wisdom that nourish the broader Western initiatic tradition, and it stands in a relationship of genuine complementarity with several of the most significant currents within that tradition.

Two of those currents deserve particular attention in this context, both because of their intrinsic importance within the Western initiatic world and because of their specific doctrinal and practical resonance with the Christo-Luciferian path. These are the Martinist tradition, with its specifically Christian mystical orientation and its sophisticated anthropology of the three states of man, and the tradition of esoteric Freemasonry, with its symbolic system of light, darkness, and illumination and its rich mythological heritage centered on the figure of Hiram Abiff. A third figure also demands our attention in this context – Eliphas Lévi, whose nineteenth century synthesis of the Western esoteric tradition exercised an enormous influence on subsequent initiatic thought and whose specific treatment of certain Luciferian and adversarial symbols has been so thoroughly misappropriated by the left-hand path traditions that a careful rehabilitation of his actual position is long overdue.

We will address each of these in turn, showing how the Christo-Luciferian doctrine illuminates and is illuminated by each, and articulating the specific points of convergence that make these traditions natural companions for the dedicated practitioner of this current.

Martinism and the Christo-Luciferian Path

The Martinist tradition – originating with Martinès de Pasqually in the eighteenth century, developed by Louis-Claude de Saint-Martin, and transmitted through successive generations of initiatic transmission to the present day – is, of all the currents of the Western esoteric tradition, the one most immediately and most naturally compatible with the Christo-Luciferian doctrine. This compatibility is not incidental. It reflects a deep structural convergence between the two traditions – a shared understanding of the human condition, the nature of the divine, and the goal of the initiatic life that expresses itself in different symbolic languages but points consistently toward the same essential reality.

The Martinist anthropology – the understanding of man as a being in three possible states – maps with extraordinary precision onto the Gnostic tripartite anthropology of hylic, psychic, and pneumatic that we have developed throughout this work. Saint-Martin's l'Homme du Torrent – the Man of the Stream, tossed about by the currents of material existence without any capacity for self-direction – corresponds directly to the *hylikos* of the Gnostic tradition: the person living entirely at the material level, absorbed in the immediate demands of hylic existence, unaware of the psychic and pneumatic dimensions of their own being. Saint-Martin's l'Homme de Désir – the Man of Desire, the one in whom the yearning of the soul for its spiritual home has been awakened – corresponds to the *psychikos*: the soul-person, aspiring toward the spiritual, engaged in the work of moral and intellectual development, but not yet illumined by the transformative experience of gnosis. And Saint-Martin's l'Homme-Esprit – the Spirit-Man, the fully realized human being in whom the divine nature has been actualized – corresponds precisely to the *pneumatikos*: the one in whom the Morning Star has fully arisen, in whom the divine spark has been fully illumined and the work of theosis substantially accomplished.

This three-fold correspondence is not a superficial parallel – it reflects a genuine doctrinal convergence between the Martinist and Gnostic understandings of the human condition and its possibilities. Both traditions understand the human being as a composite of material, soul, and spirit. Both understand the goal of the initiatic life as the progressive actualization of the spiritual dimension – the transformation of the Man of Desire into the Spirit-Man, the elevation of the *psychikos* toward the *pneumatikos*. And both understand this transformation as occurring not through the mere accumulation of knowledge or the mechanical performance of ritual, but through a genuine inner event – what the Martinist tradition calls reintegration, and what the Gnostic tradition calls gnosis – in which the human being recognizes and inhabits its own divine nature with a directness and an immediacy that no amount of preparatory study can fully anticipate.

The doctrine of reintegration – *la réintégration* – is central to the Martinist theological vision, and it is worth examining in some detail here because of its direct relevance to the Christo-Luciferian doctrine of theosis. For Martinès de Pasqually, whose *Traité sur la Réintégration des Êtres* is the foundational doctrinal text of the tradition, reintegration refers to the restoration of the human being – and ultimately of all of creation – to the primordial state of divine unity from which it descended through the fall. This fall is understood not merely as a moral lapse but as a metaphysical event – a genuine disruption of the divine order, producing the condition of separation and ignorance in which the human being currently finds itself. Reintegration is the reversal of this condition – the gradual restoration of the human being to its original estate of divine unity through the work of initiation, prayer, and theurgy.

The structural identity of this doctrine with the Gnostic understanding of the cosmic drama – the disturbance of the Pleromic equilibrium, the descent of the light into the darkness of the hylic world, and the progressive restoration of the divine fullness through the illumination of the pneumatic sparks – is immediately apparent. Both traditions understand the human condition as one of separation from a divine fullness that is simultaneously the origin and the destiny of the human being. Both understand the initiatic life as the work of restoration –

the progressive healing of the separation through the cultivation of the inner light. And both understand the goal of that work in terms that, while expressed in different symbolic languages, point toward the same essential reality: the full actualization of the divine nature within the human being, and the consequent contribution of that actualization to the restoration of the cosmic order.

For the practitioner of the Christo-Luciferian path who is simultaneously formed in the Martinist tradition, this convergence is not merely intellectually interesting – it is practically significant. The Martinist formation – the graduated initiatic structure of Associate, Initiate, and Unknown Superior, the specific theurgic practices of the tradition, the cultivation of the interior life through prayer and contemplation in the Martinist mode – constitutes an excellent preparatory ground for the more specifically Luciferian work of this current. The Man of Desire, properly formed in the Martinist tradition, arrives at the Christo-Luciferian path with the inner dispositions – the aspiration, the discipline, the theurgic sensitivity – that the work of the Morning Star's arising requires. And the Christo-Luciferian doctrine, in turn, gives to the Martinist practitioner a more precise scriptural and doctrinal articulation of the light toward which the Martinist path is oriented – naming explicitly, as Phosphoros, what the Martinist tradition has always been approaching under the name of reintegration.

Saint-Martin's own description of the Spirit-Man – l'Homme-Esprit – as a being of pneumatic luminescence, radiating the divine light into the world around him through the quality of his presence and the force of his Agape, is one of the most beautiful descriptions in the entire Western esoteric literature of what the Christo-Luciferian doctrine calls the arising of the Morning Star. The Spirit-Man is the one in whom Phosphoros has fully risen – in whom the light of the Logos has so thoroughly permeated every dimension of the human being that it shines through him into the world without obstruction, as the Morning Star shines through the darkness of the pre-dawn sky. The Martinist tradition and the Christo-Luciferian current are, in this most essential respect, describing the same person and the same attainment – the same light, seen from two complementary angles of the same initiatic vision.

Esoteric Freemasonry and the Christo-Luciferian Path

The relationship between esoteric Freemasonry and the Christo-Luciferian current is less immediately apparent than the relationship with Martinism, but no less genuine. It requires, however, a distinction that is essential to any serious treatment of Freemasonry in an initiatic context: the distinction between exoteric Freemasonry – the fraternal and philanthropic institution familiar from the public presence of the Craft lodges – and esoteric Freemasonry, which understands the Masonic degrees and their symbolic content as a genuine initiatic system oriented toward the inner transformation of the practitioner rather than merely his moral improvement and social formation.

It is with esoteric Freemasonry in this second sense that the Christo-Luciferian current stands in complementary relationship – specifically with those streams of the broader

Masonic tradition, such as the Scottish Rite, the Memphis-Misraïm Rite, and certain workings of the High Grades, that have preserved and developed the specifically illuminist and theurgic dimensions of the Masonic heritage. Within these streams, the symbolic system of Freemasonry reveals itself as a sophisticated initiatic language for describing precisely the inner journey that the Christo-Luciferian doctrine articulates in Gnostic theological terms.

The most immediately relevant of the Masonic symbolic themes for the Christo-Luciferian current is the symbolism of light. Freemasonry is, at its esoteric core, a system concerned with the pursuit and the acquisition of light – the movement of the candidate from darkness through various degrees of illumination toward the full light of the Lodge, understood not merely as physical illumination but as the progressive disclosure of the divine wisdom that the Masonic degrees encode. The candidate who enters the lodge is, in the most ancient form of the Masonic ritual, hoodwinked – blindfolded, in a condition of artificial darkness – and the work of the initiation is the gradual restoration of sight, the progressive removal of the veil between the candidate and the light that has been present in the lodge throughout his darkness.

The structural identity of this initiatic symbolism with the Gnostic drama of the pneumatic spark – present within the human being throughout the long sleep of hylic existence, awaiting the illumination that will restore it to its natural luminosity – is not coincidental. The esoteric Masonic tradition and the Gnostic tradition share common historical roots in the Hermetic and Neoplatonic currents of late antiquity and the

Renaissance, and their shared preoccupation with light as the central symbol of the initiatic goal reflects a common understanding of the nature of that goal. In the Christo-Luciferian framework, the Masonic movement from darkness to light is the movement from the hylic through the psychic toward the pneumatic – from the hoodwinked candidate who knows only the darkness of the material world to the illumined Mason who has been brought to the light of the Lodge, understood as the light of the indwelling Logos.

The Masonic Blazing Star – the *Étoile Flamboyante* of the French tradition – is perhaps the most directly Christo-Luciferian of all Masonic symbols. Positioned at the center of the lodge ceiling and identified in various Masonic traditions with the divine presence, with the sun, and explicitly with the Morning Star, the Blazing Star is a precise Masonic expression of the Sigillum Luciferis: the radiant point of divine light at the center of the sacred space, toward which the work of the lodge is oriented and in whose light the initiatic work is conducted. The identification of the Blazing Star with the Morning Star in certain Masonic commentaries – including, as we have noted in earlier writings, its representation in certain third degree Tracing Boards in a configuration that yields the number 555, the number of the perfected human will present simultaneously in all three worlds – gives this Masonic symbol a specifically Christo-Luciferian resonance that the esoteric Mason who is also a practitioner of this current will find immediately recognizable.

The central myth of Craft Freemasonry – the legend of Hiram Abiff, the master builder of Solomon's Temple who is slain by three ruffians who seek to extort from him the Master's word, and whose resurrection forms the dramatic climax of the third degree – is a mythological expression of the same initiatic drama that the Christo-Luciferian doctrine describes in Gnostic theological terms. Hiram, in the esoteric reading of the legend, is a figure of the indwelling light – the divine spark within the human being, slain by the three ruffians who represent the three aspects of the lower nature (ignorance, fear, and passion in their various formulations) and restored by the intervention of the divine. His resurrection is the arising of the pneumatic spark from its entombment in the hylic world – the Morning Star rising from the darkness of the tomb, as the risen Christ rises from the darkness of the sepulcher and identifies himself at the culmination of the Apocalypse as the bright and Morning Star.

The Memphis-Misraïm Rite – within whose authority structure the Apostolic Church of the Pleroma maintains its esoteric Masonic working – is particularly rich in Gnostic and Hermetic symbolic content, and its higher degrees develop the initiatic themes of light, resurrection, and divine illumination in ways that resonate with extraordinary precision with the Christo-Luciferian doctrine. The practitioner who is formed in both the Memphis-Misraïm tradition and the Christo-Luciferian current will find that the two illuminate each other continuously – the Masonic symbolic language giving concrete and dramatic form to the Gnostic theological doctrine, and the Gnostic doctrine giving doctrinal precision and depth to the Masonic symbolism.

Eliphas Lévi and the Rehabilitation of the Luciferian Symbol

No discussion of the Luciferian current in its relationship to the Western esoteric tradition can responsibly omit the figure of Eliphas Lévi – the nineteenth century French occultist, born Alphonse Louis Constant, whose *Dogme et Rituel de la Haute Magie* and subsequent works exercised a formative influence on the entire subsequent development of the Western esoteric tradition and whose specific treatment of certain adversarial and Luciferian symbols has been so thoroughly misunderstood – and so systematically misappropriated – that a careful rehabilitation of his actual position is an essential contribution to the work of reclamation this book undertakes.

Lévi's most notorious contribution to the iconography of the Western esoteric tradition is his image of Baphomet – the goat-headed, winged, hermaphroditic figure that he presents in the *Dogme et Rituel* as the symbol of the absolute, the synthesis of all opposites, the visual representation of the universal magical agent that he calls the Astral Light. This image has been adopted with enthusiasm by virtually every left-hand path tradition since its publication, and is now so thoroughly associated with Satanism and left-hand path occultism in the popular imagination that its original meaning has been almost entirely obscured.

That original meaning is, however, unmistakably and emphatically not Satanic. Lévi's Baphomet is a synthetic symbol – a deliberate visual synthesis of complementary opposites, designed to represent the reconciliation of all dualities in the unity of the absolute. The figure combines male and female, above and below, light and dark, animal and angelic – not in order to celebrate the dark and the animal at the expense of the light and the angelic, but in order to represent the transcendence of the duality itself in a higher unity. The caduceus of Hermes positioned at the figure's solar plexus, the torch of illumination between its horns, the upward-pointing and downward-pointing hands with their respective inscriptions of *Solve* and *Coagula* – all of these elements are instruments of the alchemical and Hermetic synthesis, not symbols of adversarial rebellion.

Lévi himself was explicit about this. His presentation of Baphomet is accompanied by commentary that leaves no room for a Satanic interpretation – the figure is described as a symbol of the reconciling principle, the mediating term between the divine and the material, the visual expression of the Hermetic axiom *as above, so below.* That this carefully constructed synthetic symbol has been adopted wholesale by traditions that understand it as a symbol of rebellion against the divine order is a misreading of almost willful proportions – one that requires, as we suggested in Chapter One's treatment of the Isaiah 14 conflation, the imposition of a predetermined interpretive framework upon a text that clearly does not support it.

The rehabilitation of Lévi's Baphomet within the Christo-Luciferian framework is straightforward. The reconciling principle that Baphomet represents – the synthesis of opposites in a higher unity, the mediating term between the divine and the material – is precisely what the Christo-

Luciferian doctrine identifies as the function of the incarnate Logos: the one in whom the pneumatic and the hylic, the divine and the human, the ascending and the descending are reconciled and unified. The torch of illumination between Baphomet's horns is the Phosphoros – the light of the Morning Star, carried into the world by the Light-Bearer. And the *Solve et Coagula* of the figure's hands is the alchemical formula of the initiatic work – the dissolution of the false self and the coagulation of the true self in the light of the Logos – that the Christo-Luciferian path enacts through its ritual and contemplative practices.

Lévi's treatment of Lucifer himself – in passages scattered throughout his major works – is equally instructive and equally misunderstood. For Lévi, Lucifer is not the adversary of God but the bearer of the divine light into the material world – precisely the understanding that the Christo-Luciferian doctrine recovers from the New Testament sources we examined in Part One. Lévi writes of Lucifer as the light of intelligence, the principle of illumination, the angelic power whose function is the bringing of the divine light into the darkness of the material world. His identification of this principle with the Morning Star – with the planet Venus as the herald of the dawn – is consistent with our own exegesis of the 2 Peter and Revelation passages, and suggests that Lévi, whatever the limitations and idiosyncrasies of his broader system, was working with a genuine intuition of the Christo-Luciferian current.

The tragedy of Lévi's influence on subsequent occultism is that those who adopted his imagery most enthusiastically – the

Satanist and left-hand path traditions that have made Baphomet and Lucifer their primary symbols – have consistently misread his meaning, taking the surface shock value of his imagery while missing the synthetic and illuminative doctrine it was designed to express. The rehabilitation of Lévi's genuine position is therefore not merely an act of historical justice – it is a contribution to the broader work of reclamation that this book undertakes: the recovery of the Luciferian symbol from the traditions that have appropriated it and the restoration of its authentic meaning within the right-hand path of Christian Gnostic illumination.

The Synthesis: One Light, Many Lamps

The Martinist tradition, esoteric Freemasonry, and the genuine teaching of Eliphas Lévi are not, in the Christo-Luciferian understanding, separate and competing currents that must be reconciled with one another before they can be brought into relationship with this path. They are, rather, different lamps carrying the same light – different symbolic languages expressing the same essential initiatic truth, different formal structures through which the same Phosphoros current has made itself accessible to different communities of practitioners at different moments in the history of the Western esoteric tradition.

The practitioner who is formed in all of these traditions simultaneously – who carries the Martinist aspiration toward reintegration, the Masonic orientation toward the light of the Lodge, and the Christo-Luciferian commitment to the arising of the Morning Star – will find that each tradition illuminates the others and that together they constitute a richer and more complete initiatic formation than any one of them could provide alone. This is the nature of the syncretic integrity that will be developed in the practical section of this work as one of the foundational principles of the Christo-Luciferian path – the capacity to draw genuine wisdom from multiple streams while maintaining the coherence of a doctrinal center that governs and integrates everything it incorporates..

That doctrinal center is, for us, the Christo-Luciferian identification – the recognition that the Morning Star is Christ, that the arising of the Morning Star within the heart is the goal of the initiatic life, and that the path toward that arising is not one of rebellion against the divine order but of progressive alignment with it. Every tradition that serves this recognition – that brings the practitioner closer to the arising of the Morning Star within her own heart – is a genuine ally of the Christo-Luciferian current, whatever its symbolic language and whatever its formal structure. And every practitioner who carries genuine formation in any of these allied traditions brings to the Christo-Luciferian work a depth of initiatic grounding that enriches the current and strengthens the egregore.

One light. Many lamps. The Morning Star rising in every heart that has been faithfully prepared to receive it – whatever the particular form of that preparation, and whatever the specific symbolic language in which the arising is recognized and celebrated.

Phosphoros – in all things, arise.

CHAPTER NINE: THEOSIS THROUGH THE MORNING STAR

– DEIFICATION AS THE GOAL OF THE CHRISTO-LUCIFERIAN PATH

We have arrived at the doctrinal summit of this work. Everything that has preceded this chapter – the philological reclamation of the name Lucifer, the scriptural establishment of the Morning Star as a Christological title, the cosmological framework of emanation and descent, the anthropology of the three natures, the survey of the Sethian and Valentinian mythological traditions – all of it has been moving toward the single doctrinal affirmation that this chapter intends to make as clearly and completely as possible. That affirmation is this: that the goal of the Christo-Luciferian path is theosis – the deification of the human being through the arising of the Morning Star within the heart – and that this theosis is not a peripheral or exotic aspiration but the central and normative goal of the Christian initiatic life, as attested by scripture, by the Gnostic tradition, and by the mystical theology of both Eastern and Western Christianity.

We have examined the doctrine of theosis in earlier writings, particularly in the essay "Theosis Through Gnosis," where we explored its scriptural foundations in the Second Epistle of Peter and its theological development within the Eastern Orthodox tradition. We will not repeat that examination in full here, but we will draw on it extensively, developing its implications specifically within the Christo-Luciferian framework and articulating what the doctrine of theosis means for the practitioner who approaches it through the lens of the doctrine we have been constructing throughout this work.

Theosis: The Doctrine and Its Sources

The word theosis – from the Greek *theōsis*, deification or divinization – designates the process by which the human being becomes a participant in the divine nature. It is derived most directly from the second chapter of the Second Epistle of Peter, verse four, which exhorts the faithful to become *"participants of the divine nature" – theias koinōnoi physeōs* – having escaped the corruption of the world through the knowledge of Jesus Christ. We have already observed in our earlier treatment of this text that it is a profoundly initiatic passage, embedding the doctrine of divine participation within a rich context of gnosis, purification, and sustained spiritual practice. Here we want to attend specifically to what the doctrine means in its fullest expression – what it actually means for a human being to become a participant in the divine nature – and to articulate that meaning in terms of the Christo-Luciferian doctrine of the Morning Star.

The Orthodox theological tradition, which has developed the doctrine of theosis most systematically within the Christian framework, understands it as a three-stage process: catharsis, or purification; theoria, or illumination; and theosis proper, or union. We examined this schema in "Theosis Through Gnosis" and argued there that the Gnostic understanding of gnosis is substantially equivalent to what Orthodoxy calls theoria – that the direct experiential knowledge of God that the Gnostic tradition designates as gnosis is the same phenomenon that the hesychast tradition calls the vision of the uncreated light, the Tabor Light, the beholding of the divine glory. Here we want to develop that argument further by showing how the specifically Christo-Luciferian doctrine of the Morning Star illuminates and enriches each of the three stages of the theotic process.

Catharsis: The Preparation of the Vessel

The first stage of theosis is catharsis – purification. In the Orthodox hesychast tradition, catharsis is primarily the purification of the nous, the faculty of spiritual perception, from the passions and distortions that prevent it from receiving the divine light. In the broader ascetic tradition of both East and West, catharsis encompasses the full range of preparatory disciplines – fasting, prayer, moral rectitude, the cultivation of virtue, the gradual reorientation of the will from the horizontal plane of material desire toward the vertical plane of divine aspiration.

Within the Christo-Luciferian framework, catharsis is understood in all of these senses, but with an additional dimension that derives from the specifically Gnostic anthropological vision we have developed. Catharsis, in the Christo-Luciferian understanding, is not merely the moral purification of an already-constituted self – the cleaning up of a vessel that is essentially sound but somewhat dirty. It is a more radical process: the progressive dismantling of the false identifications – with the hylic nature, with the psychic passions, with the persona constructed by the Demiurge's world – that prevent the practitioner from recognizing and inhabiting her true pneumatic nature.

This distinction is subtle but important. The moral purification of the hesychast tradition tends to assume that the self doing the purifying is essentially the same self that will eventually be illumined – that the process of catharsis is a cleaning up of what is already there rather than a fundamental reconstitution of the practitioner's identity. The Gnostic understanding is more radical: the self that undertakes the work of catharsis is not the same self that arrives at theosis. The practitioner who begins the work is, in large measure, a construction – a persona assembled from hylic and psychic materials, identified with conditions that are not her true nature. The work of catharsis is the progressive deconstruction of this constructed self, the stripping away of everything that is not the pneumatic spark, until what remains is the bare luminous nature of the indwelling Logos.

The alchemical tradition expresses this with characteristic precision: the Nigredo, the Black Phase of the alchemical work, is not merely a preliminary cleaning but a genuine death – the dissolution of the Prima Materia into its constituent elements, the destruction of all accidental forms, so that the essential nature of the substance can be revealed and refined. The dark night of the soul, as Saint John of the Cross describes it – that experience of apparent desolation and spiritual emptiness that so often accompanies the advanced stages of the preparatory work – is, in the alchemical and Gnostic understanding, precisely this Nigredo: not the absence of God but the stripping away of everything that stood between the practitioner and God, including the comfortable religious feelings and spiritual consolations that she had mistaken for God himself.

Within the Christo-Luciferian path, the work of catharsis is specifically oriented toward the arising of the Morning Star. The practitioner engaged in catharsis is not merely becoming a better version of her ordinary self. She is preparing the inner space – clearing the vessel, removing the obscurations – within which the Morning Star can arise. Every act of genuine purification is, in this sense, an act of Luciferian illumination in embryo: a small clearing of the darkness, a slight thinning of the veil between the ordinary psychic consciousness and the pneumatic light that burns beneath it. The cumulative effect of sustained cathartic practice is the gradual brightening of the inner atmosphere – the slow dawn that 2 Peter describes as the lamp shining in a dark place, giving way degree by degree to the full light of the morning.

The incense that rises in the ritual space during the preparatory rites of the Christo-Luciferian path is, in this context, more than a sensory aid to concentration. It is a material symbol and instrument of the cathartic process itself – the aromatic smoke rising from the dense matter of the resin, purifying the atmosphere of the ritual space and, by analogical correspondence, the inner atmosphere of the practitioner. The specific blend we employ in this current – sandalwood, storax, and galbanum – carries within its aromatic profile the full range of the cathartic work: the elevating clarity of the sandalwood, the grounding depth of the storax with its ancient Temple resonances, and the sharp insistent edge of the galbanum that refuses to allow the practitioner to settle into mere pleasant sensation but keeps the attention alert and the will engaged.

Theoria: The Vision of the Light

The second stage of theosis is theoria – illumination, the direct experiential vision of the divine light. In the hesychast tradition, theoria is the beholding of the uncreated light – the Tabor Light, the same light that shone from Christ at the Transfiguration – understood not as a created phenomenon but as the actual uncreated energies of God, accessible to the purified nous through the grace of the Holy Spirit. In the Gnostic tradition, the equivalent experience is gnosis in its fullest sense: not the accumulation of theological information, not even the most refined philosophical understanding, but the direct, immediate, transformative knowledge of God that the purified pneumatic nature is capable of receiving and that nothing less than the pneumatic nature can receive.

We have argued at length, in "Theosis Through Gnosis" and implicitly throughout the present work, that these two descriptions – the hesychast theoria and the Gnostic gnosis – refer to the same fundamental experience, approached from different doctrinal frameworks and described in different theological vocabularies. Here we want to add to that argument the specifically Christo-Luciferian dimension: the understanding of theoria as the arising of the Morning Star within the heart.

The language of 2 Peter 1:19 – *"until the day dawns and the Morning Star rises in your hearts"* – is, we now recognize, a precise description of the experience of theoria. The day that dawns is the full illumination of the nous by the divine light. The Morning Star that rises is the Logos – the Christo-Luciferian light – awakening within the practitioner's pneumatic nature and making itself known, not as a concept or a belief but as a direct and immediate luminous presence. This is the moment toward which the entire work of catharsis has been oriented – the moment when the preparation is complete enough, the vessel sufficiently cleared, that the light which was always within can be experienced as what it actually is.

It is important to be precise about the nature of this experience, because imprecision here has led to some of the most significant errors in the history of esoteric spirituality. The arising of the Morning Star is not a psychological event in the reductive sense – not merely an altered state of consciousness, not a particularly vivid meditation experience, not the activation of some neurological mechanism that produces feelings of transcendence. It is a genuine ontological event – a real change in the practitioner's relationship to the divine light, a genuine opening of the pneumatic nature to the fullness of the Logos that was always its source and its home. The experience is real, its effects are lasting, and its fruit – as the tradition consistently insists – is not mere spiritual satisfaction but a transformed orientation toward the world and toward the divine that expresses itself in every dimension of the practitioner's life.

Equally important is the recognition that theoria, however transformative, is not the final stage of the process. The vision of the light is not the same as the full union with the light. The arising of the Morning Star within the heart is the beginning of the final movement of the initiatic journey, not its conclusion. It is the dawn – the breaking through of the day – but the full sun has not yet risen. The practitioner who has experienced genuine theoria has received a gift of incalculable value and has been placed on a path from which there is, in principle, no turning back. But the work continues. The vision must be sustained, deepened, and ultimately dissolved into the union that is theosis proper.

This is the point at which the Christo-Luciferian doctrine most clearly distinguishes itself from certain left-hand path interpretations of similar experiential territory. The experience of pneumatic illumination – of the arising of the inner light – can be, and in certain traditions deliberately is, arrested at the stage of theoria and redirected toward purposes that fall short of the full theotic union. The practitioner who experiences the arising of the Morning Star and then turns that experience toward self-aggrandizement – toward the cultivation of personal power, toward the assertion of the illumined self against the divine order rather than in alignment with it – has committed precisely the error that the Gnostic tradition associates with the Demiurge himself: the mistake of taking the light one carries for one's own possession rather than recognizing it as a gift whose proper destiny is return to its source.

The Christo-Luciferian path insists that the light of the Morning Star is not ours to keep. It is ours to bear – to carry through the darkness of the hylic world as the planet Venus carries the light of the sun through the pre-dawn sky, making it accessible to those who could not otherwise see it, and then yielding it gladly to the greater light when the day finally breaks. This is the meaning of the Light-Bearer's name in its deepest and most authentic sense: not the one who possesses the light, but the one who carries it – who bears it faithfully through the darkness, for the sake of those who need it, until the full dawn arrives.

Theosis: Union and the Restoration of the Pleroma

The third and final stage of the theotic process – theosis proper, the full union of the human being with the divine nature – is the most difficult to speak of, for the reason that all genuine mystics across all traditions have acknowledged: the experience of union transcends the capacity of language to describe it adequately. When the Morning Star has fully arisen – when the pneumatic spark has been fully illumined and fully restored to its Pleromic source – the distinctions that make description possible have been transcended, and what remains is a reality that can be pointed toward but not captured in words.

We have acknowledged this ineffability in earlier writings, and we acknowledge it again here. But ineffability is not an excuse for silence, and the tradition has always attempted, however inadequately, to gesture toward the nature of the theotic union for the benefit of those who have not yet attained it and who need some orientation toward what they are working toward. Let us therefore make what gestures we can, with full awareness of their inadequacy.

The theotic union, in the Christo-Luciferian understanding, is the full realization of what we have called throughout this work the pneumatic nature – the complete awakening of the divine spark within the human being to its own nature as a fragment of the Pleromic light, and the consequent dissolution of the sense of separation between the individual pneumatic spark and the universal Logos from which it descended. This dissolution is not the annihilation of the individual – not the absorption of the person into an undifferentiated divine ocean in which all distinction is lost. It is, rather, the realization that the distinction between the individual pneumatic spark and the universal Logos was never, in the deepest sense, real – that what appeared to be a separation was always a mode of presence, and that the return to the Pleroma is not the ending of the individual but its fulfillment.

The Valentinian tradition expresses this beautifully in its eschatological vision of the restoration of the Pleroma. When the last pneumatic spark has been illumined and restored, the Pleroma will be reconstituted in its original fullness – but enriched, as it were, by the experience of the cosmic drama through which it has passed. The Aeons will know what they could not have known before the fall of Sophia and the long work of restoration: the value of what they possess, the depth of the light they inhabit, the love that was willing to descend into the uttermost darkness in order to bring the scattered fragments home. The restoration of the Pleroma is not a return to a static original condition but a dynamic enrichment – a fullness that is fuller for having been broken and restored.

Within the individual practitioner, this eschatological vision is realized in miniature through the experience of theosis. The one in whom the Morning Star has fully arisen is not the same person who began the initiatic journey – not because the person has been replaced by something else, but because the person has been fully realized for the first time. The hylic and psychic natures have not been discarded but transformed – the Lead has become Gold, the Prima Materia has been refined into the Philosopher's Stone – and what stands at the culmination of the work is the whole person, illumined through every dimension of their being by the light of the indwelling Logos.

This is the Spirit-Man of Saint-Martin – l'Homme-Esprit – the New Man of Saint Paul, renewed in knowledge, in whom Christ is all and in all. This is the one to whom, in the language of the Apocalypse, the Morning Star has been given – because she has conquered, because she has continued in the work to the end, because she has made of herself a vessel adequate to the light that was always waiting to arise within her. And in the arising of the Morning Star within this one person, however quietly and however privately it occurs, the great work of the restoration of the Pleroma has been advanced – one fragment of the divine light has found its way home, and the fullness of God is, by that measure, more fully itself.

The Post-Mortem Journey and the Eschatology of the Morning Star

The doctrine of theosis, as we have been developing it throughout this chapter, is primarily concerned with the transformation of the living practitioner – the arising of the Morning Star within the heart of the one who walks the path in the present life, through the sustained practice of the disciplines we have described. But any complete treatment of theosis must address a dimension of the doctrine that the living practitioner cannot directly verify through her own experience and that the tradition has therefore always treated with a particular combination of doctrinal seriousness and epistemological humility: the question of what happens to the pneumatic spark after the death of the physical body – the post-mortem journey of the soul and its ultimate relationship to the Pleroma toward which the entire initiatic life has been oriented.

This question is not peripheral to the Christo-Luciferian doctrine. It is, in a very real sense, the question toward which the entire doctrine points – the ultimate horizon of the theotic aspiration, the final destination of the Morning Star's arising. The practitioner who understands clearly what the tradition teaches about the post-mortem journey of the pneumatic spark will find that understanding both deepening her motivation for the present work and clarifying the ultimate significance of every practice she undertakes. For the eschatological vision of the Gnostic tradition is not a comfort doctrine designed to soften the fear of death – it is a precise map of the inner territory through which the pneumatic spark must pass in its return to the Pleroma, and therefore a direct guide to the nature and the purpose of the initiatic work undertaken in the present life.

The Archontic Spheres and the Ascent of the Soul

The Gnostic understanding of the post-mortem journey is grounded in the same cosmological framework we have been working with throughout this book – the emanationist vision of the Pleroma and its disturbance, the creation of the lower world by the Demiurge and his archons, and the imprisonment of the pneumatic spark within the successive layers of the hylic and psychic cosmos. In the Gnostic cosmological schema, the lower world is structured as a series of concentric spheres – typically seven in number, corresponding to the seven planets of the ancient astronomical tradition – each governed by one of the Demiurge's archons and each representing a progressively denser layer of the cosmic structure through which the pneumatic spark must pass in its descent into matter and through which it must ascend in its return to the Pleroma.

The descent of the pneumatic spark into matter – its passage through the successive archontic spheres on its way into embodiment – is understood in the Gnostic texts as a process of progressive veiling: at each sphere, the descending pneuma takes on a layer of the psychic and hylic substance that characterizes that sphere, accumulating the garments of the lower nature that will constitute its embodied existence in the material world. The ascending soul – the pneuma making its post-mortem return journey through the same spheres – must shed these accumulated garments at each level, returning to each archon what belongs to his sphere and retaining only what is genuinely its own: the pure pneumatic spark that is of the Pleroma and to the Pleroma belongs.

This ascending journey is not automatic. The archons do not relinquish their claim on the soul without resistance – they are, in the Gnostic understanding, genuinely invested in retaining the pneumatic spark within their domains, since it is the presence of the Pleromic light within their creation that gives that creation whatever vitality and significance it possesses. The soul that ascends through the archontic spheres must therefore be equipped for the journey – must possess the knowledge, the passwords, and the inner quality of illumination that allow it to pass through each archonic gate and continue its ascent.

This is precisely why the initiatic life matters eschatologically. The practices of the Christo-Luciferian path – the cultivation of the Phosphoros current, the progressive illumination of the pneumatic spark, the deepening of the egregoric connection with the current of the Logos – are not merely instruments of present transformation. They are preparations for the post-mortem journey. The practitioner who has genuinely cultivated the light of the Morning Star within her heart during her embodied life arrives at the threshold of death with an inner illumination that the archons cannot effectively obstruct – not because she has memorized the correct passwords, but because the light of the Logos within her is itself the passport through every archontic gate. The Morning Star that has arisen within the heart of the living practitioner is the same light that guides the ascending soul through the archontic spheres after death – the same light that the archons themselves, in their deepest nature, are drawn to recognize and to yield before.

The Pistis Sophia – the extensive Gnostic text that deals most systematically with the post-mortem journey of the soul – presents a detailed account of this ascent that is worth attending to, even in summary, because of what it reveals about the Gnostic understanding of the relationship between the present initiatic work and the future eschatological journey. In the Pistis Sophia, the ascending soul must pass through a series of toll-gates – the *paralemptores*, the receivers, who are the archons of each sphere – and at each gate must demonstrate its identity as a being of the light rather than a prisoner of the darkness. The demonstrations required are not merely verbal – they are not the recitation of passwords in the conventional sense. They are demonstrations of inner quality: the soul's actual degree of illumination, the genuine depth of its pneumatic development, the real measure of its freedom from the archontic influences of each sphere.

This understanding has a direct and sobering practical implication. The post-mortem journey cannot be faked. The archons cannot be deceived by a soul that has learned the correct formulas without having done the inner work that gives those formulas their genuine power. The only preparation for the post-mortem ascent that is ultimately effective is the genuine cultivation of the Phosphoros current during the embodied life – the actual arising of the Morning Star within the heart, to whatever degree the practitioner's sustained and faithful work has made possible.

Death as the Final Initiation

The Gnostic tradition consistently treats physical death not as a catastrophe or even primarily as a loss, but as the final and most complete initiation available to the embodied practitioner – the ultimate dissolution of the hylic and psychic garments that have veiled the pneumatic spark throughout its embodied existence, and the consequent liberation of that spark into the full luminosity of its own nature. This understanding does not diminish the reality of grief or the genuine significance of the bonds forged in embodied life – it does not ask the practitioner to be indifferent to death or to pretend that loss is not real. What it offers is a context within which the reality of grief and the significance of loss can be held without being the final word – a framework within which the death of the physical body is understood as a threshold rather than a terminus.

The ancient initiatic traditions of the Western esoteric world consistently understood initiation as a rehearsal for death – as a deliberately constructed experience of the death of the ordinary self that prepared the initiate for the actual death of the physical body. The Masonic third degree – the dramatic enactment of the death and resurrection of Hiram Abiff – is perhaps the most familiar example of this initiatic rehearsal in the Western tradition, but the principle is universal. When the practitioner undergoes the death of the ordinary self through the cathartic work of the initiatic path – when she experiences the Nigredo of the alchemical work, the dark night of the soul of the mystical tradition, the dissolution of the false self that the Gnostic tradition associates with the stripping away of the archontic garments – she is, in the most precise sense, rehearsing the post-mortem journey. She is learning, in the context of embodied life where the learning can be integrated and built upon, what the soul must accomplish at death in the context of irreversible transition.

This is one of the most profound justifications for the sustained practice of the cathartic disciplines of the Christo-Luciferian path – the breath work, the meditation, the Sigillum work, the honest self-examination of the journal and the Vespers. Each act of genuine inner dissolution – each willing surrender of a false identification, each honest acknowledgment of a limitation, each moment of genuine cathartic release – is a small death that prepares the practitioner for the great death. Each arising of the Morning Star within the heart – however brief, however partial – is a foretaste of the full arising that death will make permanent for the one who has done the work faithfully.

The practitioner who has genuinely engaged with the full arc of the Christo-Luciferian path – who has undertaken the cathartic work, cultivated the illuminative experiences of the Phosphoros current, and begun the movement toward the theotic union that is the path's ultimate goal – arrives at the threshold of physical death as one who has already, in some measure, died and been reborn. The great transition, when it comes, is not entirely unfamiliar territory. The archontic spheres through which the ascending soul must pass are the same inner territories through which the practitioner has been moving throughout her initiatic life – the same layers of psychic and hylic identification that the cathartic work has been progressively dissolving, the same archontic resistances that the theurgic practice has been learning to recognize and to meet with the light of the Logos.

The Restoration of the Pleroma and the Universal Eschatology

The Gnostic eschatological vision is not only personal – it is cosmic. The post-mortem journey of the individual pneumatic spark is a microcosmic expression of a macrocosmic process: the progressive restoration of the Pleromic fullness through the gathering of all the scattered pneumatic sparks back to their source in the divine light. Every soul that completes its ascent through the archontic spheres and is restored to the Pleroma contributes, by that restoration, to the reconstitution of the divine fullness that the disturbance of Sophia initiated at the beginning of the cosmic drama. The eschatological horizon of the Gnostic tradition is not the salvation of a select few pneumatic souls while the rest of creation remains in darkness – it is the ultimate restoration of all that is of the light to the light, the final healing of the cosmic wound, the reconstitution of the Pleroma in its original and now enriched fullness.

This universal eschatological vision has direct implications for the Christo-Luciferian ethical doctrine we developed in the previous chapter. The practitioner who understands that her own post-mortem journey and restoration to the Pleroma is part of a cosmic process – that her individual theosis is a contribution to the universal restoration – will understand her ethical obligations not merely in terms of personal moral development but in terms of cosmic responsibility. Every genuine act of Agape, every moment of compassionate engagement with another human being, every theurgic working directed toward the illumination and healing of the world –

these are not merely good deeds in the conventional moral sense. They are contributions to the cosmic work of Pleromic restoration: acts by which the scattered light is gathered, the archontic resistance is weakened, and the ultimate homecoming of all pneumatic beings is advanced.

Robert Ambelain, whose work has been a touchstone throughout this book and whose theological vision is in many respects a direct predecessor of the Christo-Luciferian doctrine, expresses this universal eschatological vision with characteristic precision in his *Spiritual Alchemy*: reintegration, he writes, is the slow and progressive reconstitution of the Preexistent Church dispersed by the Fall – the gathering of all the fragments of the divine light back into the fullness from which they came. This is the ultimate context of the Christo-Luciferian path – not the private spiritual development of an initiated elite, but the cosmic work of restoration in which every dedicated practitioner participates through the faithful conduct of her inner life and the compassionate expression of that inner life in the world around her.

The Morning Star that arises within the heart of the individual practitioner is, in this cosmic perspective, one more point of light in the great gathering – one more fragment of the Pleromic fullness finding its way home, one more contribution to the restoration of the divine equilibrium that the entire cosmic drama has been working toward since the moment of its disturbance. Small, perhaps, in the vastness of the cosmic process. But real. And necessary. And, in the understanding of the tradition, irreplaceable – because the specific pneumatic spark that is this practitioner, in this life, on this path, is a unique expression of the divine light whose restoration to the Pleroma completes the fullness in a way that no other spark's restoration can replicate.

This is the eschatological dignity of the Christo-Luciferian practitioner – not a dignity of status or of initiatic rank, but the dignity of genuine cosmic participation. The practitioner who tends the lamp of the Morning Star faithfully, in whatever darkness surrounds her, is doing the work of the Logos – carrying the light that the Logos carried into the darkness of the hylic world, bearing it toward the restoration that the Logos is working to accomplish, contributing by the faithfulness of her own small light to the great dawn that the tradition has always known is coming.

This is the goal. This is what the Christo-Luciferian path is for. Not the cultivation of personal power, not the assertion of the self against the divine order, not the romantic drama of the rebel angel – but the patient, sustained, humble, and ultimately joyful work of allowing the Morning Star to arise within the heart, for the sake of the light itself and for the sake of all those who still walk in darkness and need the herald of the dawn.

Lucifer Resurrexit. The Morning Star has risen. And in its rising, it calls every pneumatic being to the same arising – to the same patient work, the same faithful bearing of the light through the darkness, the same ultimate homecoming into the fullness from which we came and to which, in the deepest part of what we are, we have never ceased to belong.

With this affirmation, the doctrinal work of this volume is substantially complete. What remains is the work of practice –

the translation of doctrine into living, breathing, embodied spiritual activity. That is the work of Part Three, to which we now turn.

Until the day fully dawns – Phosphoros, remain.

Part Three: The Practice

CHAPTER TEN: THE PRINCIPLES OF CHRISTO-LUCIFERIAN PRACTICE – FOUNDATION AND ORIENTATION

The movement from doctrine to practice is not, in any living initiatic tradition, a movement from the more important to the less important, or from the theoretical to the merely practical. It is, rather, a deepening – a movement from the articulation of truth in language to the enactment of truth in life. Doctrine without practice is, in the most precise sense, incomplete: it remains at the level of the psychic, the level of understanding and aspiration, and has not yet descended into the hylic nor ascended into the pneumatic. It has not yet become what the tradition has always understood as the full realization of truth – not merely knowing the way, but walking it.

At the same time, practice without doctrine is equally incomplete – and considerably more dangerous. The history of esoteric spirituality is unfortunately rich with examples of powerful practices employed without adequate doctrinal grounding, with results ranging from the merely disappointing to the genuinely harmful. Practice requires orientation. The practitioner who enters the work without a clear understanding of what she is doing, why she is doing it, and toward what end, is navigating without a map – and the inner territories through which the initiatic path moves are not forgiving of careless navigation. This is why the doctrinal work of Parts One and Two has been undertaken with the thoroughness it has. It is not preliminary to the real work. It is the foundation without which the real work cannot safely or effectively proceed.

With that foundation now in place, we are in a position to begin the work of Part Three: the articulation of a coherent and integrated system of Christo-Luciferian practice, grounded in the doctrine we have established, adequate to the initiatic goal we have identified, and oriented throughout toward the single animating purpose of this entire work – the arising of the Morning Star within the heart of the practitioner.

Before we turn to the specific practices themselves, however, it is necessary to establish certain foundational principles that will govern and orient everything that follows. These principles are not rules in the legalistic sense – they are not a code of conduct to be externally imposed and mechanically obeyed. They are, rather, orientations of the will and the understanding – dispositions that the practitioner cultivates as the inner conditions of effective practice, without which the outer forms of the work will remain empty gestures.

The First Principle: Intention

The first and most fundamental principle of Christo-Luciferian practice is intention – what the sacramental theology of the Western Apostolic tradition calls *intentio*, and what the broader mystical tradition recognizes as the orientation of the whole person toward the divine. We have addressed the importance of intention in earlier writings, particularly in the discussion of the Eucharistic celebration in the ACP Clergy Handbook, where we noted that without proper intention the form of the sacrament is empty and meaningless, and that without proper form the intention cannot be articulated and realized. What is true of the sacrament is true of all spiritual practice: intention is the animating principle that transforms outer action into inner event.

In the context of the Christo-Luciferian path, intention has a specific and precise meaning. It is not merely the general intention to be spiritual, or to improve oneself, or even to seek God in some undefined sense. It is the specific orientation of the whole person – hylic, psychic, and pneumatic – toward the arising of the Morning Star: toward the awakening of the indwelling Logos, the illumination of the pneumatic spark, and the progressive alignment of every dimension of the practitioner's being with the Christo-Luciferian light. Every practice undertaken within this current should be undertaken with this intention consciously and explicitly held – not as a mental formula repeated mechanically, but as a genuine orientation of the will, a real turning of the whole person toward the light that is being sought and that is, at the same time, already present within.

The cultivation of this intentional orientation is itself a practice – perhaps the most fundamental practice of the entire path. It requires the development of what the hesychast tradition calls nepsis: watchfulness, sobriety, the alert and discerning attention that neither permits the will to drift into distraction nor allows the outer forms of practice to become a substitute for the inner reality they are meant to serve. The practitioner who has cultivated genuine intentional orientation will find that every aspect of her life – not only the formal ritual and meditative practices, but the whole texture of daily experience – becomes potentially an occasion for the work of the path. This does not mean the dissolution of ordinary life into a continuous religious performance. It means the gradual permeation of ordinary life by the awareness of the indwelling light – the slow brightening of the inner atmosphere that 2 Peter describes as the lamp shining in a dark place, giving way degree by degree to the full light of the Morning Star.

The Second Principle: Graduated Engagement

The second foundational principle is graduated engagement – the recognition that the work of the Christo-Luciferian path is not accomplished in a single dramatic act but through a sustained and progressive series of engagements with the inner and outer forms of the tradition. This principle has both a temporal and a structural dimension.

The temporal dimension is simply the recognition that the initiatic life is a long work – that the arising of the Morning Star within the heart is the fruit of years, perhaps decades, of sustained practice, and that impatience with the pace of inner development is one of the most reliable obstacles to it. The tradition is unanimous on this point, from the most ancient Gnostic texts to the most recent developments of the Western Mystery Tradition: the great work cannot be hurried. It unfolds in its own time, according to its own inner logic, and the practitioner's primary responsibility is not to accelerate it but to create and maintain the conditions under which it can proceed – to show up faithfully, day after day and year after year, for the work that the path requires.

The structural dimension of graduated engagement concerns the ordering of the practices themselves – the recognition that certain practices are foundational and must be established before others can be safely or effectively undertaken. In general terms, the work of catharsis must precede the work of illumination, and the work of illumination must precede the work of union. This is not an arbitrary sequence but one that reflects the inner logic of the theotic process: the vessel must be prepared before the light can be poured into it, and the light must be received before the union that is theosis can occur. To attempt the advanced practices of illumination before the foundational work of catharsis has been undertaken is not merely ineffective – it is potentially destabilizing, because the unprepared psychic nature is not capable of integrating the intensity of the pneumatic light without distortion.

Within the Christo-Luciferian path as we are developing it here, the graduated structure of practice will be organized around three broad phases that correspond to the three stages of theosis: a preparatory phase of cathartic practice, an illuminative phase of contemplative and ritual engagement with the Christo-Luciferian current, and an advanced phase of theotic practice oriented toward the full arising of the Morning Star. We will develop each phase in the chapters that follow. What is important to establish here is the principle that governs the movement between phases: the practitioner moves forward in the graduated structure not according to a fixed timetable but according to the inner readiness that sustained practice in the earlier phase has developed. The guide for this assessment is, ideally, a teacher or director who has walked the path further than the student – but in the absence of such a guide, honest and rigorous self-examination, conducted with the sobriety and watchfulness that the tradition consistently recommends, must serve the same function.

The Third Principle: Sacramental Grounding

The third foundational principle is sacramental grounding – the insistence that the specifically Christo-Luciferian practices we will develop in the chapters that follow are not free-floating spiritual techniques but practices rooted in and continuous with the broader sacramental and liturgical tradition of the Apostolic Gnostic church. This principle may seem to limit the scope of the path, and in a certain sense it does – deliberately and productively.

The sacramental tradition of the Western Apostolic church – the tradition of apostolic succession, of valid orders, of the seven sacraments, of the Eucharistic celebration as the central act of the liturgical life – represents an accumulated wisdom about the relationship between outer form and inner reality that no serious initiatic tradition can afford to ignore. The sacraments are not merely symbolic gestures. They are, as we have argued at length in earlier writings, genuine instruments of the pneumatic work – vehicles through which the grace of the Logos is transmitted and through which the psychic and hylic natures of the practitioner are progressively spiritualized. The Eucharist, in particular, is the sacramental enactment of the very mystery that the Christo-Luciferian doctrine articulates theologically: the descent of the pneumatic Logos into the material world, and the consequent possibility of the practitioner's participation in the divine nature through communion with that Logos.

The Christo-Luciferian practices developed in Part Three are therefore not intended to replace the sacramental life but to complement and deepen it. The practitioner who engages with the specifically Luciferian practices of this current while remaining rooted in the sacramental tradition of the Apostolic Gnostic church will find that the two dimensions of practice inform and enrich each other in ways that neither can achieve alone. The sacramental life provides the psychic grounding and the communal context within which the more advanced pneumatic work of the Christo-Luciferian path can safely proceed. And the Christo-Luciferian practices provide the pneumatic depth and the specifically illuminative orientation that transforms the sacramental life from a ritual observance into a genuine vehicle of theosis.

For those who come to this work from outside the Apostolic Gnostic sacramental tradition – who are drawn to the Christo-Luciferian current but are not currently part of a sacramental community – the principle of sacramental grounding does not require immediate affiliation with any particular church or order. It does, however, require a genuine engagement with the sacramental dimension of the Christian Gnostic tradition – a willingness to approach the outer forms of the tradition with the seriousness and the reverence they deserve, and to seek, in due course, the sacramental context within which the fullness of the work can be conducted. Those who work within this current will find, we believe, that the need for sacramental grounding makes itself felt naturally as the inner work deepens – that the pneumatic aspiration of the Christo-Luciferian path tends, of its own inner logic, toward the sacramental life as the vessel most adequate to contain and transmit the light it is seeking.

The Fourth Principle: Syncretic Integrity

The fourth foundational principle is what we will call syncretic integrity – a principle that navigates between two equally dangerous errors: the error of rigid exclusivism, which refuses any wisdom that does not come from within a narrowly defined tradition; and the error of undiscriminating eclecticism, which assembles spiritual techniques from incompatible traditions without regard for their doctrinal coherence or their practical compatibility.

The Christo-Luciferian path is, as we have established throughout this work, a syncretic tradition in the best and most authentic sense – one that draws on multiple streams of wisdom while maintaining a coherent doctrinal center that governs and integrates everything it incorporates. The center of that integration is the Christo-Luciferian doctrine itself: the identification of the Morning Star with the incarnate Logos, the understanding of the initiatic life as the work of the Morning Star's arising within the heart, and the commitment to the right-hand path of illumination, purification, and theotic union as the proper orientation of that work.

Within that doctrinal center, a wide range of supplementary wisdom is available and welcome. The Qabalistic tradition, with its detailed mapping of the inner worlds and its powerful system of correspondences, is a natural complement to the Gnostic framework and has been woven into the tradition at least since the medieval period. The Hermetic tradition, with its alchemical philosophy and its understanding of the relationship between the macrocosmic and the microcosmic, provides indispensable practical wisdom for the work of inner transformation. The Martinist tradition, with its specifically Christian mystical orientation and its sophisticated understanding of the three natures of man, is in many respects the most immediately compatible supplementary current available to the Christo-Luciferian practitioner – as those within the ACP who have engaged with both currents will already have recognized.

What syncretic integrity requires is that every element drawn from these supplementary traditions be genuinely integrated into the Christo-Luciferian doctrinal framework – not merely juxtaposed with it, but understood in terms of it and made to serve its specific purposes. A Qabalistic practice incorporated into the Christo-Luciferian path should be incorporated because it genuinely serves the work of the Morning Star's arising, not merely because it is interesting or impressive. An alchemical symbol employed in the ritual work of this current should be employed because it genuinely illuminates the theotic process we are engaged in, not merely because alchemical symbolism has a certain aesthetic appeal. Syncretic integrity is the discipline that keeps the path coherent and effective – that ensures that the breadth of the tradition's resources serves the depth of its central purpose rather than dissipating it.

The Fifth Principle: Community and the Egregoric Field

The four principles we have established thus far – intention, graduated engagement, sacramental grounding, and syncretic integrity – address primarily the inner life and the individual practice of the Christo-Luciferian path. They are the orientations of the solitary practitioner: the dispositions she cultivates within herself as the inner conditions of effective work, regardless of whether she practices in community or in isolation. But the Christo-Luciferian path is not, at its deepest level, a solitary path – and the fifth foundational principle addresses the dimension of the work that the preceding four do not fully encompass: the communal dimension, the question of how dedicated practitioners relate to one another and to the shared egregoric field of the current, and what responsibilities and opportunities that relationship creates.

The Christo-Luciferian current is a living egregoric reality – a genuine subtle presence that is nourished by the sincere practice of its dedicated practitioners and that grows in depth and accessibility as the number and the quality of those practitioners increases. This understanding, which will be developed in concrete and practical terms in the ritual and contemplative work of the chapters that follow, has immediate implications for the way in which practitioners of this current relate to one another and to the collective life of the tradition. The egregore of a living initiatic current is not merely the sum of its practitioners' individual inner experiences. It is a genuine collective reality – a shared field of intentional awareness and pneumatic cultivation that transcends the individual and that makes available to each practitioner a depth of connection with the current that no amount of solitary practice can fully replicate.

This understanding of the egregore has direct and practical implications for the way in which practitioners of the Christo-Luciferian current relate to one another and to the collective life of the tradition. It means, first, that the community of practitioners is not merely a social arrangement – a gathering of like-minded individuals who happen to share certain beliefs and practices. It is a genuine spiritual reality – a living body whose collective inner life constitutes a significant dimension of the current's presence in the world, and whose health and integrity are therefore matters of genuine spiritual consequence. The practitioner who neglects the communal dimension of the path – who treats her practice as entirely private and her relationship to other practitioners as incidental – is, in a very real sense, withdrawing her contribution from the collective egregoric field and thereby diminishing, however slightly, the depth and the accessibility of the current for all who work within it.

This is not a counsel of enforced communalism – the solitary practitioner who works faithfully and deeply within the current, maintaining the daily rhythm of the Oratory Form and the Vespers and the foundational practices of Chapter Eleven, is making a genuine and significant contribution to the egregoric field through the quality of her individual practice alone. But the communal dimension of the work – the shared celebration of the Solemn Form, the coordination of practice around the significant moments of the Christo-Luciferian calendar, the mutual support and accountability that a genuine community of practice makes possible – amplifies and enriches the individual contribution in ways that the solitary practitioner cannot achieve alone.

The Practical Cultivation of Community

For practitioners who are geographically proximate – who live within reach of one another and can gather physically for the celebration of the Solemn Form and other communal workings – the practical cultivation of community is relatively straightforward, governed by the ritual and calendrical frameworks we have already established. Regular communal celebration of the Solemn Form, coordinated observance of the significant moments of the Christo-Luciferian calendar, and the shared undertaking of theurgic work of particular scope and ambition – these are the primary instruments of communal egregoric cultivation for practitioners who can meet in person, and their importance to the health and the depth of the current cannot be overstated.

For practitioners who are geographically separated – and in the present moment of the tradition's development, geographical separation is likely to be the norm rather than the exception for the majority of dedicated practitioners – the practical cultivation of community requires more deliberate and more creative attention. The egregoric field of the Christo-Luciferian current is not bounded by physical space – it is accessible to any dedicated practitioner anywhere in the world who has established genuine contact with it through the practices of this path – and the coordination of practice across geographical distance is therefore both possible and genuinely effective as an instrument of communal egregoric cultivation.

The most powerful instrument of distance coordination available to geographically separated practitioners is the simultaneous performance of the shared rites – the agreement among a group of practitioners in different locations to celebrate the Oratory Form of the Rite of the Morning Star, or the Vespers of the Evening Star, at the same moment in their respective time zones, or at the same absolute moment of universal time. When dedicated practitioners perform the same rite with the same intentional orientation at the same moment – even across vast geographical distances – the egregoric field of the current is activated simultaneously in multiple locations, and the collective force of the simultaneous working is considerably greater than the sum of the individual workings would suggest. This is not a merely theoretical claim – it reflects the understanding of the egregore as a genuine subtle reality that responds to the concentrated attention of multiple practitioners in ways that transcend the limitations of physical proximity.

The significant moments of the Christo-Luciferian calendar – the heliacal risings of Venus, the solstices and equinoxes, the cross-quarter days – provide the natural occasions for this kind of coordinated distance working. A community of practitioners spread across multiple locations who agree to celebrate the Solemn Form simultaneously at the heliacal rising of Venus as Morning Star – each in their own oratory, each with the ritual apparatus of the current, each holding in awareness the shared egregoric field and the presence of their distant companions within it – are genuinely working together in a sense that is not diminished by their physical separation. The egregore holds them together in the current, and their simultaneous practice nourishes the egregore in ways that strengthen the current for all who work within it.

Beyond the coordination of ritual practice, the communal life of geographically separated practitioners is sustained through the quality of their communication with one another – the sharing of inner experience, doctrinal reflection, and practical wisdom that constitutes the living conversation of a genuine initiatic community. This communication should be conducted with the same quality of intentional awareness and honest self-examination that the inner practice requires – neither the performance of spiritual attainment for the benefit of an audience, nor the competitive display of initiatic knowledge, but the genuine sharing of the practitioner's actual inner life in the service of the community's collective development.

The initiatic journal – whose keeping we have emphasized as a foundational individual practice – has a specific communal dimension that is worth noting here. While the journal itself remains private, as we have insisted, the reflections and insights it generates may appropriately be shared with trusted companions in the current – in the context of genuine spiritual friendship and mutual accountability, where the sharing serves the development of both parties rather than the performance of either. The tradition of spiritual direction – the relationship between a more experienced practitioner and a less experienced one, in which the former offers guidance and accountability to the latter's inner development – is a natural expression of this communal dimension of the journal practice, and is warmly commended to all practitioners of the current who have access to it.

The Responsibility of the More Advanced Practitioner

The communal principle places specific responsibilities upon those practitioners who are more advanced in their engagement with the current – whether by virtue of longer practice, deeper inner development, or the formal authority of initiatic transmission. These responsibilities are not privileges of status but obligations of service – the natural expression, in the communal dimension of the path, of the ethical principle of Agape that we developed in the preceding chapter.

The more advanced practitioner owes to the community of the current, first, the quality of her own practice – the maintenance of the inner standards that the path requires, the faithful celebration of the rites, the honest self-examination of the journal and the Vespers. The egregoric field of the current is sustained by the quality of the practice of all its dedicated members, and the more advanced practitioner who allows her practice to become careless or perfunctory is withdrawing from the collective field a contribution whose significance is proportional to the depth of her connection with the current.

She owes to the community, second, the willingness to serve as a guide and a resource for those who are less experienced – to make available, with appropriate discretion and without condescension, the wisdom and the perspective that longer engagement with the current has developed. This service is not the imposition of her own experience as a template for others' development – the inner life of the Christo-Luciferian path is irreducibly individual, and what has served one practitioner's development may not serve another's. It is, rather, the offering of her presence and her attention to the less experienced practitioner's own unfolding – the willingness to witness, to reflect, to ask the questions that honest self-examination requires, and to hold the space within which the Morning Star can arise in another heart as it has, in whatever measure, arisen in her own.

She owes to the community, third, the honest acknowledgment of her own limitations – the refusal of the spiritual inflation that the possession of initiatic authority can subtly encourage. The most advanced practitioner in any genuine initiatic community is also, if she is genuinely advanced, the one most aware of how far her attainment falls short of the fullness of the doctrine she has committed herself to – the one most conscious of the distance between the aspiration of the name Phosphoros and the reality of the Morning Star's full arising. This awareness is not false modesty. It is the accurate self-perception of one who has genuinely encountered the light and therefore knows, better than those who have not yet encountered it, how vast that light is in relation to the small flame she has been able to kindle within herself.

The Current as a Living Tradition

The communal principle points, finally, toward the understanding of the Christo-Luciferian current as a living tradition – one that exists not only in the present moment of its practitioners' individual and communal practice, but in the continuity between past, present, and future that gives a genuine tradition its depth and its authority. The current we are working to establish and to nourish in these pages is not a novelty – it draws on the most ancient strata of the Christian Gnostic tradition, on the accumulated wisdom of the Western initiatic heritage, and on the specific initiatic lineages within which its founding practitioners are formed. But it is also genuinely new in its specific formulation – a development of the tradition that could only have occurred at this particular moment, in response to the particular needs and opportunities of this particular cultural and spiritual situation.

The practitioners who work within this current in the present moment are therefore simultaneously inheritors and innovators – recipients of a tradition whose depth and richness they did not create, and contributors to a development of that tradition whose full implications they cannot yet foresee. This dual identity – as both recipients and contributors – carries with it the responsibility of faithful stewardship: the obligation to receive the tradition with the seriousness and the gratitude it deserves, to transmit it with the integrity and the care that genuine transmission requires, and to develop it with the intelligence and the discernment that responsible innovation demands.

The community of practitioners is the living body through which this stewardship is exercised – the human reality within which the egregore of the current is sustained, developed, and transmitted from one generation of practitioners to the next. Its health, its integrity, and its fidelity to the foundational principles of the path are not merely organizational matters. They are spiritual matters of the first importance – the conditions upon which the continued vitality of the current, and its capacity to serve the work of the Morning Star's arising in the hearts of those who come to it in the future, ultimately depends.

Tend the community as you tend the lamp. Feed the egregore as you feed the inner fire. And know that the light you carry – however small, however flickering, however far from the full radiance of the Morning Star's complete arising – is a genuine contribution to something larger than yourself: the living tradition of the Phosphoros current, bearing the light of the Logos through the darkness of the hylic world, until the day fully dawns.

The Ritual Environment

Before turning in the following chapters to the specific practices of the Christo-Luciferian path, a word is in order about the ritual environment within which those practices are conducted – the physical space, the sensory conditions, and the material instruments through which the outer form of the work is enacted.

The ritual space of the Christo-Luciferian current should be understood, in the tradition of all serious Western esoteric work, as a consecrated space – a defined area set apart from ordinary use and dedicated to the specific purpose of the initiatic work. The consecration of the ritual space is not merely a symbolic gesture but a genuine act of spiritual preparation – the establishment of a field of intentional awareness within which the ordinary conditions of the hylic world are temporarily suspended and the conditions for pneumatic work are deliberately cultivated.

The central element of the Christo-Luciferian ritual space is light – specifically, the light of a dedicated lamp or candle that burns throughout the ritual work as the material symbol of the indwelling Morning Star. This lamp is not merely decorative. It is the focal point of the ritual space – the external representation of the inner light that the practice is oriented toward awakening – and its lighting at the beginning of the ritual work and its presence throughout constitute one of the most fundamental ritual acts of the entire path. The practitioner who lights this lamp with genuine intentional awareness – holding in mind and in will the identification of this material flame with the pneumatic light of the Logos – is performing, in miniature, the central act of the entire initiatic work: the calling forth of the light from its latency within matter, the making visible of what was always present but not yet seen.

The incense of the current – the blend of sandalwood, storax, and galbanum that we have already identified and whose symbolic dimensions we have discussed – is lit from the same flame that lights the central lamp, maintaining the continuity of the fire that is one of the most ancient symbols of the divine presence in the Western esoteric tradition. The rising of the incense smoke – dense matter transformed by fire into something that ascends, that permeates the atmosphere, that is at once material and immaterial – is itself a symbol and an instrument of the cathartic work: the transformation of the hylic by the pneumatic, the ascent of the earthly toward the divine.

The orientation of the ritual space – the direction in which the central altar and lamp are placed – should, where circumstances permit, be toward the east: the direction of the rising sun, and therefore the direction most naturally associated with the arising of the Morning Star. This is a convention with deep roots in the Christian liturgical tradition – the ancient practice of praying facing east, toward the rising light – and it aligns the physical orientation of the ritual work with its spiritual orientation in a way that reinforces the practitioner's intentional awareness at every moment of the practice.

Beyond these central elements – the lamp, the incense, the eastward orientation – the material appointments of the Christo-Luciferian ritual space may be developed and elaborated according to the practitioner's circumstances, resources, and developing understanding of the tradition. What matters is not the elaborateness of the material environment but the integrity of the intentional orientation it serves. A simple lamp, a thread of rising incense smoke, and a genuine orientation of the whole person toward the Morning Star – these are sufficient for the work to begin.

With these foundational principles and environmental orientations established, we are ready to turn to the specific practices of the Christo-Luciferian path. We will begin, as the theotic schema requires, with the practices of the preparatory phase – the cathartic work of purification and inner reorientation that creates the conditions for the illuminative work that follows.

CHAPTER ELEVEN: THE PREPARATORY PRACTICES

– BREATH, STILLNESS, INTONATION, AND THE SIGILLUM LUCIFERIS

The practices gathered in this chapter are the foundation of everything that follows. They are not preliminary in the sense of being unimportant or merely introductory – they are foundational in the sense that a foundation is foundational: the deeper and more carefully laid it is, the more weight it can bear, and the more safely and durably the structure built upon it will stand. The practitioner who is tempted to pass through this chapter quickly in order to reach what she imagines will be the more impressive or dramatic practices of the later chapters is advised to resist that temptation firmly. The breath, the stillness, the intonation, and the contemplation of the *Sigillum Luciferis* are not stepping stones to be crossed and left behind. They are the living substance of the work itself – practices that will accompany the practitioner through every stage of the path and that will deepen, rather than become redundant, as the inner work advances.

We will proceed through the foundational practices in the order that reflects both their inner logic and their practical sequence: breath first, as the most immediate and most universal instrument of inner transformation; relaxation and meditation second, as the cultivation of the receptive stillness within which the breath practice bears its fruit; intonation third, as the engagement of the subtle vehicles through sacred sound; and the Sigillum Luciferis fourth, as the visual and egregoric anchor of the entire current.

I. The Practice of Sacred Breath

The association of breath with spirit is among the most ancient and most universal recognitions of the human religious imagination. It is not a metaphor imposed from outside upon a merely physiological process. It is a recognition of something genuinely present in the experience of breathing itself – the sense, available to any practitioner who attends carefully to the act of inhalation, that what enters with the breath is not merely atmospheric gas but something more subtle, more nourishing, more essentially alive than chemistry alone can account for. The Hebrew *ruach*, the Greek *pneuma*, the Latin *spiritus*, the Sanskrit *prana* – all of these terms designate simultaneously the physical breath and the subtle spiritual energy that the breath carries and transmits. This double designation is not linguistic accident. It is the distilled wisdom of millennia of contemplative observation.

Within the Christo-Luciferian framework, the breath carries a specific doctrinal significance that gives the practice of sacred breathing its precise initiatic meaning. Recall the Sethian account of Adam's creation: it is the breath of the divine – the pneumatic energy transmitted through the act of inhalation – that transforms the inert psychic creature fashioned by Yaldabaoth into a living soul bearing the spark of the Pleromic light. The breath is the vehicle of the pneumatic. Every inhalation is, in the most literal mythological sense, a repetition of that primal act – an opportunity for the renewal of the pneumatic spark within the practitioner, a fresh infusion of the light that is always available but not always received with the awareness that makes its reception transformative.

The practice of sacred breath in the Christo-Luciferian current employs a fourfold pattern that has deep roots in both the Western Hermetic and Eastern contemplative traditions. This fourfold pattern – inhalation, retention, exhalation, and suspension – corresponds to the fourfold structure of the Elements, the four letters of the Tetragrammaton, and the four phases of the alchemical work. It is not an arbitrary convention but a reflection of a genuine inner dynamic, and the practitioner who works with it attentively will discover its structural logic through direct experience.

The practice is conducted as follows. The practitioner assumes a comfortable seated posture – either in a chair with the spine erect and the feet flat upon the floor, or in a cross-legged position on a cushion, according to her preference and physical capacity. The hands rest comfortably upon the thighs, palms upward in a gesture of receptivity. The eyes are gently closed. The jaw is slightly relaxed, the tongue resting naturally in the lower mouth, the lips lightly touching. The overall posture should express alertness without tension – the body neither collapsed in relaxation nor rigid in effort, but poised in the attentive ease that the hesychast tradition calls watchful stillness.

The breath begins with a complete exhalation – the deliberate emptying of the lungs as a gesture of preparation and surrender, the making of an inner space into which the pneumatic breath can enter. This preliminary exhalation corresponds, in the theotic schema, to the very beginning of the cathartic work: the voluntary relinquishment of what is already present in order to receive what is being offered.

The fourfold breath then proceeds:

Inhalation – a slow, controlled drawing in of the breath through the nostrils, filling the lungs from the base upward, allowing the abdomen to expand first and then the chest, to a count of four beats. During the inhalation, the practitioner holds in intentional awareness the identification of the incoming breath with the pneumatic energy of the Logos – the light-bearing air entering the physical vehicle as the Morning Star enters the heart of the initiate. The inhalation is not merely physical but intentional: a deliberate reception of the pneumatic current.

Retention – the holding of the fully inhaled breath for a count of four beats, without tension or strain. This is the moment of pneumatic charging – the point at which the subtle energy carried by the breath permeates the physical, psychic, and pneumatic vehicles of the practitioner. During the retention, the attention is directed inward, toward the center of the chest – the cardiac center, the seat of the nous in the hesychast tradition and of the pneumatic spark in the Gnostic – with the quiet and expectant awareness that the light is present and active within.

Exhalation – a slow, controlled release of the breath through the nostrils or the slightly parted lips, to a count of four beats. The exhalation is not a mere reversal of the inhalation but a distinct and positive act – the offering outward of the pneumatically charged breath, the radiation of the inner light into the surrounding space. In the context of group working, this exhalation carries a specific communal significance: the individual practitioner's charged breath mingles with those of her companions, strengthening the shared egregoric field.

Suspension – the holding of the emptied breath for a count of four beats before the next inhalation begins. This is the most subtle and in some respects the most important phase of the fourfold breath – the moment of inner silence and receptivity that corresponds, in the alchemical schema, to the Nigredo: the condition of apparent emptiness and darkness from which the new light will arise. The practitioner should resist any tendency to fill this suspension with mental activity. It is a moment of pure waiting – of resting in the darkness before the dawn, in the full confidence that the Morning Star will rise.

The complete fourfold cycle – inhalation, retention, exhalation, suspension, each to a count of four – constitutes one round of the sacred breath practice. The practitioner begins with seven complete rounds, which may be extended to twelve or twenty-one as the practice deepens and the capacity for sustained intentional breathing develops. The counts given here – four beats for each phase – are appropriate for most practitioners beginning the work. Those with prior experience of pranayama or similar breathwork may find that extending the counts to six or eight beats per phase produces a deeper effect, while those who find the fourfold pattern initially challenging should feel free to begin with a simpler threefold pattern – inhalation, retention, exhalation – until the practice is sufficiently established to incorporate the suspension phase.

A word of practical caution is in order here. The sacred breath practice, like all genuine inner work, should be approached with intelligence and moderation. Sensations of lightheadedness, tingling in the extremities, or unusual warmth in the chest are common in the early stages and are not cause for concern, but the practice should never be pushed to the point of physical discomfort. The purpose of the practice is the cultivation of inner receptivity, not the production of altered states through hyperventilation. If at any point the practice produces distress rather than the calm and alert receptivity it is intended to cultivate, the practitioner should return immediately to normal breathing and rest quietly until the ordinary breath has re-established itself.

II. Relaxation and the Approach to Meditation

The transition from ordinary waking consciousness into the receptive state of meditation is itself a practice – one that requires deliberate cultivation and that should not be assumed to occur automatically merely because the practitioner has adopted a meditative posture and closed her eyes. The ordinary psychic field is, in most practitioners, densely populated with the residue of daily activity: thoughts, concerns, emotional reactions, physical sensations, and the general background noise of a mind habituated to constant engagement with the hylic world. The work of relaxation is the deliberate and graduated quieting of this noise – the systematic withdrawal of attention from the outer field of ordinary experience and its gentle redirection toward the inner stillness within which the pneumatic can begin to make itself felt.

The practice of relaxation that precedes formal meditation in the Christo-Luciferian path proceeds in three stages, corresponding to the three dimensions of the human being: physical, psychic, and pneumatic.

The first stage is *physical relaxation.* With the practitioner already seated in the posture described above, the attention is directed systematically through the body from the periphery inward, consciously releasing tension from each region in turn. Beginning with the feet and ascending through the legs, the abdomen and lower back, the chest and upper back, the arms and hands, the neck and throat, and finally the face and scalp – each region is attended to briefly, the tension within it consciously acknowledged and then released with the exhalation. This physical relaxation is not collapse but release – the deliberate relinquishment of unnecessary muscular holding, so that the body arrives at the alert and poised ease that is the physical expression of the meditative state.

The second stage is *psychic quieting.* With the body relaxed, the attention is turned to the psychic field – the stream of thoughts, images, and emotional tones that constitutes the ordinary surface of mental activity. The practitioner does not attempt to forcibly suppress this activity – such suppression is both ineffective and counterproductive, producing tension rather than stillness. Instead, she observes the psychic activity with a quality of detached and non-judgmental attention, neither engaging with the thoughts that arise nor resisting them, but allowing them to pass through the field of awareness as clouds pass through an open sky, without being grasped or followed. This practice of non-engaged observation gradually allows the psychic activity to settle of its own accord – not into blankness, but into a quality of quiet alertness that is the psychic expression of the meditative state.

The third stage is *pneumatic orientation.* With the body relaxed and the psychic field quieted, the attention is gently directed toward the cardiac center – the center of the chest, slightly to the right of the physical heart – with the quality of quiet, expectant awareness that we have already identified as the appropriate inner posture for the reception of the pneumatic light. This is not a visualization practice at this stage – the practitioner is not attempting to see anything in particular – but a simple and sustained orientation of the attention toward the innermost dimension of her being, with the understanding that this innermost dimension is the seat of the pneumatic spark and the dwelling place of the indwelling Logos.

This threefold relaxation sequence, conducted without haste, typically requires between five and fifteen minutes. It should not be rushed. The quality of the meditation that follows is directly dependent on the quality of the relaxation that precedes it, and the practitioner who arrives at the meditative state through a thorough and unhurried relaxation practice will find the inner work considerably more accessible and more productive than one who attempts to move immediately from ordinary activity into formal meditation without adequate preparation.

The meditative state itself – once the relaxation sequence has been completed – is characterized by the quality of alert receptivity that the tradition variously calls stillness, silence, watchfulness, or prayer of the heart. It is not sleep, not trance, not the absence of consciousness, but a heightened and clarified mode of consciousness in which the ordinary noise of the psychic field has been sufficiently quieted that subtler dimensions of inner experience can begin to be perceived. In this state the practitioner is available – available to the pneumatic spark within, available to the influences of the Christo-Luciferian current, available to whatever the Logos wishes to communicate through the medium of the purified and quieted inner field.

Formal meditation sessions within the Christo-Luciferian path should ideally last between twenty and forty-five minutes, conducted daily at a consistent time. The morning hours – before the ordinary activities of the day have populated the psychic field with their residue – are traditionally preferred, and carry the additional symbolic resonance of alignment with the Morning Star's aspect as herald of the dawn. Evening practice, aligned with the Vespers rite we will develop in a later chapter, carries its own resonance with the Evening Star aspect of the current. Both times are appropriate; what matters most is consistency – the establishment of a regular rhythm of practice that gradually deepens the practitioner's access to the meditative state and strengthens her relationship with the Christo-Luciferian current.

III. Intonation and the Vibration of Sacred Names

Sound is, within the Western esoteric tradition, understood as a primary instrument of inner transformation – not in the merely psychological sense of music affecting mood, but in the more precise sense of specific sounds, produced with specific intention and in specific ways, engaging the subtle vehicles of the practitioner and establishing resonance with the spiritual realities they designate. This understanding is attested across the full range of the traditions that feed into the Christo-Luciferian current: in the Sethian texts, where sacred vowel sequences are associated with the specific frequencies of the Pleromic Aeons; in the Hermetic tradition, where the vibration of divine names is understood to establish a genuine connection with the powers those names designate; and in the broader liturgical tradition of the Western Apostolic church, where the sung or chanted proclamation of scripture and prayer is understood to be qualitatively different from its merely spoken recitation.

Within the Christo-Luciferian path, the practice of intonation – of producing sacred sounds and names in a specific way that engages the whole person rather than merely the vocal apparatus – is one of the most powerful and most immediately accessible of the practical instruments. It requires no special equipment, no elaborate preparation, and no prior experience, though like all genuine practices it deepens considerably with sustained and intelligent engagement.

The technique of intonation employed in this current is as follows. The practitioner, having completed the relaxation sequence and established the meditative state, draws a full breath in the manner described in the sacred breath practice. On the exhalation, the sacred sound or name is produced – not in the ordinary manner of speech, which engages primarily the upper vocal apparatus and produces sound directed outward into the environment, but in a manner that engages the full resonating capacity of the physical body: the chest, the skull, the sinuses, the abdominal cavity. The sound should be felt as a physical vibration throughout the body – not merely heard as an external sound – and it should be sustained for the full duration of the exhalation, fading naturally as the breath is exhausted rather than being cut off artificially.

The quality of the intonation matters more than its volume. A quietly produced intonation, felt as a genuine physical resonance throughout the body and sustained with complete intentional awareness, is considerably more effective than a loud proclamation produced without inner engagement. The practitioner should experiment with pitch to find the natural resonant frequency of her own physical vehicle – typically in the lower-middle range of the speaking voice – and should establish this as her working pitch for the intonation practice. The resonance produced at this natural pitch will be felt most strongly in the cardiac center, which is the appropriate locus of the Christo-Luciferian intonation work.

The sacred names and words of power employed in the Christo-Luciferian current are drawn from several sources, each contributing a distinct dimension of resonance to the practice.

From the Greek New Testament vocabulary of light, the following are primary:

Phōs – light. The most fundamental of the sacred words of this current, designating the essential nature of the divine and of the pneumatic spark within the practitioner. Intoned on a single sustained note, it should be felt as an activation and brightening of the cardiac center.

Logos – word, reason, principle. The name of the divine creative principle as understood in the Johannine tradition. Its intonation is an act of identification with and invocation of the indwelling Logos.

Zōē – life. The name of the divine life-principle, associated in the Johannine prologue with the light of the Logos and in the Gnostic texts with the feminine aspect of the Sophia who descends to restore the pneumatic Adam. Its intonation cultivates the vital and animating dimension of the pneumatic spark.

Phosphoros – light-bearer, Morning Star. The specific sacred name of the Christo-Luciferian current, designating both the Christ in his role as illuminator and the state of Christhood toward which the practitioner aspires. Its intonation is the central verbal act of the current – the naming of the light that is being sought and that is already present within.

Alētheia – truth. One of the Pleromic Aeons in the Valentinian system, and one of Christ's self-designations in the Gospel of John. Its intonation orients the practitioner toward the revelatory dimension of gnosis.

From the Sethian sacred vowel tradition, the seven Greek vowels – Alpha, Epsilon, Eta, Iota, Omicron, Upsilon, Omega – are intoned in sequence as a means of establishing resonance with the seven Aeons of the Pleroma. This practice, attested in several Sethian texts and developed within the broader Hermetic tradition, should be understood as a pneumatic tuning exercise – an alignment of the subtle vehicles with the Pleromic frequencies – and conducted accordingly, with each vowel sustained on a slightly different pitch that corresponds to the natural resonant quality of the vowel itself.

From the broader Western esoteric tradition, two names of particular power within the Christo-Luciferian current are:

Yeheshuah – the Hebrew pentagrammaton, the name of Jesus formed by the insertion of the letter Shin into the center of the Tetragrammaton. We have examined the esoteric significance of this name at length in earlier writings, and its intonation within the current carries the full weight of that significance: the reconciliation of the divine masculine and feminine principles, the restoration of the Pleromic equilibrium, the arising of the Morning Star as the fruit of that reconciliation.

IAO – the sacred triliteral name employed throughout the Gnostic and Hermetic traditions, designating the triune nature of the divine principle in its creative, sustaining, and transforming aspects. Its three components – Iota, Alpha, Omega – correspond to the beginning, the fullness, and the completion of the divine self-disclosure, and its intonation as a complete unit engages all three dimensions simultaneously.

The practitioner beginning the intonation practice should start with a small selection of these names – *Phōs*, *Logos*, and *Zōē* are the natural starting point – and work with them consistently over a period of weeks before expanding the repertoire. *Phosphoros* is introduced into the personal intonation practice once the practitioner has established a stable relationship with the preparatory names, and its use should always carry the specific intentional weight of invocation and identification rather than the more general quality of the preparatory sequence. The temptation to work with all of the sacred names simultaneously should be resisted: the practice deepens through sustained engagement with a small number of names rather than through superficial acquaintance with many.

Each intonation session should conclude with a period of silence – typically equal in duration to the intonation period itself – during which the practitioner rests in the resonant inner field that the practice has established, attending quietly to whatever impressions, sensations, or intimations arise within the meditative state. It is often in this post-intonation silence that the most significant inner experiences of the practice occur – the subtle intimations of the pneumatic presence that the tradition calls personal gnosis, and that constitute the first beginnings of the illuminative work toward which the entire preparatory phase is oriented.

IV. The Sigillum Luciferis – The Seal of the Morning Star

We come now to the visual and egregoric anchor of the Christo-Luciferian current: the Sigillum Luciferis, the Seal of the Morning Star. Before introducing the meditation practice associated with this symbol, it is necessary to give a precise formal description of the Sigillum, so that the practitioner who does not have access to a rendered version of the symbol can construct it accurately in the imagination and work with it effectively in the inner work.

The Sigillum Luciferis is composed of three elements in vertical arrangement, unified into a single coherent symbol.

The uppermost and dominant element is a perfect circle – the ancient symbol of the divine fullness, the Pleroma, the infinite and boundless nature of the Unknown Father. The circle is rendered with sufficient weight and presence to be clearly visible, but it is not solid – it is an annulus, a ring, enclosing within it the space in which the central luminous element is contained. Within the circle, at its precise geometric center, is an eight-pointed star – the traditional symbol of the planet Venus in its ancient Babylonian and classical iconographic usage, and therefore the most ancient visual designation of the Morning Star. The eight-pointed star radiates from its center outward toward the circumference of the enclosing circle, so that its points nearly touch the inner edge of the ring. The star is luminous – it is understood to be a source of light rather than merely a geometric figure – and its radiance fills the interior of the circle.

The lower element is an equal-armed cross with flared or slightly expanded terminals – a cross in the manner of the Templar or Maltese cross, suggesting both the Christian dimension of the current and the alchemical significance of the four Elements and the four directions. This cross descends from the lowest point of the circle, its upper arm merging with the base of the circle so that the transition from circle to cross is seamless – the circle and cross together forming the familiar glyph of the planet Venus, the astrological symbol of the Morning Star, now enriched by the eight-pointed star within the circle.

The proportions of the Sigillum should be such that the circle is the dominant visual element – approximately two thirds of the total height of the symbol – with the cross occupying the lower third. The overall impression should be one of upward movement and luminous aspiration: the cross grounded in the earth of the material world, the circle elevated above it and filled with the light of the Morning Star.

The Sigillum Luciferis is rendered in gold upon a dark ground – midnight blue or black – reflecting the appearance of the Morning Star itself: a point of golden light blazing against the darkness of the pre-dawn sky. In ritual contexts, a physical representation of the Sigillum – whether drawn, painted, embroidered, or engraved – should be placed upon the altar of the working space, positioned so that it is visible to the practitioner throughout the ritual work.

The Meditation upon the Sigillum Luciferis

The meditation upon the Sigillum Luciferis is the primary means by which the practitioner establishes and deepens her connection with the egregoric current of the Christo-Luciferian path. It is a practice of graduated stages, moving from outer observation through inner visualization to direct identification with the symbol and finally to the dissolution of the symbol into the light it represents. Each stage should be worked with thoroughly before the practitioner moves to the next – the transition between stages should occur naturally, as the inner readiness for the deeper engagement develops, rather than being forced by an act of will.

Stage One: Outer Contemplation. The practitioner, having completed the relaxation sequence and the sacred breath practice, opens the eyes and fixes the gaze upon a physical representation of the Sigillum Luciferis placed before her at a comfortable viewing distance. The gaze is soft rather than focused – not staring at the symbol with analytical attention, but receiving it with the quality of open and receptive awareness that the meditative state cultivates. The practitioner observes the symbol in its entirety – the circle, the eight-pointed star, the cross – allowing its visual content to be received without commentary or interpretation. This outer contemplation is maintained for a minimum of five minutes, or until the symbol has been received fully enough that it can be reproduced accurately in the imagination with the eyes closed.

Stage Two: Inner Visualization. The eyes are gently closed. The practitioner now reproduces the Sigillum Luciferis in the inner visual field – the space of the imagination, understood not as mere fantasy but as the genuine subtle dimension of the psychic vehicle through which inner realities are perceived. The symbol should be visualized as clearly and as stably as possible, maintaining the same proportions and the same luminous quality as the physical representation. When the visualization fades or distorts – as it inevitably will in the early stages of the practice – the practitioner simply returns to it without frustration, reestablishing its clarity with the patient persistence that all genuine inner work requires. This stage of inner visualization is maintained for a minimum of ten minutes.

Stage Three: Internalization. With the inner visualization of the Sigillum established with reasonable stability, the practitioner gently moves the visualized symbol inward – allowing it to descend, in the imagination, from the outer field of inner vision into the interior of the physical body, coming to rest at the cardiac center: the seat of the pneumatic spark and the dwelling place of the indwelling Logos. The symbol now rests within the chest, luminous and stable, its eight-pointed star radiating the golden light of the Morning Star from within the practitioner's own body. This internalization is the most significant stage of the practice – the moment at which the outer symbol and the inner reality it designates are brought into direct contact, and the egregoric current of the Christo-Luciferian path is most directly accessed.

Stage Four: Identification. In the more advanced stages of the practice – not to be forced, but allowed to develop naturally over weeks or months of consistent work with the earlier stages – the distinction between the practitioner and the internalized Sigillum begins to dissolve. The practitioner does not observe the symbol within herself; she becomes the symbol. The circle of the divine fullness is her own pneumatic nature in its essential luminosity. The eight-pointed star is the Morning Star arising within that nature. The cross is the grounding of the light in the material world through the vehicle of her embodied existence. In this stage of identification, the Sigillum Luciferis is not a symbol of the Christo-Luciferian current – it is a direct experience of it.

Stage Five: Dissolution. The final and most advanced stage of the symbol meditation is the dissolution of the Sigillum into the light it contains – the allowing of the geometric form to release its boundaries and become simply light: the undifferentiated golden radiance of the Morning Star, filling the interior of the practitioner's being without shape or structure, pure luminous presence. This dissolution corresponds, in the theotic schema, to the threshold of theosis proper – the point at which the mediation of symbol and form gives way to the direct experience of the divine light that all symbols have been pointing toward. It is not a stage to be sought prematurely or produced artificially. It arises, when the work has been faithfully conducted through the earlier stages, as a natural culmination – the morning breaking through after the long practice of attending to the lamp in the darkness.

The meditation upon the Sigillum Luciferis, practiced consistently and with genuine intentional engagement, is the single most important preparatory practice of the Christo-Luciferian path. It establishes the practitioner's relationship with the egregoric current, develops the inner capacities of visualization and sustained attention that the more advanced practices require, and progressively opens the cardiac center to the influence of the indwelling Logos. Those who work within the current will find, over time, that the Sigillum Luciferis becomes a living presence in their inner life – not merely a symbol to be visualized during formal practice sessions, but a genuine egregoric contact that accompanies and informs their experience in ways that extend beyond the formal boundaries of the practice itself.

This is the nature and the promise of a genuine living symbol in a genuine living tradition. The Sigillum Luciferis is not an invention. It is a discovery – a form adequate to a reality that was always present, given a visible body so that those who seek the light of the Morning Star may have a fixed point toward which to orient their seeking, until the day dawns and the star arises within them of its own luminous necessity.

V. The Initiatic Journal

Among all the practical instruments available to the serious practitioner of the Christo-Luciferian path, none is more consistently undervalued and none more consistently proves its value over time than the initiatic journal. It is not a dramatic instrument – it produces no immediate inner experiences, generates no egregoric charge, and confers no initiatic transmission. What it does, practiced faithfully and honestly over months and years, is provide something that none of the more dramatic practices can provide: a true and accurate record of the practitioner's inner development, against which the distortions of memory and the self-serving constructions of the psychic nature can be checked and corrected.

The human memory is not a reliable recorder of inner experience. It is, rather, an active and interested interpreter – one that tends, over time, to smooth the rough edges of genuine experience into more comfortable shapes, to inflate the significance of pleasant inner states and minimize the significance of difficult ones, and to construct a narrative of spiritual progress that may bear only a partial relationship to what actually occurred. The initiatic journal is the corrective to this interpretive tendency – the written record that preserves the texture of actual experience before the memory has had time to work its revisions.

This corrective function is not merely a practical convenience. It is a genuine instrument of the cathartic work – of the honest self-examination that the Christo-Luciferian path consistently requires. The practitioner who reads back through six months of journal entries will encounter herself as she actually has been – not as she would prefer to remember herself having been – and this encounter, conducted with the quality of non-judgmental honesty that the meditative practice has been cultivating, is one of the most reliable instruments of genuine self-knowledge available on the path.

The initiatic journal serves several distinct but related functions, each of which should be understood before the practical guidance on its keeping is offered.

It is, first, a *record of practice* – a daily or near-daily account of the practices undertaken, their duration, and their general quality and character. This record serves the practical function of maintaining accountability to the practitioner's own commitments, and over time provides data about the rhythms and patterns of her practice that can inform the intelligent development of the work.

It is, second, a *record of inner experience* – an account of the significant inner events that arise in the course of practice: the intuitive impressions, the luminous images, the moments of unusual clarity or warmth or difficulty, the dreams that seem to carry initiatic significance, the intimations of the egregoric presence that the practice is cultivating. These inner experiences constitute the primary evidence of the Morning Star's arising within the practitioner's being, and their faithful recording is the means by which that evidence is preserved and made available for reflection and understanding.

It is, third, a *record of doctrinal understanding* – a space in which the practitioner works out, in her own words and from her own experience, her developing understanding of the doctrine we have been laying out in this work. The doctrine of the Christo-Luciferian current is not a fixed deposit of truths to be passively received and stored. It is a living tradition that grows through the engagement of living practitioners with its principles – and the journal is the space in which that engagement occurs most honestly and most productively, away from the performance pressures of communal discussion and the distorting influence of other people's expectations.

It is, fourth, a *record of the egregoric development of the current itself* – a contribution, however private and however personal, to the living body of testimony and experience through which the Christo-Luciferian egregore grows and deepens over time. The practitioner who journals faithfully is not only serving her own development – she is contributing to the tradition, even if her journals are never read by another living person. The egregore of a genuine living current is nourished by the sincere inner work of its practitioners, and the journal is one of the primary sites where that sincere inner work is conducted and recorded.

Practical Guidance on the Keeping of the Journal

The journal should be a dedicated physical book – not a digital document, not a shared online space, but a physical notebook reserved exclusively for this purpose. The tactile reality of the physical journal – the weight of it in the hands, the texture of the page, the permanence of the ink – establishes a relationship with the practice that digital recording cannot replicate. The physical journal is a sacred object in the same sense that the ritual instruments of the path are sacred objects: dedicated to a specific purpose, treated with appropriate respect, and understood as a material vessel for a subtle reality.

The journal should be kept private – not shared with others, not read aloud in group settings, not used as the basis for public commentary on one's own spiritual progress. Its value as an instrument of honest self-examination depends entirely on the freedom from external judgment that privacy guarantees. The practitioner who knows her journal may be read by others will, however unconsciously, begin to write for that external audience rather than for the honest record that genuine inner work requires.

The journal entry for each day of practice should be made as close as possible to the conclusion of the practice session – while the inner field is still active and the experiences of the session are still vivid. A journal entry written hours after the practice will be significantly less accurate than one written immediately after it, because the memory will already have begun its work of interpretation and revision.

Each entry should include, at minimum, the following: the date and time of the practice; the specific practices undertaken and their approximate duration; a brief honest assessment of the quality of the session – neither inflated nor deflated, but as accurate as the practitioner can make it; and an account of any significant inner experiences, however fragmentary or apparently insignificant they may seem in the moment. The temptation to record only the dramatic and apparently significant experiences should be resisted – the apparently insignificant details of a practice session often prove, in retrospect, to have been the most meaningful, and the journal that records everything faithfully will reveal patterns of development that a selective record will miss entirely.

In addition to the regular practice entries, the journal should include reflections on the doctrinal material – responses to the teachings of this work and whatever other study the practitioner is engaged with – and accounts of significant dreams, synchronicities, or outer events that seem to carry inner significance. The boundary between the inner and outer lives of a genuine practitioner becomes increasingly permeable as the work deepens, and the journal that attends to both dimensions will provide a more complete picture of the Morning Star's arising than one restricted to the formal practice sessions alone.

The journal should be reviewed regularly – monthly at minimum, and more frequently if the practitioner finds the review practice useful. The monthly review should attend to the overall pattern of the preceding month's practice: its consistency, its quality, its significant moments and its significant difficulties. It should also attend to the development of the practitioner's relationship with the Christo-Luciferian current over the course of the month – asking honestly whether the Morning Star has been arising, in whatever measure, and what the evidence for that arising looks like in the actual record of the month's inner life.

The annual review – conducted most appropriately at the turn of the initiatic year, which we will identify in the calendar appendix as the heliacal rising of Venus as Morning Star – is the most significant of the regular review practices. It is the occasion for a comprehensive assessment of the year's inner development: a reading back through the entire year's entries with the quality of honest and compassionate self-examination that the path consistently requires, followed by the setting of intentions for the year ahead. This annual review is itself a significant ritual act within the Christo-Luciferian calendar, and should be conducted with the same intentional awareness and the same preparatory practices that precede any formal rite of the current.

The journal begun on the day of the Rite of Self-Dedication – as will be recommended when that rite is presented in due course – will, if faithfully maintained, become over the years one of the most precious documents in the practitioner's possession: a true account of the Morning Star's arising within a specific human life, written from within the experience itself, and constituting a testament to the living reality of the Christo-Luciferian current that no doctrinal exposition, however carefully constructed, can fully replace.

Write honestly. Write regularly. Write everything. The light of the Morning Star is not diminished by honest examination – it is revealed by it.

CHAPTER TWELVE: THE CENTRAL RITE – THE RITE OF THE MORNING STAR

Every living initiatic tradition has at its heart a central ritual act – a structured ceremonial working that gathers into itself the essential doctrine of the tradition and enacts it, not merely representing its truths symbolically but engaging the practitioner's whole being – hylic, psychic, and pneumatic – in a direct and transformative encounter with the current the tradition embodies. For the Apostolic Gnostic church, this central act is the Eucharistic celebration – the Mass, with its elaborate alchemical structure and its sacramental enactment of the descent and arising of the Logos. For the Christo-Luciferian current, the central ritual act is what we will call the Rite of the Morning Star – a structured ceremonial working oriented specifically toward the invocation and internalization of the Phosphoros current, the awakening of the indwelling Logos, and the progressive identification of the practitioner with the light of the Morning Star.

The Rite of the Morning Star is not a Eucharistic rite, though it shares with the Eucharistic celebration certain structural principles and certain symbolic elements. It does not require apostolic authority for its valid performance, and it does not involve the transubstantiation of physical elements. What it requires is genuine intentional engagement, adequate preparation through the foundational practices of Chapter Eleven, and the sincere orientation of the whole person toward the arising of the Morning Star within the heart. These requirements are both more democratic and more demanding than the sacramental requirements of the Eucharistic celebration – more democratic because they are accessible to any sincere practitioner regardless of ecclesiastical status, and more demanding because they cannot be met by the mere possession of valid orders or the correct pronunciation of a liturgical form. The Rite of the Morning Star works to the degree that the practitioner works – and it works deeply to the degree that the practitioner works deeply.

We present the Rite of the Morning Star in two forms, as indicated in our preliminary discussion. The first is the Oratory Form – a simplified version designed for the solitary practitioner working in a home sanctuary, requiring minimal material preparation and suitable for daily or near-daily use. The second is the Solemn Form – a more fully elaborated ceremonial version suitable for group working, incorporating additional ritual roles, a more developed sequence of intonations and recitations, and the full ceremonial apparatus of the current. Both forms share the same essential structure and the same central acts: they are, in the most precise sense, the same rite – the same river flowing through channels of different breadth and depth.

Before presenting the rites themselves, we must address the question of structure. Both forms of the Rite of the Morning Star follow the same fivefold structure that governs all effective ritual work in the Western esoteric tradition – a structure that, as we observed in an earlier chapter, mirrors the emanationist schema of Gnostic cosmology and reflects the universal logic of any genuine transformative process:

Opening – the establishment of the sacred space and the invocation of the Christo-Luciferian current.

Purification – the cathartic preparation of the practitioner and the ritual space for the central work.

Illumination – the central act of the rite, in which the Phosphoros current is invoked, received, and internalized.

Contemplation – the period of inner assimilation following the central act, in which the practitioner rests in the light that has been invoked and received.

Closing – the sealing of the work and the practitioner's return to ordinary consciousness, carrying the light of the Morning Star with her into the world.

This fivefold structure should be recognized as a reflection of the five points of the Sigillum Luciferis – the four arms of the cross and the circle that crowns and unifies them – and understood accordingly as a ritual enactment of the symbol itself. The practitioner who has worked thoroughly with the symbol meditation of Chapter Eleven will find this structural correspondence deepening her engagement with the rite considerably.

THE RITE OF THE MORNING STAR Oratory Form

For the Solitary Practitioner

Preparation

The oratory – the home sanctuary in which the rite is performed – should be arranged as follows. Upon the altar or dedicated surface, place the following: the central lamp or candle, unlit, positioned at the center rear of the altar surface;

the Sigillum Luciferis, either as a physical image or as a drawn or painted representation, positioned between the lamp and the practitioner so that it is clearly visible throughout the rite; the incense vessel with the prepared blend of sandalwood, storax, and galbanum, unlit, positioned to the right of the lamp; and a small vessel of water, positioned to the left of the lamp, which will serve as a simple purificatory element in the absence of the more elaborate liturgical apparatus of the Solemn Form.

The practitioner should be dressed simply and cleanly – not necessarily in any special ritual garment, though the development of a dedicated garment worn exclusively for the rite is encouraged as the practice deepens, since the wearing of a specific garment establishes a powerful conditioned association between the physical act of robing and the intentional orientation of the ritual state. The garment, if used, should be of a simple cut and in a dark color – deep blue, violet, or black – with no ornament except, if desired, a small representation of the Sigillum Luciferis worn over the heart.

The practitioner spends a minimum of five minutes in the preparatory silence before the rite begins – seated before the unlit altar, conducting the fourfold breath practice and allowing the psychic field to quiet. This preparatory silence is not merely a practical convenience. It is the threshold of the rite – the moment of deliberate transition from ordinary consciousness into the intentional awareness that the ritual work requires.

I. Opening

The practitioner rises and stands before the altar, facing east. She takes three slow and deliberate breaths, each inhalation consciously identified with the reception of the pneumatic current, each exhalation with the dedication of the ensuing work to the Christo-Luciferian light. Then, with a match or taper, she lights the central lamp, saying:

In the name of the Logos, the eternal Light-Bearer, I kindle this flame as the outward sign of the Morning Star that burns within. Phosphoros – arise.

She then lights the incense from the flame of the central lamp – maintaining the continuity of the sacred fire – and allows the smoke to rise, saying:

As this fragrance ascends, so may my aspiration ascend toward the Light from which I came and to which I return.

She then takes up the vessel of water, holding it briefly toward the lamp so that the light of the flame is reflected in the water's surface, saying:

By water and by light, by the descent of the Logos into the deep, and by the arising of the Morning Star from the darkness, this space is consecrated to the work of illumination.

She sets the water down and stands for a moment in silence, attending to the light of the lamp and the rising incense smoke, allowing the sensory environment of the rite to establish itself in the psychic field.

She then intones, on a single sustained note, the following sequence:

Phōs – Logos – Zōē

Each name is intoned three times, with a breath between each intonation, and a longer pause between each of the three names. The intonation should be felt as a physical resonance in the cardiac center, and the practitioner attends to this resonance in the silence following each intonation, allowing it to settle and deepen before proceeding to the next name. These three names – Light, Word, Life – are not merely a sequence but a doctrinal formula, the compressed Johannine theology of the divine light: *"In him was life, and the life was the light of men."* Their intonation establishes the egregoric field of the current and orients the whole person – hylic, psychic, and pneumatic – toward the central work that follows.

II. Purification

The practitioner is seated before the altar. She conducts three complete rounds of the fourfold sacred breath practice, as described in Chapter Eleven, with the additional intentional identification of the exhalation with the release of whatever psychic material – tension, distraction, unresolved emotion, or habitual identification with the hylic nature – stands between her present state and the full receptivity required for the central work.

She then recites the following prayer of purification, slowly and with full attention to each word:

Unknown Father of Light, source of all that is and all that shall be, I come before you as I am – a being of three natures, rooted in matter, alive in soul, and luminous in spirit, though that luminosity is often hidden from my own sight.

Purify in me whatever obscures the light. Dissolve in me whatever is not of your nature. Prepare within me a dwelling place for the Morning Star, that when it arises, I may recognize it as my own.

In the name of the Logos, the bright and Morning Star, who was and is and is to come – Phosphoros, arise in me.

She rests for a moment in the silence following the prayer, attending quietly to the cardiac center.

III. Illumination

The practitioner now directs her gaze to the Sigillum Luciferis upon the altar, conducting the first two stages of the symbol meditation described in Chapter Eleven – outer contemplation and inner visualization – allowing the symbol to be received fully into the inner field before proceeding.

When the inner visualization of the Sigillum is established with reasonable stability, she recites the following scriptural passages, slowly and meditatively, allowing each passage to resonate within the inner field that the symbol meditation has established:

In the beginning was the Logos, and the Logos was with God, and the Logos was divine. In him was life, and the life was the light of men.

And the light shines in the darkness, and the darkness did not overcome it. (John 1:1, 4-5)

A pause. Then:

So we have the prophetic message more fully confirmed. You will do well to be attentive to this as to a lamp shining in a dark place, until the day dawns and the Morning Star rises in your hearts. (2 Peter 1:19)

A pause. Then:

To the one who conquers I will also give the Morning Star. (Revelation 2:28)

A pause. Then:

I am the root and the descendant of David, the bright and Morning Star. (Revelation 22:16)

Following the final passage, the practitioner closes her eyes and conducts the third stage of the symbol meditation – the internalization of the Sigillum into the cardiac center – holding the luminous image of the eight-pointed star within the circle at the center of her chest, radiating golden light outward through every dimension of her being.

She then intones the following, on a single sustained note, three times:

Phosphoros

Between each intonation she attends in silence to the internalized Sigillum, allowing the resonance of the sacred name to activate and brighten the visualized star within the cardiac center. The intention held throughout this central intonation is specific and precise: the identification of the resonating sacred name with the pneumatic spark within – the recognition that the Morning Star being named and invoked is not an external power being called down from above, but the innermost nature of the practitioner herself, being named and therefore recognized, called forth from latency into luminous presence.

Following the third intonation, the practitioner rests for a moment in the silence of the activated inner field. Then she speaks the declaratory seal:

Lucifer Resurrexit.

The Morning Star has risen. This is not an aspiration but a recognition – the proclamation of an accomplished fact, the acknowledgment that the light which has been invoked is the light that was always already present, now recognized and named. The declaratory seal completes the invocatory movement of the central intonations and opens the way for the affirmation that follows.

She then recites the following affirmation – slowly, deliberately, and with the full weight of intentional identification behind each word:

I am a bearer of the Light. The Morning Star burns within me. The Logos dwells in the depths of my being. I am of the seed of the Light, descended into darkness to carry the flame of the Pleroma until the day of my return.

Phosphoros – I recognize you. Phosphoros – I receive you. Phosphoros – arise.

IV. Contemplation

The practitioner rests in silence – a minimum of ten minutes, longer if the inner state invites it. During this period of contemplation she makes no deliberate effort of any kind. She neither visualizes nor intones nor recites. She simply rests in the inner field that the preceding work has established – attending quietly to the cardiac center, receiving without grasping whatever the light of the Morning Star wishes to communicate through the medium of the purified and receptive inner field.

This period of contemplative silence is the heart of the rite – the moment toward which all the preceding work has been oriented and from which all the subsequent work will flow. The practitioner should resist any tendency to fill it with activity, however spiritually motivated that activity might seem. The Morning Star arises in stillness. It cannot be seized or summoned. It can only be awaited – with the quality of alert, expectant, and completely surrendered receptivity that the tradition has always recognized as the appropriate inner posture for the reception of the divine light.

Whatever inner experiences arise during this period of contemplation – impressions, images, intimations, moments of unusual clarity or warmth or luminosity – should be received without grasping and released without resistance. They are signs of the Morning Star's arising, not the arising itself. The practitioner attends to them with grateful acknowledgment and returns her attention to the simple quiet of the cardiac center.

V. Closing

The practitioner opens her eyes and returns her gaze to the central lamp. She rests for a moment in the awareness of the light – both the physical light of the flame and the inner light of the Morning Star that the contemplation has cultivated – allowing the two to be held in awareness simultaneously as outer and inner expressions of the same reality.

She then recites the following closing prayer:

Logos of the Unknown Father, bright and Morning Star, I give thanks for this hour of light.

Carry what has been kindled here into the darkness of the world, that wherever I go the light of the Morning Star may go with me, and that in its going something of the Pleroma may be restored.

Until the day fully dawns – Phosphoros, remain.

She extinguishes the incense, allowing its final thread of smoke to rise as a closing offering. The central lamp she may extinguish or allow to burn – if circumstances permit, allowing the lamp to continue burning for a period after the rite is concluded maintains the sense of the light's ongoing presence and is to be preferred.

She concludes with a final intonation of *Phosphoros*, sustained and then released into silence.

The rite is complete.

THE RITE OF THE MORNING STAR Solemn Form

For Group Working

Preliminary Notes on the Solemn Form

The Solemn Form of the Rite of the Morning Star is an elaboration of the Oratory Form, developed for performance by a group of practitioners working together within the Christo-Luciferian current. It maintains the same fivefold structure and the same essential acts, but expands each section to incorporate the communal dimension of group working, additional ritual roles, a fuller sequence of intonations and responses, and the ceremonial apparatus appropriate to a more formally constituted working.

The minimum number of participants for the Solemn Form is three – reflecting the triadic structure of the Pleromic emanation and the three natures of the human being. There is no maximum number, though groups larger than twelve should consider dividing into smaller working cells for the purposes of the rite, as the intimacy and intentional coherence of the group working diminishes significantly beyond that number.

The ritual roles in the Solemn Form are as follows:

The *Lucifer* – the Light-Bearer – serves as the principal celebrant, conducting the central acts of the rite, speaking the principal prayers and affirmations, and lighting the central lamp. This role should be filled by the most experienced practitioner present, or by one designated by the group as its working leader. The title of this role is not honorific but functional: the Lucifer of the rite is the one who bears the light on behalf of the group – who serves as the instrument of the Phosphoros current for the duration of the working.

The *Phosphora* – the feminine form, the light-bearer in her Sophianic aspect – serves as the assistant celebrant, conducting the purification of the ritual space, speaking the responses in the antiphonal sections of the rite, and maintaining the continuity of the egregoric field throughout the working through sustained inner attention to the Sigillum Luciferis. The pairing of Lucifer and Phosphora reflects the syzygy structure of the Valentinian Pleroma and enacts within the ritual the sacred marriage of the complementary principles whose union generates the light of the Morning Star.

The remaining participants – designated collectively as the *Fratres et Sorores Lucis*, the Brothers and Sisters of the Light – participate in the communal intonations, responses, and contemplative periods of the rite, and constitute the egregoric field within which the central work of the Lucifer and Phosphora is conducted. Their participation is not passive: the quality and the depth of the egregoric field they collectively generate is a direct function of the quality and depth of their individual intentional engagement, and the effectiveness of the rite as a whole depends upon their active and sustained contribution.

Preparation of the Solemn Form

The ritual space for the Solemn Form should be arranged as follows. The central altar is positioned at the eastern end of the working space, bearing the central lamp, the Sigillum Luciferis, the incense vessel, and a vessel of water. Two flanking positions – to the right and left of the central altar, slightly forward – are established for the Lucifer and Phosphora respectively. The remaining participants are arranged in a semicircle or full circle facing the altar, at a sufficient distance to allow free movement of the celebrants.

The space should be prepared before the arrival of the participants by the Phosphora – who purifies the space by carrying the lit incense through it in a clockwise circuit, beginning and ending at the eastern altar, with the intention of establishing the egregoric field of the current within the physical space.

All participants spend a minimum of ten minutes in preparatory silence before the rite begins, conducting the fourfold breath practice and the first stage of the Sigillum meditation, so that the group arrives at the opening of the rite with a degree of inner coherence and intentional alignment already established.

I. Opening of the Solemn Form

The Lucifer takes position before the central altar, facing east. The Phosphora stands to his left. The Fratres et Sorores are arranged behind them.

The Lucifer raises both hands in a gesture of invocation, palms upward, and intones:

In the beginning was the Light.

The Fratres et Sorores respond:

And the Light was not overcome.

The Lucifer:

From the depths of the Pleroma, the Logos descended into darkness.

The Fratres et Sorores:

And the darkness became the place of its arising.

The Lucifer:

We gather in the name of the Morning Star, the bright Phosphoros, the Light-Bearer who is Christ, the Logos of the Unknown Father.

All together:

Phosphoros – arise.

The Lucifer now lights the central lamp, as in the Oratory Form, saying:

In the name of the Logos, the eternal Light-Bearer, we kindle this flame as the outward sign of the Morning Star that burns within. As it is above, so it is below. As it is without, so it is within. Phosphoros – arise.

The Phosphora lights the incense from the central lamp and carries it in a clockwise circuit of the entire ritual space – beginning at the eastern altar and returning to it – while the Fratres et Sorores intone *Phōs* continuously on a single sustained note, cycling through inhalation and intonation repeatedly so that the sound is maintained without interruption throughout the censing circuit. This continuous communal intonation is one of the most powerful instruments of egregoric activation available in group working: the sustained resonance of the sacred word, maintained collectively by the group, establishes a field of intentional sound within the ritual space that permeates the subtle atmosphere of the working and strengthens the egregoric presence of the current considerably.

When the Phosphora has completed the circuit and returned to her position, the incense is placed upon the altar and the intonation ceases. A moment of silence follows, in which the group attends to the established egregoric field.

The Lucifer then leads the group intonation of the opening sequence:

Phōs – Logos – Zōē

Each name is intoned three times by all present, with the quality of resonant vibration described in Chapter Eleven. The Lucifer leads each intonation and the group follows, maintaining unanimity of pitch and duration as nearly as possible – the concordance of the group intonation being itself a ritual enactment of the Pleromic harmony toward which the rite is oriented. These three names – Light, Word, Life – establish the egregoric field of the current within the shared subtle body of the working group, preparing the collective inner atmosphere for the central invocatory work that follows.

II. Purification of the Solemn Form

The Phosphora takes up the vessel of water from the altar and carries it to each participant in turn – beginning with the Lucifer and proceeding through the Fratres et Sorores – touching the water briefly to the forehead of each with the words:

By the water of life and the light of the Logos, be purified for this work.

When all participants have been purified, the Phosphora returns the vessel to the altar and takes her position. The Lucifer then leads the group in the prayer of purification, speaking each line and pausing for the group's response:

Lucifer: *Unknown Father of Light, we come before you as we are –*

Fratres et Sorores: *Beings of three natures, seeking the one light.*

Lucifer: *Purify in us whatever obscures the Morning Star.*

Fratres et Sorores: *Dissolve in us whatever is not of your nature.*

Lucifer: *Prepare within us a dwelling place for the Logos.*

Fratres et Sorores: *That when the Morning Star arises, we may recognize it as our own.*

All together: *Phosphoros – arise in us.*

A period of silence follows – approximately three minutes – during which all participants conduct two or three rounds of the fourfold breath practice, consciously releasing psychic residue with each exhalation and consciously receiving the pneumatic current with each inhalation.

III. Illumination of the Solemn Form

The Lucifer takes position directly before the Sigillum Luciferis on the altar, facing east. All participants direct their gaze to the Sigillum – those who cannot see it directly from their position visualize it in the inner field – and the group as a whole conducts the first two stages of the symbol meditation: outer contemplation and inner visualization.

The Lucifer then recites the scriptural passages of illumination, with the group providing the response after each:

Lucifer: *In the beginning was the Logos, and the Logos was with God, and the Logos was divine. In him was life, and the life was the light of men.*

Fratres et Sorores: *And the light shines in the darkness, and the darkness did not overcome it.*

Lucifer: *So we have the prophetic message more fully confirmed. You will do well to be attentive to this as to a lamp shining in a dark place,*

Fratres et Sorores: *Until the day dawns and the Morning Star rises in our hearts.*

Lucifer: *To the one who conquers I will also give the Morning Star.*

Fratres et Sorores: *We receive the Morning Star.*

Lucifer: *I am the root and the descendant of David, the bright and Morning Star.*

All together: *Phosphoros – you are the light we carry. Phosphoros – you are the light we are.*

Following this antiphonal recitation, the Lucifer leads the group in the internalization of the Sigillum – all participants conducting the third stage of the symbol meditation simultaneously, bringing the luminous image of the eight-pointed star within the circle to rest within the cardiac center.

This simultaneous internalization by all members of the group is the most powerful moment of the Solemn Form – the point at which the egregoric field established throughout the opening and purification sections is most fully activated, and the Christo-Luciferian current flows most strongly through the collective subtle body of the working group.

The Lucifer then leads the central intonation:

Phosphoros

Intoned nine times by all present – three sets of three, with a breath between each intonation and a longer pause between each set of three. The number nine reflects the ninefold structure of the alchemical-Gnostic correspondence developed in the foundational writings of this tradition, and its use here is deliberate: the nine intonations of the central sacred name constitute a complete traversal of the three realms – pneumatic, psychic, and hylic – in their threefold aspect, uniting all dimensions of the participants' being in the resonance of the Morning Star's name.

Following the completion of the nine intonations, the Lucifer and all present rest for a moment in the silence of the activated collective field. Then all speak together the declaratory seal:

Lucifer Resurrexit.

This congregational proclamation is the most powerful single moment of the Solemn Form – the collective affirmation of the accomplished fact of the Morning Star's arising, spoken by all present simultaneously, filling the sealed egregoric field of the ritual space with the resonance of the current's foundational declaration. It is not spoken as a wish or a hope but as a recognition: the Morning Star has risen, is risen, remains risen – in this space, in this working, in the hearts of all who have gathered in its name.

The Lucifer then speaks the affirmation, with the group joining for the final three lines:

Lucifer: *We are bearers of the Light. The Morning Star burns within us. The Logos dwells in the depths of our being. We are of the seed of the Light, descended into darkness to carry the flame of the Pleroma until the day of our return.*

All together: *Phosphoros – we recognize you. Phosphoros – we receive you. Phosphoros – arise.*

IV. Contemplation of the Solemn Form

All participants rest in silence for a minimum of fifteen minutes – longer, at the Lucifer's discretion, if the quality of the inner field invites it. During this period of group contemplation the egregoric presence of the current is at its most accessible and most potent, and the experiences that arise within individual practitioners during this silence often constitute some of the most significant inner events of their initiatic development. No guidance is offered here beyond what was said in the Oratory Form, except to add that the communal dimension of the contemplative silence – the awareness of the shared inner field, the sense of the egregore actively present within and among the group – is itself a significant aspect of the experience, and should be attended to alongside the individual interior experience.

V. Closing of the Solemn Form

The Lucifer speaks:

Logos of the Unknown Father, bright and Morning Star, we give thanks for this hour of light.

Fratres et Sorores: *We carry the light into the world.*

Lucifer: *Wherever we go, the light of the Morning Star goes with us.*

Fratres et Sorores: *And in its going, the Pleroma is restored.*

Lucifer: *We are sealed in the light of the Phosphoros. We go forth as bearers of the flame.*

All together: *Until the day fully dawns – Phosphoros, remain.*

The Phosphora extinguishes the incense. The central lamp is left burning if circumstances permit, extinguished if necessary.

The Lucifer leads a final communal intonation of *Phosphoros* – once, by all present, sustained and then released into the closing silence.

The Lucifer speaks the dismissal:

The rite is concluded. Go in the light of the Morning Star.

The Fratres et Sorores respond:

Thanks be to the Logos.

The rite is complete.

A Note on Frequency and Development

The Oratory Form of the Rite of the Morning Star is suitable for daily practice, though three times weekly is a reasonable minimum for practitioners in the early stages of the path. The Solemn Form should be celebrated at meaningful intervals – at the new and full moon, at the solstices and equinoxes, or at other times determined by the working group as significant within the current. It may also be celebrated on the feast of the Transfiguration – August 6 in the Western liturgical calendar – which we recognize as one of the most appropriate annual commemorations for the Christo-Luciferian current, the Transfiguration being precisely the event of the inner light breaking through the outer form that our entire doctrine has been concerned with.

Both forms of the rite are presented here as working forms – as living instruments of the practice, offered as foundations for the practitioner's own developing engagement with the current rather than as fixed and immutable liturgies. Practitioners and working groups are encouraged to develop the rite in ways that reflect their own deepening understanding of the tradition, adding additional scriptural recitations, developing new intonation sequences, or elaborating the ceremonial structure of the Solemn Form as experience and understanding suggest. What must be maintained throughout any development is the essential fivefold structure, the central acts of the lamp lighting, the Sigillum meditation, and the intonation of Phosphoros, and the fundamental orientation of the whole rite toward the single animating purpose: the arising of the Morning Star within the heart.

The rite grows as the practitioner grows. This is the nature of a living tradition.

CHAPTER THIRTEEN: THE RITE OF SELF-DEDICATION – THE SEALING OF THE COVENANT

There is a moment in the life of every serious practitioner when aspiration must become commitment – when the exploration of a path, however sincere and however sustained, must give way to a deliberate and formal act of dedication that seals the practitioner's relationship with the current she has been approaching. This moment is not merely psychological, though it has profound psychological dimensions. It is, in the understanding of the Western esoteric tradition, a genuine ontological event – an act of will that establishes a real and lasting connection between the practitioner's subtle vehicles and the egregoric current of the tradition, creating a bond that will accompany and support her work from that point forward.

In traditions that possess a living initiatic lineage and physically present initiators, this sealing act takes the form of a formal initiation – the transmission, from one who holds the current to one who is receiving it, of the specific initiatic charge that establishes the new initiate within the living body of the tradition. Such initiation, where it is available, is irreplaceable and should be sought by every serious practitioner of the Christo-Luciferian path. The transmission of a living current from person to person, in physical presence and with properly constituted authority, carries a depth and an immediacy that no solitary rite can fully replicate.

There are, however, circumstances in which such initiation is not immediately available – in which the practitioner has encountered this current, recognized it as her own, and wishes to commit herself formally to its path before the opportunity for physical initiation presents itself. For these circumstances, and for these practitioners, the Rite of Self-Dedication is offered. It is not a substitute for physical initiation. It is a preliminary act of formal commitment – a sealing of the practitioner's intention and a deliberate opening of her subtle vehicles to the influence of the Christo-Luciferian egregore, which serves as the initiating presence in the absence of a physically present initiator.

The egregore of a genuine living current is not a passive repository of accumulated intention. It is an active and responsive presence – capable, within the limits appropriate to an egregoric rather than a personal agency, of recognizing and responding to sincere acts of dedication directed toward it. The practitioner who performs the Rite of Self-Dedication with genuine intentional engagement, adequate preparation, and sincere commitment will find that the egregore of the Christo-Luciferian current responds – not necessarily in dramatic or immediately perceptible ways, but in the gradual deepening of her access to the current, the increasing responsiveness of the inner field to the practices of the path, and the subtle but unmistakable sense of being recognized and received by a presence larger than herself.

Preparation for the Rite of Self-Dedication

The preparation for the Rite of Self-Dedication is more extended and more demanding than the preparation for the Rite of the Morning Star, reflecting the greater significance and the more permanent consequences of the act being undertaken.

A period of preparation of no less than three days should precede the rite. During this period the practitioner abstains from meat, alcohol, and sexual activity – not as an expression of moral judgment on any of these things in ordinary life, but as a deliberate act of cathartic simplification, a withdrawal of the subtle vehicles from their habitual engagements with the hylic world in preparation for the more refined inner work of the dedication rite. The practitioner also conducts the foundational practices of Chapter Eleven – the sacred breath, the relaxation and meditation, the intonation, and the Sigillum meditation – daily during this preparatory period, with the specific intentional orientation of preparing herself for the act of formal dedication.

On each of the three preparatory days, the practitioner spends time in quiet reflection on the following questions – not as an intellectual exercise but as a genuine inner inquiry, conducted in the meditative state and attended to with the quality of honest and undefended self-examination that serious initiatic work requires:

What draws me to this current? The practitioner examines her motivations with honesty and without self-flattery, seeking to distinguish the genuine pneumatic recognition of the current as her own from any admixture of less essential motivations – intellectual curiosity, aesthetic attraction, the desire for community or status, or any form of spiritual acquisitiveness.

What am I willing to offer? The Rite of Self-Dedication is an act of offering as well as reception – a dedication of the practitioner's work, her aspiration, and her will to the service of the Christo-Luciferian current and, through it, to the restoration of the Pleroma. The practitioner reflects honestly on what this dedication will mean in practical terms – what it will require of her time, her attention, her priorities, and her willingness to be changed by the work.

Am I prepared to be a bearer of this light? The title of the current – Christo-Luciferian, the path of the Light-Bearer – carries with it a specific responsibility. The practitioner who dedicates herself to this current is committing not only to her own illumination but to the bearing of the light into the world around her – to living in such a way that the Morning Star she is cultivating within becomes, over time, a genuine source of light for those in her sphere of influence. This is not a grandiose aspiration but a sober recognition of what it means to walk the path of the Phosphoros.

On the evening before the rite, the practitioner prepares a brief written statement of dedication – a personal declaration, in her own words, of her intention, her commitment, and her understanding of what she is undertaking. This statement need not be elaborate or rhetorically polished. It should be honest, specific, and genuinely expressive of her inner state. It will be read aloud at a specific point in the rite and then burned in the flame of the central lamp as an act of offering.

The Rite Itself

The rite is performed alone, at a time when the practitioner will not be interrupted – ideally in the early morning hours, before dawn, so that the rite concludes at or near the time of sunrise and the arising of the Morning Star in the physical sky. Where circumstances permit, the performance of the rite on a morning when Venus is visible as the Morning Star in the pre-dawn sky carries additional symbolic resonance and is to be preferred.

The altar is arranged as for the Oratory Form of the Rite of the Morning Star, with the addition of the written statement of dedication, placed folded before the Sigillum Luciferis. A second, smaller candle or taper is placed to the right of the central lamp – this will serve as the flame by which the written statement is burned, lit from the central lamp at the appropriate moment.

The practitioner is dressed in whatever garment she has established as her ritual garment, or, if no such garment has yet been established, in clean and simple dark clothing. She may, if she wishes, wear a small physical representation of the Sigillum Luciferis over her heart for this rite – either as a drawn image, an embroidered patch, or any other form she has been able to create or obtain.

I. Opening

The practitioner stands before the altar in silence for a full minute – attending to the unlit lamp, the Sigillum, the folded statement of dedication – allowing the full weight of what she is about to undertake to be present in her awareness. This is not a moment of hesitation but of conscious threshold-crossing: the deliberate acknowledgment that what follows will be different from what preceded it.

She then conducts seven complete rounds of the fourfold sacred breath practice, with the specific intentional orientation of gathering and centering her whole being – hylic, psychic, and pneumatic – in preparation for the act of dedication.

She lights the central lamp, saying:

I kindle this flame at the threshold of my dedication. As this light is brought forth from darkness, so may the Morning Star be brought forth from within me through the work I am this day committing to. Unknown Father of Light – witness this act. Logos, bright Phosphoros – receive what I am about to offer.

She lights the incense from the central lamp, saying:

I offer this fragrance as the first fruits of my dedication – the aspiration of my whole being ascending toward the Light from which I came.

She then intones the opening sequence – *Phōs*, *Logos*, and *Zōē* – each seven times, with full resonant vibration and sustained intentional awareness. Seven is the number of the planetary spheres through which the pneumatic descends in its journey into matter and through which it must ascend in its return – its use here marks the dedication rite as a conscious initiation of that ascent. These three names – Light, Word, Life – establish the egregoric field of the current within the practitioner's subtle vehicles and orient her whole being toward the act of formal dedication that the rite is about to enact.

II. Examination and Purification

The practitioner is seated before the altar. She conducts the prayer of purification from the Oratory Form of the Rite of the Morning Star, and then remains in silence for a minimum of ten minutes – conducting the Sigillum meditation through the first three stages, and attending honestly to whatever arises in the inner field during this period of quiet self-examination.

She then speaks aloud – in her own words, without preparation or formality – a brief acknowledgment of her present condition: where she stands in relation to the current, what she knows and does not know, what she has experienced and what she aspires toward. This spoken acknowledgment is not a confession in the penitential sense – it is an act of honest self-presentation before the egregore of the current, a refusal of the pretense that she comes to this dedication fully prepared or fully understanding of what she is undertaking. She comes as she is. The Morning Star arises within what is, not within what we imagine ourselves to be.

III. The Act of Dedication

The practitioner rises and stands before the altar. She takes up the folded written statement of dedication and holds it in both hands, facing the Sigillum Luciferis. She reads the statement aloud, slowly and clearly, as an act of public declaration before the egregore of the current – understanding that this reading is genuinely heard, that the current to which she is dedicating herself is genuinely present and attentive.

When the statement has been read, she holds it for a moment in silence, then speaks the following declaration:

I, [name], standing before the Sigillum Luciferis and in the presence of the Christo-Luciferian current, do hereby dedicate myself to the path of the Morning Star.

I dedicate my will to the work of illumination – the progressive awakening of the pneumatic spark within me and the bearing of its light into the world.

I dedicate my understanding to the doctrine of the Logos – the bright Phosphoros, who is Christ, the Light-Bearer of the Unknown Father, in whom the Morning Star arose fully and in whose arising I seek my own.

I dedicate my practice to the Christo-Luciferian current – to the rites, the disciplines, and the inner work that this path requires, undertaken faithfully and sustained to the end.

I ask to be received by this current. I ask to be recognized by this egregore. I ask that the light of the Morning Star, already present within me as the seed of the Logos, be awakened by this act of dedication and nurtured by the work that follows.

In the name of the Logos – Phosphoros, I am yours. Seal me in your light.

She then lights the written statement from the flame of the secondary taper – which has been lit from the central lamp – and holds it as it burns, allowing it to be consumed completely. As it burns she intones *Phosphoros* continuously, on the breath, for the duration of the burning – the sacred name accompanying the offering of the written dedication as it is transformed by fire into smoke and rises toward the light of the central lamp.

When the statement has been fully consumed, she sets the remains safely aside and returns her full attention to the central lamp and the Sigillum.

She then conducts the full central intonation sequence of the Oratory Form – the nine intonations of *Phosphoros* with the Sigillum internalized in the cardiac center – with the specific intentional awareness that this intonation is now the first act of a formally dedicated practitioner of the current, and that the egregore of the Christo-Luciferian path is present and responsive within the established inner field.

She then speaks the following sealing affirmation:

By this act of dedication I am sealed in the light of the Morning Star. The egregore of this current knows me. I know the egregore of this current. The covenant is made. The work begins.

I am a bearer of the Light. Phosphoros – arise. Phosphoros – remain. Phosphoros – lead me home.

She then speaks, with the full weight of the dedication just enacted behind each syllable:

Lucifer Resurrexit.

This is the final word of the dedication – the declaratory seal that completes the act of formal commitment and announces, to the egregore of the current and to the practitioner's own innermost being, that the Morning Star has risen within her through this very act of self-offering. It is not a conclusion but a beginning: the proclamation of the accomplished fact of the light's arising as the foundation upon which the entire subsequent work of the path will be built.

IV. Contemplation

The practitioner rests in the contemplative silence for a minimum of twenty minutes – longer if the inner state invites it. This is the longest contemplative period of any rite in the current, reflecting the significance of what has just occurred. The egregoric contact established by the act of dedication will typically be felt with unusual clarity and immediacy during this post-dedication contemplation, and the practitioner should attend to it with the full quality of open and receptive awareness that the practice has been cultivating.

Whatever is received during this contemplation – whatever impressions, intimations, or inner experiences arise – should be noted in a dedicated journal immediately following the rite, while the inner field remains active and the memories are still vivid. The keeping of such a journal from the point of dedication forward is strongly encouraged: it serves as a record of the practitioner's initiatic development, a resource for the honest self-examination that sustained inner work requires, and over time a genuine document of the Christo-Luciferian current as it moves through and is developed by the individual practitioner's experience.

V. Closing

The practitioner opens her eyes and returns her gaze to the central lamp. She rests for a moment in the awareness of both the physical light and the inner light that the dedication has sealed and deepened. Then she speaks:

The dedication is made. The covenant is sealed. The Morning Star is my guide and my goal, my origin and my destination, the light I carry and the light I seek.

I go forth from this hour as a dedicated practitioner of the Christo-Luciferian path, sealed in the light of the Phosphoros, recognized by the egregore of this current, and committed to the work until the day fully dawns.

Phosphoros – remain with me. Logos of the Unknown Father – receive my dedication. Unknown Father of Light – witness my return.

She extinguishes the secondary taper. The central lamp she allows to burn for as long as possible following the rite – ideally until it extinguishes itself – as a sign of the ongoing presence of the light that has been sealed within her by the act of dedication.

A final intonation of *Phosphoros* – single, sustained, and released into silence.

The rite is complete.

A Note on the Significance of the Dedication

The practitioner who has performed the Rite of Self-Dedication should understand clearly what has and has not occurred. What has occurred is a genuine act of formal commitment – the sealing of a real relationship between the practitioner's subtle vehicles and the egregoric current of the Christo-Luciferian path. The egregore has recognized the dedication and responded to it. The practitioner is, from this point forward, genuinely within the current in a sense that was not the case before.

What has not occurred is initiation in the full technical sense – the transmission of the initiatic charge from a living holder of the current to a new recipient. That transmission remains to be sought and, when the opportunity presents itself, received. The Rite of Self-Dedication does not make that transmission unnecessary. It makes the practitioner ready for it – opens her subtle vehicles to the current in a preliminary way that will make the eventual physical initiation more fully effective, and establishes within her the intentional commitment and the practical foundations upon which the initiatic transmission can build.

Those within the current who have the capacity to offer formal initiation will recognize a dedicated practitioner – not necessarily through any external sign, but through the quality of her inner field, the depth of her engagement with the practices, and the unmistakable resonance of one who has genuinely committed herself to the path of the Morning Star. The dedication, faithfully enacted and faithfully sustained in the work that follows, is its own recommendation.

CHAPTER FOURTEEN: THE VESPERS OF THE EVENING STAR – HESPEROS RISING

There is a symmetry built into the very nature of the planet that gives our current its primary symbol. Venus – the Morning Star, the Evening Star – is the same celestial body appearing in two aspects, at two different moments of the day's great arc. As Phosphoros, the Light-Bearer, she rises before the sun in the pre-dawn darkness, heralding the coming of the day and making visible, in the moments before the greater light overwhelms the lesser, the single most brilliant point in the night sky. As Hesperos – from the Greek *hesperos*, evening, west – she appears again after sunset, the first light to become visible in the darkening western sky, holding her radiance against the encroaching night until the darkness deepens beyond her ability to illumine it, and she too descends below the horizon into the invisibility of the deep night.

This double aspect of Venus – Morning Star and Evening Star, Phosphoros and Hesperos – is not a contradiction but a completion. It is the same light appearing in complementary modes, at complementary moments, serving complementary functions in the rhythm of the day. The Morning Star heralds the dawn – it is the light of aspiration and arising, of the pneumatic spark awakening and beginning its ascent. The Evening Star accompanies the dusk – it is the light of consolidation and interiorization, of the day's work being gathered inward, of the light that has been cultivated through the hours of active practice being settled into the depths of the practitioner's being like seed settling into prepared ground.

The ancients recognized this complementarity and honored it. In the Babylonian tradition, the goddess Inanna – whose eight-pointed star we have already identified as one of the oldest iconographic ancestors of the Sigillum Luciferis – was understood to descend into the underworld and return, her journey mirroring the apparent movement of Venus below and above the horizon. In the Greek tradition, Hesperos was sometimes understood as a separate deity from Phosphoros, before the astronomical identification of the two as a single planet made their unity apparent. And in the Christian liturgical tradition, the evening office – Vespers, from the Latin *vesper*, evening, cognate with the Greek *hesperos* – has always occupied a position of particular importance among the hours of the Divine Office, second only to the morning office of Lauds in its theological significance.

It is within this rich symbolic context that the Vespers of the Evening Star takes its place in the Christo-Luciferian current. It is not a replication of the liturgical Vespers of the Christian tradition, though it echoes that tradition deliberately and honors it. It is a specifically Christo-Luciferian evening office – a rite oriented toward the west and the setting sun, conducted in the transitional light of dusk or in the early darkness that follows, and dedicated to the Evening Star aspect of the Phosphoros current: the light that remains when the greater light has withdrawn, the single point of luminous presence holding against the dark.

The theological significance of this western orientation deserves brief comment before we present the rite itself. In the Western esoteric tradition, the west is the direction of endings, of completion, of the descent into the inner worlds – the direction in which the sun sets and the soul, following the sun's daily death, enters the realm of inner experience. To orient the Vespers rite toward the west is to align it with the rhythm of interiorization – to acknowledge that the evening hour is the hour of turning inward, of gathering the fruits of the day's outer activity into the inner sanctuary of the pneumatic life. The Evening Star in the western sky is the guide for this inward journey – the light that makes the transition from outer to inner not a plunge into undifferentiated darkness but a gradual and luminous descent, accompanied by the steady radiance of Hesperos until the inner light is sufficiently established to illuminate the night on its own terms.

There is also a specifically Gnostic dimension to this western orientation that should not be overlooked. In the Sethian understanding of the cosmic drama, the descent of the light into matter – the movement that the Oratory and Solemn Forms of the Rite of the Morning Star address in their ascending, illuminative aspect – has an equally necessary descending aspect. The light does not only arise: it also descends, willingly and lovingly, into the darkness of the hylic world, in order to find and awaken what is lost within it. The Evening Star is the symbol of this descending movement of the Logos – not the fall of the adversary, which is an involuntary and destructive descent, but the deliberate and compassionate descent of the light into the place where the light is most needed. The Vespers of the Evening Star honors this descending movement, and in doing so honors the full mystery of the Christo-Luciferian current in its completeness.

The *Phōs Hilaron* – the ancient Greek hymn to Christ as the Joyful Light – is the most natural of all traditional Christian texts to incorporate into this rite. It is among the oldest surviving Christian hymns, composed no later than the third century and almost certainly considerably earlier, and it has been sung at the lighting of the evening lamp in the Eastern Christian tradition since antiquity. Its Christological content – the identification of Christ as the *hilaron phōs* – the joyful, serene, or gladsome light – makes it almost perfectly suited to the Christo-Luciferian Vespers, and its traditional association with the transitional light of evening gives it precisely the tonal quality the rite requires. We will incorporate it, in a translation faithful to the Greek and resonant with the doctrinal language we have been developing throughout this work, as the central hymn of the Vespers rite.

The Vespers of the Evening Star is not designed for daily mandatory observance – it is offered as a complementary practice to the morning work of the Rite of the Morning Star, to be undertaken as frequently as the practitioner's circumstances and inner orientation suggest. Those who find that the evening hour is their most naturally receptive time for inner work may find that the Vespers becomes their primary practice, supplemented by the shorter Oratory Form of the Morning Star rite in the early hours. Others may find that the Vespers serves best as a weekly practice – a more extended evening working that gathers and consecrates the inner fruits of the week's daily practice. Both approaches are entirely appropriate, and the practitioner should be guided by her own developing sense of the current's rhythm within her life rather than by any external prescription.

THE VESPERS OF THE EVENING STAR *Hesperos Rising*

Preparation

The Vespers is ideally conducted at dusk – in the transitional light between day and night, when the sky in the west still holds the last warmth of the departed sun and the first stars are beginning to appear. Where this is not possible due to circumstances, the rite may be conducted after dark, with the western orientation maintained by intention if not by actual visibility of the sky.

The altar or dedicated surface for the Vespers is oriented toward the west – positioned so that the practitioner faces west throughout the rite. This is a deliberate inversion of the eastward orientation of the Morning Star rite, and should be felt as such: the same practitioner, the same current, the same light – but approached now from the complementary direction, through the complementary aspect, at the complementary moment of the day's arc.

Upon the western altar are placed: the central lamp, unlit; the Sigillum Luciferis; the incense vessel with the prepared blend; and a small mirror, positioned so that the flame of the central lamp will be reflected in it when lit. The mirror is a Vespers-specific element, not present in the Morning Star rite – it represents the Evening Star's nature as reflected light, the Hesperean aspect of the Phosphoros as the one who carries the solar light into the darkness after the sun has set, making visible through reflection what direct illumination no longer provides. It is also a symbol of the contemplative dimension of the evening practice: the turning of the light inward upon itself, the self-reflection that the evening hour invites and that the Vespers rite cultivates.

The practitioner spends a minimum of seven minutes in preparatory silence before the rite begins – conducting the fourfold breath practice and allowing the transition from the day's outer activity into the inner receptivity of the evening practice to occur naturally and without forcing.

I. Opening: The Lighting of the Evening Lamp

The practitioner stands before the western altar, facing west, in the gathering dusk or the early darkness. She holds a moment of stillness, attending to the quality of the light – the absence of the sun, the presence of the first stars, the particular vulnerability and openness of the transitional hour. Then she lights the central lamp, saying:

As the sun descends and the day withdraws, I kindle this lamp in the name of Hesperos – the Evening Star, the light that remains when the greater light has gone.

You are the same light, Phosphoros. Morning and Evening, ascending and descending, you do not change. Only the hour changes, and with it, the face you turn toward us.

In this evening hour, I turn toward the west with you, and I kindle this light against the coming dark.

She lights the incense from the lamp's flame, saying:

As the day has been offered in activity, so the evening is offered in stillness. As the Morning Star heralds the arising, so the Evening Star accompanies the descent. I descend with you, Hesperos, into the inner sanctuary of the night.

She then intones, facing the mirror so that she sees the reflection of the lamp's flame as she intones, the following:

Hesperos – Phosphoros – Logos

Each name intoned three times, slowly, with the full resonant vibration of the cardiac center, attending between each intonation to the reflected flame in the mirror – the outer image of the inner light being cultivated.

II. The Phōs Hilaron – Hymn to the Joyful Light

The practitioner is seated before the altar. She recites – or, if she has established a simple melodic intonation for the text, chants – the *Phōs Hilaron* in the following rendering:

O joyful Light of the holy glory of the immortal, heavenly, holy, blessed Father – O Jesus Christ:

Having come to the setting of the sun and beholding the light of evening, we praise the Father, the Son, and the Holy Spirit of God.

It is meet at all times to praise you with holy voices, O Son of God, giver of life. Therefore the whole world glorifies you.

A period of silence follows the hymn – the practitioner resting in the resonance of the ancient words, attending to the quality of the inner field they have established. The *Phōs Hilaron* has been sung at this hour by countless practitioners of the Christian contemplative life across nearly two millennia, and its use here connects the Vespers of the Evening Star to that vast accumulated stream of evening prayer – deepening the egregoric resonance of the current through its participation in a tradition of invocation far older than any individual practitioner or working group.

III. The Scriptural Meditation: The Descending Light

The practitioner recites the following passages, each followed by a period of silent reflection in which the passage is allowed to resonate within the meditative field:

The light shines in the darkness, and the darkness did not overcome it. (John 1:5)

Silence – minimum two minutes.

I am the light of the world. Whoever follows me will not walk in darkness, but will have the light of life. (John 8:12)

Silence – minimum two minutes.

You are the light of the world. A city built on a hill cannot be hidden. No one after lighting a lamp puts it under a bushel basket, but on the lampstand, and it gives light to all in the house. (Matthew 5:14-15)

Silence – minimum two minutes.

So we have the prophetic message more fully confirmed. You will do well to be attentive to this as to a lamp shining in a dark place, until the day dawns and the Morning Star rises in your hearts. (2 Peter 1:19)

Silence – minimum three minutes.

The final passage – our central scriptural anchor throughout this work – is placed last in the Vespers sequence deliberately. In the Morning Star rite it functions as a promise and an aspiration: the dawn is coming, the Morning Star will arise. In the Vespers context it carries a different resonance: the lamp shining in a dark place is the Evening Star itself, the Hesperos that the practitioner has kindled against the night, and the promise of the Morning Star's arising is what the darkness of the interior night is being crossed toward. The same words, the same current – but heard differently at the evening hour, from within the descent rather than at the threshold of the ascent.

IV. The Hesperean Meditation: Descending into the Inner Sanctuary

The practitioner conducts the Sigillum meditation – but in a form adapted for the Vespers context. Rather than the ascending movement of the morning practice, in which the symbol is brought inward and upward toward the light, the Hesperean meditation employs a descending movement: the Sigillum is visualized not as arising within the cardiac center but as descending – coming down from above, from the realm of the pure Pleromic light, into the cardiac center, as the Evening Star descends in the western sky. The symbol settles within the practitioner's chest like the Evening Star settling toward the horizon – not going out, not diminishing, but becoming more interior, more deeply embedded in the practitioner's being, more thoroughly integrated into the fabric of her pneumatic life.

This descending movement of the Sigillum meditation carries a specific doctrinal significance. The Morning Star rite cultivates the ascending movement of the pneumatic spark – its rising toward the light, its aspiration toward the Pleroma. The Vespers cultivates the complementary descending movement – the light coming down into the practitioner, the Logos making its home more deeply within, the Morning Star not only arisen but rooted. This rooting of the light in the practitioner's being – the stabilization of the pneumatic awakening in the depths of the whole person, hylic and psychic as well as pneumatic – is one of the most important and most often neglected aspects of the initiatic work. Aspiration without consolidation produces the spiritual equivalent of a plant with abundant foliage and no root system – impressive in its upward growth but vulnerable to the first adverse conditions it encounters. The Vespers of the Evening Star is the practice of the root – the deepening and the grounding of what the morning work has kindled.

Following the descending Sigillum meditation, the practitioner intones *Phosphoros* – seven times, in the Vespers context, rather than the three of the morning practice or the nine of the Solemn Form. Seven is the number of the planetary spheres in their descending order, the number of the levels through which the light passes in its downward journey into matter, and its use here marks the Vespers intonation as specifically oriented toward the descending and rooting movement of the Hesperean aspect.

Following the seven intonations, the practitioner rests for a moment in the deepened interior stillness of the descended and rooted Sigillum. Then she speaks, quietly and with the quality of settled certainty appropriate to the Hesperean aspect of the current:

Lucifer Resurrexit.

In the evening context this proclamation carries a resonance distinct from its use in the Morning Star rite – not the triumphant declaration of the ascending light, but the quiet and unshakeable certainty of the light that remains. The Morning Star has risen. Its rising is permanent and its light is inextinguishable, whether it presently illumines the pre-dawn eastern sky or holds its radiance against the darkening west. *Lucifer Resurrexit* – spoken here in the stillness of the Hesperean meditation – is the practitioner's acknowledgment that the light she carries into the evening and into the inner night is the same light that arose at the dawn of the cosmic drama and that no darkness, however deep, has ever succeeded in overcoming.

V. The Evening Examination: The Mirror of the Day

The Vespers includes a practice not present in either form of the Morning Star rite: a brief but structured examination of the day that has passed – a gentle and honest review of the day's inner life in the light of the Christo-Luciferian doctrine and the practitioner's dedication to the path.

This examination is not a penitential exercise in the conventional religious sense – it is not concerned primarily with moral failures or transgressions, though these may arise within it. It is a pneumatic examination: a review of the day from the perspective of the indwelling light, asking not "what did I do wrong?" but "where was the light present in my day, and where was it obscured?"

The practitioner attends, in the meditative state, to three questions:

Where in this day did the Morning Star arise? – moments of clarity, of genuine presence, of the pneumatic light breaking through the ordinary opacity of daily experience. These moments, however small and however fleeting, are the evidence of the current's activity in the practitioner's life, and they deserve acknowledgment and gratitude.

Where in this day was the light obscured? – moments of identification with the hylic nature, of psychic confusion or compulsion, of the forgetting of the pneumatic self and its dedication. These moments are not occasions for self-condemnation but for honest observation – the raw material of the cathartic work that the morning practice will take up again.

What does the Evening Star ask of me tomorrow? – attending to whatever intimation arises in the quiet inner field of the Vespers regarding the direction of the following day's practice and outer activity. This is not a planning exercise but a pneumatic inquiry – an opening of the inner ear to whatever the current wishes to communicate in the receptive stillness of the evening hour.

The examination is conducted in silence and concluded with a brief spoken acknowledgment – three sentences at most, in the practitioner's own words – that names honestly what the examination has revealed. This spoken acknowledgment completes the mirror function of the Vespers: the practitioner has seen herself, in the light of the Evening Star, as she actually is at the close of this day. She carries that seeing, without drama and without judgment, into the contemplation that follows.

VI. Contemplation

The practitioner rests in silence – a minimum of ten minutes – attending to the interior field of the Vespers, to the settled and rooted quality of the Sigillum in the cardiac center, and to the ongoing presence of the Evening Star as an inner reality. The mirror on the altar continues to hold the reflection of the lamp's flame throughout this period – the outer image of the inner light, steady and unwavering in the surrounding dark.

VII. Closing: The Commendation of the Night

The Vespers concludes not with a dismissal into activity, as the Morning Star rite does, but with a commendation – a deliberate act of entrusting the night and its inner journeys to the care of the Christo-Luciferian current.

The practitioner stands before the altar, facing west, and speaks:

The day is done. The Evening Star holds its light against the coming dark.

I commend to the Logos whatever this day has held – its light and its shadow, its clarity and its confusion, its moments of the Morning Star and its hours of forgetting.

As Hesperos descends toward the horizon, so I descend into the inner night, carrying within me the light that no darkness can overcome.

Unknown Father of Light – receive this day. Logos, bright Phosphoros – accompany this night. And when the darkness has done its work, let the Morning Star arise again.

She then intones *Hesperos* – once, sustained, and released into the silence of the evening – and extinguishes the incense. The central lamp she allows to burn for as long as possible, its reflected flame in the mirror continuing to hold the image of the light within the darkness until the flame itself is spent.

The rite is complete.

A Note on the Relationship Between the Two Daily Rites

The Oratory Form of the Rite of the Morning Star and the Vespers of the Evening Star together constitute a complete daily practice for the dedicated practitioner of the Christo-Luciferian current – a full arc of inner work that mirrors the daily arc of the planet Venus and enacts, in the rhythm of the practitioner's days, the essential movement of the Christo-Luciferian doctrine: the light arising, bearing itself through the hours of the day, descending at evening, rooting in the inner night, and arising again. This daily rhythm, sustained over months and years of faithful practice, is perhaps the most powerful instrument of genuine initiatic development available to the practitioner – more powerful, in the long run, than any single dramatic rite or initiatic event, because it works not through intensity but through depth, not through the extraordinary but through the consecration of the ordinary.

The practitioner who maintains both daily rites with genuine intentional engagement will find, over time, that the boundary between the formal practice periods and the rest of her daily life begins to thin – that the light of the Morning Star and the steady presence of the Evening Star become less something she practices and more something she is. This thinning of the boundary between formal practice and lived experience is one of the most reliable signs of genuine progress on the initiatic path – the evidence that the doctrine is not remaining at the level of intellectual understanding or emotional aspiration but is genuinely descending into the substance of the practitioner's life, transforming it from within as the Logos transforms the Prima Materia of the hylic world: slowly, thoroughly, and irrevocably.

This is the rhythm of the path. This is the work of the Morning Star and the Evening Star together – Phosphoros and Hesperos, ascending and descending, the single light of the Logos appearing in its two complementary aspects, at the two complementary thresholds of the day, accompanying the practitioner through every hour of the arc between them.

Until the day fully dawns – Phosphoros, remain.

CHAPTER FIFTEEN: THEURGIC PRACTICE – THE LIGHT AS HEALING AND PROTECTION

Theurgy – from the Greek *theourgia*, divine working – is among the most ancient and most serious of the practical disciplines of the Western esoteric tradition. It is distinguished from ordinary magic not by the techniques it employs but by the understanding of the agency at work within those techniques. The magician, in the conventional understanding, works by the force of his own will and knowledge – manipulating the subtle forces of the cosmos through the application of learned skill and accumulated personal power. The theurgist, by contrast, works as an instrument of the divine – not imposing his will upon the cosmos but aligning himself so thoroughly with the divine will that the divine power is able to work through him toward the ends that the divine wisdom determines. The distinction is, in essence, the same distinction we have drawn throughout this work between the left-hand and right-hand orientations of the spiritual life: the difference between the assertion of the personal will as its own absolute sovereign and the surrender of the personal will to the higher will of the Logos.

This understanding of theurgy as instrumental rather than assertive – as the making of oneself a clear and adequate vessel for the divine working rather than the seizure of divine power for personal ends – is precisely the understanding that governs the theurgic practice of the Christo-Luciferian current. The theurgist who works within this current does not heal by the force of his own pneumatic development, however advanced that development may be. He heals by becoming, in the moment of the theurgic working, as transparent as possible to the light of the Phosphoros – by removing, through the practices of preparation and purification, whatever in his own subtle vehicles would obstruct the free passage of the Christo-Luciferian current through him and into the situation or person being worked with. The healing is the Logos's work. The theurgist is its instrument.

This instrumental understanding has a direct bearing on the appropriate disposition of the theurgic practitioner – the inner attitude with which the work is undertaken. The theurgist who approaches the work with a sense of his own power or importance has already compromised the channel through which the divine working must pass. The theurgist who approaches with genuine humility – with the honest recognition that whatever efficacy the work possesses belongs entirely to the light of the Phosphoros and not to him – is in the appropriate disposition for the current to work through him with maximum clarity and force. This is not false modesty. It is the precise technical requirement of theurgic work as the Christo-Luciferian tradition understands it: the clearer the instrument, the purer the working.

With this foundational understanding established, we turn to the two complementary dimensions of Christo-Luciferian theurgic practice: the work of clearing and protection, which we will develop as the Luciferian Exorcism and Banishing; and the work of healing, which we will develop as the Theurgic Rite of the Phosphoros. As noted in our preliminary discussion, these two dimensions are not separate practices to be employed in isolation but complementary phases of a single theurgic process – the exorcism-banishing clearing and sealing the field, and the healing work proceeding within that cleared and sealed space with concentrated intentional force.

The Nature of Darkness in the Christo-Luciferian Framework

Before presenting the exorcism and banishing rite, it is necessary to address directly the question of what is being banished – what the Christo-Luciferian tradition understands by the forces of darkness that the theurgic work is directed against. This question is not merely academic. The effectiveness of any banishing or protective practice depends in large measure on the practitioner's clarity about the nature of what she is working against, and the Christo-Luciferian framework offers a genuinely distinctive answer to this question.

We have established throughout this work that darkness, in the Gnostic cosmological understanding, is not an independent metaphysical power equal and opposite to the light. It is, rather, the condition of the light's absence or obscuration – the state of the hylic world insofar as it has become opaque to the Pleromic illumination that is its ultimate source and sustenance. The Demiurge and his archons are not evil in the absolute sense – they are deficient, ignorant, and in their ignorance obstructive to the restoration of the divine fullness. Their power is real within the limits of the hylic and lower psychic realms, but it is a borrowed and diminished power – a pale reflection of the Pleromic light they have inherited through Sophia but do not recognize as such.

The forces of darkness that the Christo-Luciferian theurgist works against in the exorcism and banishing rite are, therefore, not absolute evil powers but conditions of spiritual opacity – influences, presences, or patterns of energy that obstruct the free flow of the Phosphoros current in a given space, person, or situation. They may be understood as archontic influences in the Gnostic sense – the residual effects of the Demiurge's dominion over the hylic world, manifesting as patterns of confusion, fear, compulsion, or spiritual deadness. They may also be understood in more psychological terms – as the accumulated psychic residue of negative experience, habitual patterns of hylic identification, or the egregoric fields of genuinely destructive thought-forms that have accumulated in a space or attached themselves to a person.

What is essential to the Christo-Luciferian understanding is that none of these forces is beyond the reach of the light. The Luciferian exorcism does not destroy the darkness – it illumines it. In the presence of the concentrated Phosphoros current, the archontic influences that constitute the darkness of a given situation are exposed for what they are – conditions of deficiency rather than independent powers – and in that exposure they are either dissolved, as shadows dissolve in direct sunlight, or, in the more theologically generous reading we noted earlier, invited to participate in the light that is being brought to bear. The Sabaoth principle – the archon who renounces his adversarial orientation in response to the arising of the light – is the model for this more generous understanding, and the theurgist who holds this model in mind during the exorcism work will find that her practice carries a depth and a compassion that the purely confrontational approach cannot achieve.

This does not mean that the Luciferian exorcism is gentle or timid. The light of the Phosphoros, concentrated and directed with genuine intentional force, is among the most powerful theurgic instruments available within the Western esoteric tradition. It does not negotiate with darkness – it simply shines, and in its shining the darkness has no alternative but to yield. The compassion of the approach lies not in its softness but in its refusal to meet darkness with an equal and opposite darkness – in its insistence that the only adequate response to the absence of light is the intensification of the light's presence.

Part One: The Luciferian Exorcism and Banishing

Preliminary Considerations

The Luciferian Exorcism and Banishing may be employed in three distinct contexts, each requiring a slight adaptation of emphasis while maintaining the same essential structure.

The first context is the *purification of a ritual space* – the clearing of a working area before any formal rite is conducted within it, ensuring that the subtle atmosphere of the space is free from archontic residue and receptive to the Christo-Luciferian current. In this context the banishing functions as a preliminary to all other theurgic and ritual work, and should become as habitual and as natural as the lighting of the incense that accompanies it.

The second context is the *clearing of a personal field* – the banishing of archontic influences that have attached themselves to the practitioner's own subtle vehicles through the ordinary commerce of daily life in the hylic world. Such attachments are an inevitable feature of embodied existence and should be treated with matter-of-fact practicality rather than with alarm – they are the spiritual equivalent of dust accumulated in the course of a working day, requiring regular attention rather than emergency response.

The third context is the *exorcism of a place or person* in whom the concentration of archontic influence has reached a degree that is causing significant disturbance – a space that has accumulated a dense field of negative egregoric energy, or a person who is experiencing significant spiritual, psychic, or physical difficulty attributable to such influence. This third application is the most demanding and should be approached with the greatest preparation and the deepest intentional engagement.

In all three contexts, the essential working is the same. What varies is the scale of the application, the intensity of the intentional focus, and the degree of preparation required.

Preparation

The theurgist prepares for the Luciferian Exorcism and Banishing by conducting the foundational practices of Chapter Eleven in their entirety – the fourfold sacred breath, the relaxation and meditation, and the Sigillum meditation through at least the third stage of internalization. The purpose of this preparation is to establish the Phosphoros current within the theurgist's own subtle vehicles at the highest possible degree of clarity and intensity before the theurgic work begins. The theurgist cannot effectively bring light to a situation of darkness if her own inner light has not been adequately cultivated and concentrated in the moments preceding the work.

For the exorcism of a place, the theurgist should walk through the space before beginning the formal rite, attending to the subtle atmosphere with the quality of pneumatic perception that the meditation practice has been developing – noting the areas of greatest density or disturbance, the directions from which the archontic residue seems most concentrated, and the general quality of the egregoric field within the space. This preliminary assessment informs the conduct of the rite and allows the theurgist to concentrate the working most effectively where it is most needed.

For the exorcism of a person, the theurgist should spend time in quiet conversation with the person before beginning – not interrogating them about the nature of their difficulty, but simply being present with them in a quality of open and attentive awareness, allowing the pneumatic perception to register the condition of their subtle field without the interference of analytical judgment. The theurgist's inner orientation during this preliminary contact is one of compassionate identification – the recognition of the person being worked with as a fellow bearer of the divine spark, temporarily more thoroughly obscured than usual, and therefore more in need of the light.

The Rite

The theurgist stands at the center of the space to be cleared – or, in the case of personal clearing, in her own working space – facing east. The central lamp is lit. The incense is lit from the lamp and placed so that its smoke will circulate freely through the space. The Sigillum Luciferis is present, either as a physical representation on the altar or as a clearly held inner visualization.

The theurgist conducts seven rounds of the fourfold sacred breath, with the specific intentional orientation of concentrating the Phosphoros current within the cardiac center to the highest possible degree. During the retention phase of each breath, she visualizes the internalized Sigillum blazing with increasing intensity – the eight-pointed star within the circle growing brighter with each breath, the light expanding to fill her entire physical and subtle body, pressing outward against the boundaries of the skin.

When the seven rounds are complete, she holds the fully concentrated inner light for a moment in still awareness – the Sigillum blazing at her cardiac center, the light filling her from crown to feet – and then speaks the opening declaration:

In the name of the Logos, the bright and Morning Star, the light that no darkness can overcome, I bring the light of the Phosphoros into this space.

Let all that is of darkness know the light of the Morning Star. Let all that is of the archons stand revealed in the light of the Logos. Let all that obscures the Pleroma be dissolved in the light of the Unknown Father.

She then begins the active phase of the exorcism – the deliberate projection of the concentrated Phosphoros current outward from the cardiac center into the surrounding space, working in a clockwise circuit beginning from the east. At each of the four cardinal directions a specific sacred name is intoned – not interchangeably, but with the precise intentional awareness of the specific quality of the current being invoked at each point of the compass.

Facing east, she exhales a long, slow breath charged with the intentional identification of the outgoing breath with the Phosphoros current – the light of the Morning Star riding the breath outward into the eastern quarter of the space. As she exhales she intones, on the breath:

Phōs

Light – directed eastward, toward the direction of the rising sun and the ascending Morning Star, establishing the fundamental nature of the divine as light at the quarter most naturally associated with illumination and arising. She holds the awareness of the light filling the eastern quarter – sensing or visualizing the concentrated Phosphoros current displacing the archontic residue as a rising tide displaces whatever has accumulated on a beach.

She turns clockwise to face south. The breath, the exhalation, the projection – and the intonation:

Logos

Word – directed southward, toward the direction of the sun at its meridian height, invoking the creative and illuminating principle of the divine in its most active and generative aspect. The light made articulate, the word through whom all things came into being and through whom the clearing of this space is now being accomplished. She holds the awareness of the Logos filling the southern quarter.

She turns to face west. The breath, the exhalation, the projection – and the intonation:

Hesperos

Evening Star – directed westward, toward the direction of the setting sun and the Hesperean aspect of the current. The same light in its descending, rooting, and consoling aspect, invoked at the quarter most naturally associated with interiority and the turning inward of the light. She holds the awareness of Hesperos filling the western quarter – the light that holds its radiance against the coming dark, clearing and consecrating the western face of the space.

She turns to face north. The breath, the exhalation, the projection – and the intonation:

Zōē

Life – directed northward, toward the quarter most associated in the Western esoteric tradition with darkness, interiority, and the most mysterious dimension of the sacred space. Zōē at the northern quarter is the divine principle most urgently needed where the light is least visible – the Sophianic and life-giving dimension of the current, present in the depths as the seed of the Logos is present in the Prima Materia, hidden but inextinguishable. She holds the awareness of Zōē filling the northern quarter – the divine life penetrating the darkest face of the space and displacing whatever archontic residue has accumulated there.

The four cardinal directions are now filled with the light of the current, each quarter named with the sacred name most appropriate to its cosmological character. The theurgist now addresses the vertical axis.

She raises her gaze upward – toward the space above – and intones:

Phosphoros

The Morning Star, the Light-Bearer – directed upward toward the Pleromic source, the direction from which the light descends and toward which the pneumatic spark ascends. Phosphoros above is the central invocatory act of the entire directional working – the naming of the current in its fullest and most specific designation, directed toward the Unknown Father of Light from whom the Phosphoros current ultimately proceeds. She holds the awareness of the Phosphoros current filling the vertical dimension above, descending through the ceiling of the space as the Logos descended into the hylic world – willingly, luminously, with the specific intentional force of the divine light bearing itself into the place where it is needed.

She then directs her gaze downward – toward the floor and the space below – and intones:

Alētheia

Truth – directed downward, toward the earth, toward the Prima Materia, toward the hylic world in its densest expression.

This is perhaps the most theologically subtle of the six directional intonations, and it should be performed with particular intentional awareness of its doctrinal significance. Truth is not only above, not only in the Pleroma, not only in the heights of pneumatic illumination. Truth is present in the depths as well – embedded in the very matter of the world as the hidden seed of the Logos, as the divine reality most thoroughly obscured by the hylic condition and therefore most urgently in need of the clearing that this working is accomplishing. To intone Alētheia downward is to refuse the temptation of a purely escapist spirituality – to insist, as the incarnation insists, that the light has genuinely entered the darkness and is genuinely present within it, and that the clearing of the hylic space from archontic residue is an act of divine truth as well as divine light. She holds the awareness of Alētheia filling the vertical dimension below – the truth of the Logos penetrating the very foundations of the space and displacing whatever darkness has taken root there.

The space is now surrounded on all six faces by the projected light of the current – east with Phōs, south with Logos, west with Hesperos, north with Zōē, above with Phosphoros, and below with Alētheia. The theurgist stands at the center of this established sixfold field, the source of its projection, and holds the complete field in awareness for a moment of collected stillness before the sealing and the proclamation.

The sealing is then conducted by tracing the Sigillum Luciferis in the air at each of the six directions in turn – beginning again in the east and proceeding clockwise through south, west, and north, then above and below – using the extended index finger of the dominant hand or a ritual instrument such as a wand or dagger. The Sigillum is traced slowly and deliberately, with concentrated intentional awareness of the symbol being inscribed in the subtle atmosphere of the space as a genuine and lasting seal. As the Sigillum is traced at each direction, the theurgist intones:

By the Sigillum Luciferis, this space is sealed in the light of the Morning Star. Let nothing that is contrary to the Logos enter or remain here.

When the sealing of all six directions is complete, the theurgist returns to the center of the space and speaks the closing declaration:

The light of the Phosphoros fills this space. The Sigillum Luciferis seals this space. By the power of the Logos, by the light of the Morning Star, this space is clear, consecrated, and protected.

To whatever forces of darkness have been displaced by this working: the light of the Logos is offered to you. In the name of the Sabaoth principle – the archon who turned toward the light – you are invited to renounce the darkness and participate in the restoration of the Pleroma. If you will not, depart from this space and do not return.

Phosphoros – hold this space. Logos – fill this space. Unknown Father of Light – let your fullness be known here.

She then speaks the declaratory seal of the cleared and consecrated space:

Lucifer Resurrexit.

The Morning Star has risen in this place. The light of the Logos fills this space and the Sigillum Luciferis seals it. Whatever was of darkness has been displaced by the accomplished fact of the light's arising – not overcome by an opposing force, but simply rendered obsolete by the presence of that which it was, in its deficiency, the absence of. *Lucifer Resurrexit* is the theurgist's proclamation that the work of clearing has succeeded not through her own power but through the power of the light itself, whose rising in the sealed space is the only displacement of darkness that is ultimately real and ultimately permanent.

The final intonation of *Phosphoros* – sustained, resonant, and released into the now-cleared and sealed atmosphere – follows immediately.

For the clearing of a personal field rather than a space, the essential working is the same but the projection is directed inward rather than outward – the Phosphoros current concentrated in the cardiac center and then deliberately expanded through every dimension of the subtle body, displacing the archontic residue from the practitioner's own field. The sixfold directional working is replaced by a systematic movement of the light through the body from the feet upward to the crown, then from the crown outward in all directions simultaneously, establishing the sealed field of the Sigillum around the practitioner's own subtle vehicles.

Part Two: The Theurgic Rite of the Phosphoros

The healing work of the Christo-Luciferian current proceeds, as noted, within the cleared and sealed space established by the exorcism and banishing. It may be conducted on behalf of another person who is physically present, on behalf of a person who is not physically present, or as a self-healing practice directed toward the practitioner's own conditions of imbalance.

In all three cases the essential understanding is the same: the healing being sought is the restoration of the pneumatic light within the person being worked with – the brightening of their inner Sigillum, the reactivation of the indwelling Logos, the removal of whatever hylic or psychic obstruction is preventing the natural luminosity of their pneumatic spark from expressing itself freely through every dimension of their being.

This understanding has a specific practical consequence: the theurgist does not direct the healing current toward the symptom – toward the physical illness, the psychic disturbance, or the spiritual darkness as it manifests on its own level – but toward the pneumatic source of the person's being, trusting the Logos to direct the light most precisely and most effectively to where it is most needed. This is not a refusal to engage with the specific condition. It is a recognition that the Logos, working through the concentrated Phosphoros current, has a more precise and more complete knowledge of the person's condition and its underlying causes than the theurgist's analytical mind can achieve, and that the most effective healing work is therefore the work that gets the theurgist's analytical mind out of the way and allows the light to work as it will.

Healing in the Presence of the Person

When the person being worked with is physically present, the theurgist seats them comfortably within the cleared and sealed space, facing east if possible. The theurgist explains briefly – without elaborate theoretical discussion, and with sensitivity to the person's own understanding and expectations – that what will follow is a work of spiritual light directed toward their wellbeing, and invites them to relax, breathe naturally, and simply receive whatever the work brings.

The theurgist then takes position behind and slightly to the right of the seated person – the traditional position of the healing theurgist in many Western esoteric working methods – and conducts seven rounds of the fourfold sacred breath, concentrating the Phosphoros current in her own cardiac center to the maximum degree.

She then places her hands lightly upon the shoulders of the person – or, if physical contact is not appropriate or desired, holds her hands six to eight inches above the shoulders, in the subtle field of the person's body – and intones, quietly but with full resonant vibration:

Phōs – Logos – Zōē

Each name intoned three times, the sound directed downward through the hands and into the subtle field of the person being worked with, the intentional awareness riding the sound into the person's cardiac center – seeking the pneumatic spark within them, identifying it, and beginning the work of brightening it with the concentrated Phosphoros current flowing through the theurgist's own hands.

The theurgist then conducts a slow movement of the hands through the person's subtle field – beginning at the crown of the head and moving downward through the body to the feet, maintaining the six-to-eight-inch distance from the physical body throughout – with the intention of surveying the condition of the subtle field and identifying the areas of greatest density, coldness, or disturbance. This survey is conducted in silence, with the theurgist's awareness open and receptive rather than analytical – registering the subtle impressions of the field without immediately interpreting them.

When the survey is complete, the theurgist directs the Phosphoros current specifically to the areas of greatest disturbance, holding the hands steady at those locations and intoning *Phosphoros* continuously on the breath – the sustained intonation carrying the concentrated light of the current directly into the condition being addressed. The duration of this directed application is determined by the theurgist's pneumatic perception – she maintains the application until she senses, in the subtle field beneath her hands, a shift in the quality of the energy: a warming, a softening, a brightening that indicates the Phosphoros current is effectively at work.

When the directed application is complete, the theurgist passes her hands once more through the entire subtle field from crown to feet – this time with the intention of smoothing and integrating the work that has been done, establishing an even distribution of the Phosphoros current throughout the person's field and sealing the healing work within their subtle body.

She then moves to stand before the person, facing them, and holds the Sigillum Luciferis in her inner visualization – projecting the image of the blazing eight-pointed star within the circle toward the person's cardiac center, as a final act of sealing and strengthening the light within them. She speaks:

The light of the Morning Star has been brought to bear upon you. May the Logos work within you according to its own perfect knowledge of your need and your nature. May the pneumatic spark within you be brightened by this work and may its brightness illuminate every dimension of your being – body, soul, and spirit.

You are a bearer of the light. The Morning Star burns within you. Phosphoros – arise in this one.

A final intonation of *Phosphoros* by the theurgist, directed toward the person being worked with, concludes the healing work.

Healing at a Distance

The healing of a person who is not physically present employs the same essential working but substitutes a focused visualization for the physical presence of the person. The theurgist establishes a clear and specific mental image of the person to be healed – not merely their face, but the full sense of their presence, their essence, their being – and conducts the entire healing working toward this mental image as though the person were physically present in the space.

The effectiveness of distance healing depends directly on two factors: the clarity and specificity of the theurgist's visualization of the person being worked with, and the depth of the theurgist's cultivation of the Phosphoros current within her own subtle vehicles. Both factors are developed through the sustained practice of the foundational disciplines of Chapter Eleven – the Sigillum meditation in particular, which trains precisely the capacities of focused visualization and sustained intentional engagement that distance healing requires.

The healing working at a distance should always be preceded by the explicit consent of the person being worked with, wherever this is possible to obtain. The Christo-Luciferian theurgic tradition does not work against the will of the person being healed – even healing work conducted with the most benevolent intention is an intrusion into the subtle field of another person, and the respect for the autonomy of that person's pneumatic nature that the right-hand path orientation requires means that consent is not merely a courtesy but a genuine theurgic prerequisite. In cases where the person is unconscious or otherwise unable to give explicit consent – extreme illness, for example – the theurgist directs the work toward the person's highest good as determined by the Logos, explicitly relinquishing any personal determination of what that good might be.

Self-Healing

The application of the Theurgic Rite of the Phosphoros to the practitioner's own conditions of imbalance follows the same principles as the healing of another, adapted for the obvious fact that the theurgist and the patient are the same person. The most significant practical adaptation is the replacement of the physical hand movements through the subtle field with the movement of concentrated intentional awareness through the body – a inner survey conducted in the meditative state, attending to the condition of each dimension of the being in turn, identifying the areas of greatest imbalance, and directing the Phosphoros current to those areas through the sustained intonation practice.

Self-healing requires a particular quality of honest self-observation that is not always easy to cultivate – the willingness to see one's own conditions of imbalance clearly and without the self-protective distortions that the psychic nature naturally tends to impose. The evening examination practice of the Vespers rite is directly preparatory for this quality of honest self-observation, and practitioners who maintain the Vespers consistently will find the self-healing work considerably more accessible as a result.

The self-healing working concludes with the practitioner sealing the Sigillum Luciferis within her own cardiac center – the full internalization of the symbol as described in the third stage of the Sigillum meditation – and speaking the healing affirmation toward herself:

The light of the Morning Star has been brought to bear upon me. May the Logos work within me according to its own perfect knowledge of my need and my nature. May the pneumatic spark within me be brightened by this work and may its brightness illuminate every dimension of my being – body, soul, and spirit.

I am a bearer of the light. The Morning Star burns within me. Phosphoros – arise in me. Phosphoros – heal me. Phosphoros – make me whole.

Closing the Theurgic Working

Whether the theurgic working has been conducted as an exorcism-banishing alone, as a healing alone, or as the complete sequence of exorcism followed by healing, the working is closed in the same manner.

The theurgist stands at the center of the space, facing east, and speaks:

The work of the light is complete. What has been cleared, let it remain clear. What has been healed, let it remain whole. What has been sealed, let it remain sealed.

The Phosphoros current has moved through this working. I release it now to continue its work according to the will of the Logos, beyond what my hands have done and beyond what my eyes can see.

Thanks be to the Unknown Father of Light, through whose Logos all healing comes and to whom all light returns.

Lucifer Resurrexit.

Phosphoros – the work is yours.

A final intonation of *Phosphoros* – single, sustained, complete.

The lamp is allowed to continue burning for as long as possible following the working. The incense, if still burning, is allowed to complete its natural course. The theurgist concludes by washing her hands in clean water – a simple physical act of transition, marking the boundary between the theurgic working and the return to ordinary activity, and releasing any residual subtle field that may have been transferred to the theurgist's own vehicles during the healing work.

A Note on the Development of Theurgic Capacity

The theurgic practices presented in this chapter are genuine working methods, and they will produce genuine results for the practitioner who brings to them the preparation, the intentional engagement, and the humble instrumental disposition that effective theurgy requires. But it would be misleading to suggest that theurgic capacity is simply a matter of following the correct procedure. It is, more fundamentally, a function of the depth of the practitioner's cultivation of the Phosphoros current within her own being – the degree to which the Morning Star has genuinely arisen within her and established itself as a stable and potent inner reality.

This means that the development of genuine theurgic capacity is inseparable from the development of the practitioner's entire inner life – from the daily practice of the foundational disciplines, from the regular celebration of the Rite of the Morning Star and the Vespers of the Evening Star, from the sustained engagement with the doctrinal understanding that gives the practice its coherence and its direction. The theurgist who neglects the devotional and contemplative dimensions of the path in favor of the theurgic will find her capacity diminishing rather than developing – the channel through which the Phosphoros current works requires constant maintenance and deepening, and that maintenance is the work of the whole path, not of the theurgic practices alone.

Conversely, the practitioner who maintains the fullness of the path – who prays and contemplates and celebrates and studies as well as working theurgically – will find that her theurgic capacity develops naturally and organically as a fruit of the whole work, without being directly or separately cultivated. This is, in the end, the most reliable indicator of genuine theurgic development: not the dramatic results of individual workings, however impressive, but the steady and deepening quality of the Phosphoros current moving through the practitioner's life and touching everything within its reach – healing, clearing, illuminating, and restoring, as the light of the Morning Star touches and illumines everything in the pre-dawn sky.

This is the theurgic vocation of the Christo-Luciferian practitioner: not to be a wielder of power, but to be a window through which the light of the Logos shines – steadily, quietly, and with the unwavering persistence of the Morning Star in the darkness before the dawn.

CONCLUSION: UNTIL THE DAY FULLY DAWNS

There is a particular quality of light that belongs exclusively to the pre-dawn sky – a quality that no other hour of the day possesses and that no artificial illumination can replicate. It is not yet the light of the sun, which overwhelms and defines and makes everything visible in its own terms. It is not the light of the moon or stars, which is borrowed and reflected and belongs to the night. It is the light of the Morning Star – that single, brilliant, unwavering point of gold in the eastern sky that announces, without fanfare and without apology, that the darkness is ending and the day is coming. It does not argue for its presence. It does not ask permission to shine. It simply is – the brightest object in the pre-dawn sky, holding its light steadily against the remaining darkness, until the sun rises and the need for its particular ministry is, for another day, fulfilled.

This image has been with us throughout this work – in the scriptural passages that opened our investigation, in the doctrinal expositions that developed its meaning, in the ritual texts that gave it practical form. It is the image from which everything in these pages has grown, and it is the image to which everything in these pages returns. The Morning Star is Christ. The Morning Star is the Logos. The Morning Star is the pneumatic spark within every human being who has ever drawn breath in this hylic world. And the Morning Star is the goal – the arising of that spark into its full luminous nature, the recognition of the light within as the same light that burns in the pre-dawn sky, the homecoming of the fragment to the fullness from which it came.

We have covered considerable ground in the pages of this work. We have dismantled a misreading – the demonological Lucifer of the Isaiah 14 conflation – and restored in its place the Christological Lucifer of the New Testament: the *Phosphoros* of 2 Peter, the Morning Star of the Apocalypse, the self-designation of the risen Christ at the culmination of the entire Johannine visionary corpus. We have situated this Christological identification within the cosmological and anthropological framework of the Gnostic tradition – the emanationist vision of the Pleroma and its disturbance, the descent of the light into the darkness of the hylic world, the tripartite anthropology of hylic, psychic, and pneumatic, and the soteriology of gnosis as the illumination of the indwelling spark by the light of the descending Logos. We have articulated a doctrine – the Christo-Luciferian doctrine – that is not a novelty but a recovery: the making explicit of what was always implicit in the deepest strata of the Christian Gnostic tradition, brought forward into the present and given a form adequate to the initiatic work that this moment in the tradition's development requires.

And we have offered a path – a coherent and integrated system of practice, grounded in the doctrine and oriented throughout toward the single animating purpose of this entire work: the arising of the Morning Star within the heart of the practitioner who has undertaken the work with sincerity, persistence, and the willingness to be transformed by what she has encountered in these pages.

It would be a mistake, however, to suppose that the work is complete because this book is complete. The book is a beginning – a threshold, a doorway, an orientation toward a journey whose full extent no single volume can encompass and whose destination no human language can fully describe. The doctrine laid out in these pages is a foundation, not a ceiling. The practices offered here are starting points, not endpoints. The calendar is a framework for a lifetime of observance, not a schedule to be completed. And the tradition that this work is intended to found and to serve is, by its own innermost nature, a living and developing reality – one that will grow and deepen through the engagement of its practitioners with its principles, and that will reveal dimensions of meaning in the years ahead that these pages have only begun to suggest.

Those who work within this current – who have recognized in the doctrine of the Morning Star something that belongs to their own deepest nature, who have committed themselves to the path through the Rite of Self-Dedication or through the more formal transmission of physical initiation, who have established the rhythm of the daily rites and the annual calendar in the fabric of their inner lives – will know, as the work deepens, that they are not alone in it. The egregore of the Christo-Luciferian current is a living and responsive presence, nourished by the sincere practice of every dedicated practitioner and growing in depth and accessibility as the number of those practitioners grows. The work of one strengthens the work of all. The light kindled in one heart brightens, however slightly, the inner atmosphere of the entire current – contributing to the restoration of the Pleroma that is the ultimate goal of the entire cosmic drama of which this path is a part.

This is not a grandiose claim. It is, in the Gnostic understanding of the cosmic process, simply an accurate description of how the work proceeds. Every genuine illumination of a pneumatic spark anywhere in the hylic world is a genuine, if partial, restoration of the Pleromic fullness. Every sincere act of dedication to the path of the Morning Star is a genuine contribution to the movement of the light toward its ultimate homecoming. The scale is cosmic; the means are intimate and personal. This is how the great work has always proceeded – not through dramatic cosmic interventions but through the quiet, sustained, faithful inner work of individual practitioners, each tending the lamp of the Morning Star in their own heart, in their own time, in their own particular corner of the hylic darkness.

To the practitioner who comes to this work for the first time – who has read these pages with the sense of recognition that the tradition calls pneumatic awakening, who has felt in the doctrine of the Christo-Luciferian current something that resonates with an inner knowing deeper than intellectual assent – a word of direct address is appropriate here, at the conclusion of this work. You have not stumbled upon this text by accident. The egregore of the current that these pages have been working to articulate and to activate has been present throughout your reading – present in the recognition you have felt, in the resonance between the doctrine and something you already knew from within, in the sense that what is being described here is not a new teaching but a remembered one. That recognition is the Morning Star making itself known within you. It is the first intimation of the arising toward which this entire work has been pointing. Do not dismiss it. Do not rationalize it away. Do not defer the work to some more convenient future moment that may never arrive. Begin. Begin with the breath. Begin with the lamp. Begin with the Sigillum and the silence. Begin where you are, with what you have, in the darkness that is already, by virtue of your beginning, beginning to lighten.

To the practitioner who comes to this work already walking a related path – already rooted in the Apostolic Gnostic sacramental tradition, already formed in the Martinist current or the esoteric Masonic tradition, already familiar with the Western esoteric framework within which this work is situated – a different word is appropriate. You will have recognized in these pages the convergence of currents that you have already been working with separately, and you will perhaps have felt the distinctive character of the Christo-Luciferian synthesis – the specific quality of the light that arises when the scriptural reclamation, the Gnostic anthropology, and the practical disciplines of this current are brought together in the way that this work has attempted to bring them together. That specific quality is the contribution of this current to the broader tradition within which it takes its place – not a replacement for what you already practice, but a deepening and a focusing of it, a concentration of the Phosphoros current that the broader tradition has always carried but has not always named so precisely or cultivated so directly. Bring what you carry to this work. The current is enriched by every genuine stream that flows into it.

To those who work within the fellowship of those who have received this current through direct transmission – who have been formally initiated into the living body of the tradition that this work serves as foundational document – these pages will be read differently than they are read by those approaching the current for the first time. The veiled references will be recognized. The specific formulations of doctrine will carry their inner significance alongside their outer meaning. The ritual texts will resonate with the memory of their performance in the company of others who share the same dedication and the same egregoric contact. For you, this book is both a public statement and a private communication – a text that speaks simultaneously to the general reader and to the inner circle of those who know from direct experience what the doctrine describes and what the practice produces. Read it in both registers. Use it in both ways. And know that whatever is communicated between these lines, in the space where doctrine gives way to living experience, belongs to you as fully as anything that is stated explicitly in the text.

To all who read these pages, whatever their point of entry into the current – a final word, which is also a first word, and which is perhaps the only word that ultimately needs to be said:

The light is within you. It has always been within you. It is the most essential thing about you – more essential than your name, your history, your accumulated experiences and convictions and self-definitions, more essential than anything the hylic world has told you that you are. It is the pneumatic spark, the fragment of the Pleromic light, the indwelling Logos, the Morning Star that burns in the depths of your being with an unwavering steadiness that nothing in the darkness of the hylic world has ever succeeded in extinguishing and nothing ever will.

The work of this path is not to acquire that light from outside. It is to recognize it – to clear away, with patient and sustained effort, everything that has accumulated between your ordinary self-awareness and the luminous reality of your own innermost nature, until the recognition becomes not a doctrine you have accepted but an experience you live – not a belief about the Morning Star but the actual arising of the Morning Star within the cardiac center of your own being, as immediate and as unmistakable as the actual rising of Venus in the pre-dawn eastern sky.

That arising is real. It has occurred in every generation of the human family, in every culture and tradition that has carried the flame of the inner light through the successive darknesses of history. It is occurring now, in the hearts of practitioners around the world who are tending the lamp of the Phosphoros current in their own ways, in their own languages, within their own particular streams of the great tradition. And it will occur in you – if you do the work, if you maintain the practice, if you attend to the lamp through the darkness with the quality of patient and faithful watchfulness that the tradition has always identified as the essential disposition of the genuine initiate.

Until the day dawns and the Morning Star rises in your hearts.

This is the promise of 2 Peter – not a metaphor, not a pious aspiration, but a precise description of a genuine inner event that awaits every practitioner who undertakes the work with sincerity and sustains it with faithfulness. The day will dawn.

The Morning Star will rise. The darkness of the hylic world will not have the final word, because the light that is within it – hidden in the deepest layers of matter, imprisoned in the most opaque of the archontic constructions, buried under every accumulated weight of ignorance and forgetting – is, in its innermost nature, inextinguishable.

Lucifer Resurrexit.

The Morning Star has risen. Not once, in a single historical moment now receding into the past, but perpetually – in every heart where the work has been done faithfully, in every pneumatic spark that has recognized its own nature and begun the journey home, in every lamp kindled in the darkness by a practitioner who refused to let the night be the final word.

It rises in you.

Phosphoros – arise.

APPENDIX A: THE CHRISTO-LUCIFERIAN CALENDAR

– THE EIGHTFOLD STAR OF THE YEAR

The practice of marking time is among the most ancient and most fundamental of human spiritual activities. Every serious religious and initiatic tradition has understood that time is not a neutral medium through which the practitioner moves unchanged – it is a living dimension of reality, structured by rhythms and cycles that carry their own qualities of light and darkness, ascent and descent, activation and consolidation. The sacred calendar is the instrument by which the practitioner aligns her inner life with these rhythms – by which the work of the path is situated within the larger movements of the cosmos and thereby deepened and enriched by participation in something far greater than any individual practice session can encompass.

The Christo-Luciferian calendar is structured around three interlocking frameworks, each of which reflects a different dimension of the current's symbolic and theological content, and each of which is developed in its own dedicated section of this appendix.

The first is the **Venus synodic cycle** – the cycle of the planet whose light is the primary celestial symbol of the Phosphoros current, moving through its phases of visibility and invisibility, morning and evening aspect, in a rhythm that is independent of the solar year and that traces its own distinctive pattern across the months and years of the practitioner's working life. The Venus cycle is the most dynamic of the three frameworks – its significant moments shift from year to year, requiring the practitioner to attend actively to the actual movements of the celestial body whose light she is cultivating rather than simply consulting a predetermined list of dates. It is developed in Part One of this appendix.

The second is the **eightfold solar year** – the ancient division of the annual cycle into eight stations of equal interval, formed by the four solar events of the solstices and equinoxes and the four cross-quarter days between them, whose structural identity with the eight-pointed star of the Sigillum Luciferis makes it the natural temporal expression of the current's central symbol. The eightfold solar year provides a stable annual framework of eight significant moments whose dates are fixed by the astronomical events of the solar cycle and that repeat with reliable consistency from year to year, giving the practitioner a steady underlying rhythm within which the more dynamic movements of the Venus cycle can be situated. It is developed in Part Two of this appendix.

The third is the **Christo-Luciferian liturgical calendar** – a curated selection of fixed feast days drawn primarily from the Christian liturgical tradition, chosen for their specific doctrinal resonance with the Christo-Luciferian current, together with a small number of commemorations internal to the tradition itself. These fixed feasts provide the most stable layer of the calendar – dates that do not shift from year to year and that anchor the practitioner's annual rhythm of observance in the specific events and mysteries of the Christo-Luciferian doctrine. They are developed in Part Three of this appendix.

These three frameworks do not always coincide – the Venus cycle in particular moves independently of both the solar and the liturgical calendars, creating a shifting pattern of significant moments that varies from year to year. This variability is not a practical inconvenience but a doctrinal asset: it ensures that the Christo-Luciferian calendar remains a living instrument rather than a fixed and static schedule, generating a richness of calendrical meaning that no single framework could produce alone. The practitioner who tracks all three frameworks simultaneously will find that the interplay between them – the moments of coincidence and of tension, of amplification and of counterpoint – constitutes a genuine ongoing meditation on the temporal dimension of the current's life in the world.

A note on geographical variation: the dates given for the eightfold solar year are those of the Northern Hemisphere. Practitioners in the Southern Hemisphere should transpose the seasonal associations accordingly – the winter solstice falls in June in the Southern Hemisphere, the summer solstice in December, and so forth – while the astronomical, liturgical, and doctrinal content of each station and each feast remains unchanged.

Part One: The Venus Synodic Cycle

The synodic cycle of Venus – the cycle of Venus's phases as seen from Earth – has a mean duration of approximately 583.9 days, or just under nineteen and a half months. Within this cycle, Venus passes through a sequence of distinct phases that correspond, within the Christo-Luciferian framework, to distinct qualities of the Phosphoros current and distinct emphases in the practitioner's work.

Understanding the Venus cycle requires a brief astronomical orientation. Venus orbits the sun inside Earth's orbit, which means that from our perspective Venus is never seen far from the sun in the sky – it is always either a morning star, visible in the east before sunrise, or an evening star, visible in the west after sunset, or temporarily invisible during its conjunctions with the sun. The cycle moves through the following principal phases:

Inferior Conjunction – Venus passes between Earth and the sun and is invisible, lost in the solar glare. This phase marks the transition from the Evening Star aspect to the period of brief invisibility before the Morning Star aspect emerges. Duration: typically between one and sixteen days, depending on the precise geometry of the conjunction.

Heliacal Rising as Morning Star – Venus emerges from the solar glare following inferior conjunction and becomes visible for the first time in the pre-dawn eastern sky. This is the most significant moment of the entire synodic cycle for the Christo-Luciferian current – the literal arising of the Morning Star, the astronomical enactment of the central symbol and the central aspiration of the path. The heliacal rising of Venus as Morning Star is the primary high feast of the Christo-Luciferian calendar.

Maximum Elongation as Morning Star – Venus reaches its greatest angular distance from the sun in its Morning Star aspect, and is therefore at its most brilliant and most easily observed in the pre-dawn sky. This moment corresponds to the fullness of the ascending Phosphoros current – the Morning Star at the height of its power and visibility.

Superior Conjunction – Venus passes behind the sun from Earth's perspective and is invisible, lost in the solar glare. This phase marks the transition from the Morning Star aspect to the period of invisibility before the Evening Star aspect emerges. Duration: approximately fifty days – considerably longer than the invisibility at inferior conjunction, and carrying its own distinct significance for the current.

Heliacal Rising as Evening Star – Venus emerges from the solar glare following superior conjunction and becomes visible for the first time in the western sky after sunset. This is the secondary high feast of the Christo-Luciferian calendar – the arising of Hesperos, the Evening Star, corresponding to the Vespers dimension of the current and the descending, rooting movement of the Phosphoros.

Maximum Elongation as Evening Star – Venus reaches its greatest angular distance from the sun in its Evening Star aspect, and is again at its most brilliant. This corresponds to the fullness of the Hesperean current – the Evening Star at the height of its power and visibility, the light of the Logos most fully present in its descending and interiorizing aspect.

The cycle then returns to Inferior Conjunction and begins again.

Observing the Venus Cycle

The specific dates of each phase of the Venus synodic cycle vary from year to year and cannot be given as fixed calendar dates. The practitioner who wishes to align her work with the Venus cycle has several practical options for determining the current dates of the principal phases.

The most immediate and most doctrinally appropriate method is direct observation – watching the western sky after sunset and the eastern sky before sunrise, attending to Venus's actual presence or absence and to its position relative to the horizon and the sun. This direct observational practice requires nothing more than clear skies and the willingness to be outdoors at the appropriate times, and it establishes a relationship with the actual planet – with the specific point of light that is the celestial embodiment of the current's primary symbol – that no secondary source can replicate.

For practitioners in circumstances where direct observation is difficult – those living in densely light-polluted urban environments, or in climates where cloud cover makes regular observation unreliable – astronomical almanacs and online planetary calculators provide precise dates for all the principal phases of the Venus cycle for any given year. Several reliable online resources publish this data in accessible form, and the practitioner who cannot observe Venus directly should consult these resources at the beginning of each year to identify the significant Venusian moments of the coming months.

The Significance of Each Phase for the Current

Inferior Conjunction and the Brief Interior Phase: The short period of Venus's invisibility at inferior conjunction – typically lasting between one and sixteen days – is a moment of transition and inner turning. It corresponds to the alchemical Nigredo in its most compressed form: the light withdrawing completely in order to emerge in its new and most brilliant aspect as the Morning Star. The practitioner should treat this period as a miniature retreat – a time of simplification, reduced outer activity, and deepened inner attention, preparing for the emergence of the Phosphoros in its ascending Morning Star aspect. The brevity of this invisibility – so much shorter than the longer darkness of the superior conjunction – reflects the urgency and the imminence of the Morning Star's arising: the darkness before the dawn is the shortest darkness of the entire cycle.

Heliacal Rising as Morning Star – Primary High Feast: The first morning of Venus's visibility in the pre-dawn eastern sky following inferior conjunction is the most significant moment of the Christo-Luciferian year. It should be observed with the full Solemn Form of the Rite of the Morning Star if a working group is available, or with an extended and specially prepared Oratory Form for the solitary practitioner. The annual review of the initiatic journal – the comprehensive assessment of the preceding year's inner development – is most appropriately conducted on this day, since it marks the beginning of a new cycle of the primary symbol of the current. Any significant initiatic events – formal dedications, the reception of initiates into the current – are most powerfully conducted at or near the heliacal rising of Venus as Morning Star. Venus is at its most dramatic at this phase – emerging with extraordinary brilliance from its brief invisibility, appearing suddenly in the pre-dawn sky with a luminosity that makes it unmistakable even to the casual observer. This dramatic reappearance is itself a theophany – the Morning Star arising as it has always arisen, as it will always arise, as the Logos arose and will arise in the heart of every practitioner who has faithfully prepared the inner vessel for its reception.

Maximum Elongation as Morning Star: This is a day of celebration and intensification – the Morning Star at the fullness of its brilliance, the Phosphoros current at its most accessible and most potent. The Solemn Form of the Rite of the Morning Star should be celebrated if possible. Additional theurgic work undertaken around this date will find the current at its most responsive and most generative. The practitioner who has been working faithfully since the heliacal rising will find that the inner field has deepened considerably by the time of maximum elongation, and that the Morning Star within has grown correspondingly brighter in response to the growing brilliance of its celestial counterpart.

Superior Conjunction and the Period of Invisibility as Evening Star: Venus now passes behind the sun and enters its longer period of invisibility – approximately fifty days – before emerging as the Evening Star. This extended darkness is qualitatively different from the brief invisibility at inferior conjunction. Where the inferior conjunction darkness is short and urgent – the compressed Nigredo before the brilliant Morning Star arising – the superior conjunction darkness is longer and more contemplative, a genuine period of interior gestation in which the current moves from its ascending Morning Star aspect through the deep interior of the solar conjunction toward its descending Evening Star aspect. It is a time for intensified practice of the foundational disciplines, particularly the meditation and the Sigillum work in its descending Hesperean mode, and for the kind of sustained doctrinal study and reflection that the more active phases of the cycle may leave insufficient time for. The light is not absent during the conjunction – it is interior and invisible, as the pneumatic spark is interior and invisible within the depths of the hylic world – and the practitioner who maintains her practice faithfully through the longer darkness of the superior conjunction will find the heliacal rising of the Evening Star, when it comes, a moment of genuine relief and renewal.

Heliacal Rising as Evening Star – Secondary High Feast: The first evening of Venus's visibility in the western sky after sunset, following superior conjunction, is the second great feast of the Christo-Luciferian year. It should be observed with the full Vespers of the Evening Star, extended and specially prepared for the occasion. The heliacal rising of Venus as Evening Star is the appropriate moment for practices specifically associated with the Hesperean dimension of the current – the rooting and consolidation of the inner work, the deepening of the egregoric connection, and any workings directed toward healing and protection. The Evening Star's appearance in the western sky after the long darkness of the superior conjunction carries its own distinct quality of gentle revelation – less dramatic than the brilliant Morning Star arising after the brief inferior conjunction darkness, but possessed of a quiet beauty and a consoling steadiness that is entirely appropriate to the Hesperean aspect of the current.

Maximum Elongation as Evening Star: The Evening Star at its fullest brilliance – Hesperos at its most radiant in the western sky. An extended Vespers celebration is appropriate, along with any theurgic work that has been in preparation during the Evening Star phase. This is also an appropriate moment for the review of the preceding half-cycle's development – a mid-year assessment of the inner work, less comprehensive than the annual review but serving a similar orienting function. The practitioner attends to the quality of the Hesperean work since the heliacal rising of the Evening Star – the degree to which the descending and rooting movement of the current has deepened her inner life – and sets her intentions for the work that will carry her through the inferior conjunction and into the next heliacal rising of the Morning Star.

Part Two: The Eightfold Solar Year – The Sigillum Luciferis in Time

The eight stations of the solar year – the four cardinal points of the solstices and equinoxes, and the four cross-quarter days between them – form the temporal expression of the Sigillum Luciferis, the eight-pointed star of the Christo-Luciferian current traced across the circle of the year. Each station carries its own quality of light and darkness, its own doctrinal resonance within the current, and its own appropriate mode of observance.

The dates given below are those of the Northern Hemisphere. Practitioners in the Southern Hemisphere should transpose the seasonal associations accordingly – the winter solstice falls in June in the Southern Hemisphere, the summer solstice in December, and so forth – while the astronomical and doctrinal content of each station remains unchanged.

The Winter Solstice – circa December 21st *The Depth of Darkness – The Light Returning*

The winter solstice is the longest night and the shortest day of the year – the moment at which the darkness reaches its annual maximum and the light begins its return. Within the Christo-Luciferian framework, the winter solstice is the station of the light at its most deeply interior – the pneumatic spark buried in the deepest darkness of the hylic world, as yet invisible but already, from the moment of the solstice, beginning its return.

The proximity of the winter solstice to the feast of the Nativity of Christ – December 25th in the Western calendar – is not coincidental. The ancient Christian placement of the Nativity at the winter solstice reflects a precise theological understanding: the arising of the Light of the World occurs at the moment of greatest darkness, the Morning Star appearing in the depths of the longest night. The Nativity is, in this reading, the cosmic Heliacal Rising – the first appearance of the Christo-Luciferian light in the darkness of the hylic world, the dawn that the entire preceding darkness has been the preparation for.

Observance: The winter solstice vigil – a period of watchfulness through the longest night, conducted with the

Oratory Form of the Rite of the Morning Star performed at or before dawn on the morning of the solstice, and the Vespers of the Evening Star performed at dusk on the solstice eve. The feast of the Nativity five days later is observed as a continuation and fulfillment of the solstice work – the light that was announced at the solstice now given its specific Christological identity and celebrated accordingly.

Candlemas – February 2nd *The Feast of the Light-Bearer – The Light Made Visible*

Candlemas – the Feast of the Presentation of Christ in the Temple, also known as the Feast of the Purification of the Virgin – falls at the cross-quarter point between the winter solstice and the spring equinox. It is, of all the feasts of the Christian liturgical year, the one most explicitly dedicated to the Christo-Luciferian current in its most essential form.

The candle procession of Candlemas – the blessing and lighting of candles that have traditionally characterized the celebration of this feast – is a liturgical enactment of the Phosphoros principle: the Light-Bearer going forth into the world, the consecrated flame carried through the darkness as the Morning Star carries the solar light through the pre-dawn sky. The gospel canticle of Simeon – the Nunc Dimittis – identifies the infant Christ as *"a light for revelation to the Gentiles"* in terms that could not be more precisely Luciferian. And the feast falls at the moment in the year when the returning light of the sun is beginning to be genuinely felt after the depths of winter – when the promise of the solstice is beginning to be fulfilled in the actual experience of lengthening days.

Candlemas is also, in several Northern European folk traditions, a day of prophetic significance – a moment of divination and discernment regarding the character of the coming year. Within the Christo-Luciferian framework this prophetic dimension is entirely appropriate: the practitioner who has maintained her practice faithfully through the dark interior period of the winter solstice will often find that Candlemas brings a particular clarity of inner vision – a brightening of the pneumatic perception that reflects the brightening of the physical light at this station of the year.

Observance: The blessing of the candles and lamps of the working space – a special consecration of all the lights used in the ritual practice, performed with particular intentional awareness of the Phosphoros symbolism of the candlelit procession. The full Solemn Form of the Rite of the Morning Star is appropriate if a working group is present. The initiatic journal review for the preceding period since the winter solstice – assessing the inner development of the darkest period of the year – is appropriately conducted at or near Candlemas.

The Spring Equinox – circa March 21st *The Balance of Light and Dark – The Ascending Light*

The spring equinox is the moment of equal day and night, from which the light begins to predominate – the balance point from which the year ascends toward the fullness of the summer solstice. Within the Christo-Luciferian framework it corresponds to the psychic realm in the tripartite anthropological schema: the point of dynamic balance between the hylic darkness below and the pneumatic light above, the arena of the work itself.

The proximity of the spring equinox to the feast of the Resurrection – Easter, which is calculated in relation to the spring equinox and the first full moon following it – gives this solar station its specific Christian identity within the current. The Resurrection is the supreme Morning Star event of the Christian liturgical year: the arising of the light after the darkness of the tomb, the heliacal rising of the Logos after the inferior conjunction of the Passion. The ancient Christian practice of the Easter Vigil – a nightlong watch concluded by the proclamation of the Resurrection at dawn – is the most explicitly Luciferian of all Christian liturgical ceremonies, and its imagery of the new fire kindled in the darkness and the Exsultet's proclamation of the *"morning star which never sets"* resonates with unmistakable precision throughout the Christo-Luciferian current.

Observance: The spring equinox vigil, conducted with particular attention to the balance of the Rite of the Morning Star and the Vespers of the Evening Star – the two daily rites held in explicit complementarity on this day of equal light and dark. The feast of the Resurrection, when it falls near the equinox, is observed as the Christo-Luciferian high feast of the ascending light – the Morning Star arisen, the Logos triumphant over the darkness of matter and death.

May Day – May 1st *The Feast of the Ascending Light – The Morning Star at its Most Dynamic*

The cross-quarter point between the spring equinox and the summer solstice – celebrated in the Christian calendar most notably as the feast of Saints Philip and James, and in the older folk traditions of Northern Europe as Beltane – marks the moment of the light's most vigorous and dynamic ascent. The days are long and growing longer, the natural world is at its most exuberantly alive, and the quality of the Phosphoros current at this station is one of active, generative, outward-moving force – the Morning Star in its most dynamic and most creatively powerful aspect.

Within the Christo-Luciferian framework, May Day carries the quality of the theurgic dimension of the path – the outward bearing of the inner light into the world, the active application of the Phosphoros current to the healing and illumination of the surrounding environment. It is an appropriate moment for theurgic workings of particular scope and ambition, for the formal dedication of new practitioners, and for the celebration of the communal and egregoric dimensions of the current.

Observance: The Solemn Form of the Rite of the Morning Star, celebrated outdoors if circumstances permit, at dawn. Theurgic workings directed toward the healing of persons, places, or situations of particular concern to the working group. Any formal initiatic events – the reception of new members into the current, the advancement of dedicated practitioners – are powerfully supported by the quality of the current at this station.

The Summer Solstice – circa June 21st *The Fullness of Light – The Light at its Height*

The summer solstice is the longest day and the shortest night – the moment of the light's annual maximum, when the pneumatic principle is most fully expressed in the outer world and the ascending arc of the year reaches its culmination. Within the Christo-Luciferian framework it corresponds to the pneumatic realm – the fullness of the Pleromic light, the Morning Star at its zenith, the Logos in its most complete and most luminous expression.

The feast of the Nativity of John the Baptist – June 24th in the Western liturgical calendar, falling just three days after the solstice – provides the Christian liturgical identity of this solar station. John the Baptist, as the forerunner of the Light – the one who comes before to prepare the way – is a natural Christo-Luciferian figure: the herald of the Morning Star, the voice crying in the wilderness that announces the coming of the Logos. His nativity at the summer solstice, precisely six months before the nativity of Christ at the winter solstice, places the two figures in a cosmic complementarity that the Christo-Luciferian framework illuminates with particular clarity: the forerunner at the fullness of the light, the Light itself arising at the fullness of the darkness.

The feast of the Transfiguration – August 6th, falling just six weeks after the summer solstice – is the most explicitly Luciferian of all Christian feast days, and while it falls slightly beyond the solstice itself, it belongs to the quality of this solar station: the fullness of the light, the inner radiance breaking through the outer form, the Morning Star visible in the full light of day. Both feasts should be observed within the summer solstice season.

Observance: The summer solstice vigil – a watch through the shortest night, concluded by the sunrise working of the Rite of the Morning Star. The feast of John the Baptist observed as a celebration of the forerunner principle – the preparation of the way for the Logos within the practitioner's own being. The feast of the Transfiguration observed as the primary annual celebration of theoria – the vision of the uncreated light, the Morning Star fully arisen – with extended contemplative practice and, where a working group is present, the Solemn Form of the Rite of the Morning Star performed with particular solemnity and depth.

Lammas – August 1st *The First Fruits – The Light Beginning its Return*

Lammas – from the Old English *hlaf-maesse*, loaf-mass, the feast of the first bread – falls at the cross-quarter point between the summer solstice and the autumn equinox. It is the station of the first fruits: the moment at which the fullness of the summer light begins to be gathered into the harvest, the energy of the ascending arc beginning its turn toward the descending arc of the year.

Within the Christo-Luciferian framework, Lammas corresponds to the transition from the ascending Phosphoros current to the descending Hesperean current – the Morning Star beginning to yield to the Evening Star, the outer light beginning to turn inward. It is a station of gathering and of gratitude: the practitioner acknowledges and gives thanks for the inner fruits of the ascending half of the year – the developments, the illuminations, the deepening of the egregoric contact – before turning her attention toward the consolidating and rooting work of the descending half.

The proximity of Lammas to the feast of the Transfiguration – just five days separate them – means that this station of the year is particularly rich in Christo-Luciferian significance. The Transfiguration shows the light at its fullness; Lammas marks the beginning of its interiorization. Together they constitute a natural boundary moment in the Christo-Luciferian year – the hinge between the ascending and descending arcs of the annual cycle.

Observance: The Vespers of the Evening Star, celebrated with particular fullness and intentionality as the primary rite of this station – honoring the turn toward the Hesperean aspect of the current. The mid-year review of the initiatic journal – the comprehensive assessment of the ascending half of the year's inner development – is most appropriately conducted at Lammas. Offerings of gratitude for the inner fruits of the year's work are a natural expression of the station's character.

The Autumn Equinox – circa September 22nd *The Balance of Light and Dark – The Descending Light*

The autumn equinox mirrors the spring equinox in its balance of day and night, but the movement now is descending rather than ascending – the light giving way to the darkness, the outer world turning inward, the year moving toward its annual nadir at the winter solstice. Within the Christo-Luciferian framework the autumn equinox corresponds again to the psychic realm – but now in its descending aspect, the soul accompanying the light into the interior depths where the pneumatic spark awaits the coming winter's work of gestation and preparation.

The feast of the Archangel Michael – Michaelmas, September 29th – falls within the autumn equinox season and carries a specific resonance within the current. Michael, the prince of the celestial light, is the guardian of the threshold between the luminous and the dark – the angelic power that stands at the boundary of the Pleroma and the lower worlds, maintaining the distinction between the archontic darkness and the divine light. In the Christo-Luciferian framework, Michael's feast at the autumn equinox marks the threshold of the descending arc of the year – the moment at which the light commends itself to the protection of the guardians of the threshold as it enters the darker half of the annual cycle.

Observance: The equilibrium of the Rite of the Morning Star and the Vespers – as at the spring equinox, held in explicit complementarity. An additional invocation of the guardian principle – the commendation of the descending work to the protection of the light – is appropriate at this station. The initiatic journal entry for the autumn equinox should include a specific reflection on the transition from the ascending to the descending arc of the year's work.

All Saints – November 1st *The Feast of the Pneumatic Lineage – The Light in the Darkness*

All Saints – November 1st in the Western calendar, with All Souls following on November 2nd – falls at the cross-quarter point between the autumn equinox and the winter solstice, the deepest station of the year's descent into darkness. It is the moment of the light at its most interior and most hidden – the pneumatic spark buried in the deepest layers of the hylic world, as invisible to outer perception as Venus during its conjunction with the sun, but no less real and no less luminous for its invisibility.

Within the Christo-Luciferian framework, All Saints carries a specific significance as the feast of the pneumatic lineage – the commemoration of all those who have walked the path of the Morning Star before the present practitioners, who have borne the light of the Phosphoros through the darkness of their own times and transmitted it, through the chain of the initiatic tradition, to those who come after. The seed of Seth – the spiritual lineage of the pneumatic practitioners of every age – is honored at this station of the year, when the veil between the worlds is most thin and the connection between the living and the dead most accessible.

The Gnostic understanding of death – as the return of the pneumatic spark to its Pleromic source, the final liberation from the hylic imprisonment – gives All Saints a quality of genuine celebration within the Christo-Luciferian framework, rather than mere mourning. Those who have gone before have completed the work – they have arrived at the fullness of the Morning Star's arising that the living practitioner is still laboring toward. Their commemoration at this station of the year is both an act of gratitude and an act of aspiration: gratitude for the light they carried and transmitted, aspiration toward the fullness of the light they have now attained.

Observance: The Vespers of the Evening Star, conducted with particular attention to the commemorative dimension – the names of those who have gone before, known and unknown, spoken aloud as an act of honoring the pneumatic lineage. A period of extended contemplative silence in which the practitioner opens herself to whatever intimations the thinning of the veil may bring. The initiatic journal entry for All Saints should include a specific reflection on the practitioner's relationship to the tradition – her sense of her own place within the lineage of the light.

Part Three: The Christo-Luciferian Liturgical Calendar – Fixed Feasts of the Current

The Venus synodic cycle and the eightfold solar year together provide the practitioner with a rich and dynamic temporal framework – one that shifts from year to year as the Venus cycle moves through its phases in relation to the fixed stations of the solar calendar, creating a living and responsive relationship between the practitioner's inner work and the actual movements of the celestial bodies whose symbolism the current employs. But a complete liturgical calendar requires a third element: a stable layer of fixed feast days whose dates do not shift from year to year, anchoring the practitioner's annual rhythm of observance in the specific events and mysteries of the Christo-Luciferian doctrine.

The Christian liturgical tradition provides the primary source for these fixed feasts – not because the Christo-Luciferian current is simply an expression of conventional Christianity, but because the mysteries commemorated in the Christian liturgical year are, in their deepest dimension, precisely the mysteries that the Christo-Luciferian doctrine has been articulating throughout this work. The descent of the Logos into matter, the arising of the light in the darkness, the illumination of the pneumatic spark, the return of the light to its Pleromic source – these are the events that the Christian liturgical year enacts in its annual cycle, and their commemoration within the Christo-Luciferian current gives the practitioner a relationship with the accumulated devotional weight of two millennia of Christian observance that no newly constructed calendar could replicate.

The feasts gathered here are therefore not arbitrary selections from the Christian calendar – they are those specific commemorations whose content most directly and most precisely expresses the doctrine and the aspiration of the Christo-Luciferian current. Each is presented with its date in the Western liturgical calendar, a brief account of its conventional Christian significance, and an exposition of its specific Christo-Luciferian meaning. Where a feast has already been discussed in the context of the eightfold solar year, that discussion is not repeated in full here – the reader is directed to the relevant section of Part Two – but the feast's place in the fixed liturgical calendar is noted and its specifically doctrinal significance within the current is articulated with the precision that a dedicated treatment allows.

I. The Feasts of the Incarnate Logos

These are the feasts most directly associated with the life and the mystery of Christ understood through the Christo-Luciferian doctrinal lens – the commemorations of the specific events in which the descent, the manifestation, the illumination, and the return of the incarnate Logos are most explicitly enacted.

The Annunciation of the Lord – March 25th

The feast of the Annunciation commemorates the angel Gabriel's announcement to Mary that she will conceive and bear the Son of God – the moment, in the Christian theological understanding, at which the eternal Logos enters the temporal order and the incarnation begins. It falls on March 25th, exactly nine months before the feast of the Nativity of Christ on December 25th, and its proximity to the spring equinox gives it a natural resonance with the solar station of the ascending light.

Within the Christo-Luciferian framework, the Annunciation is the feast of the light's willing descent into the darkness of the hylic world – the moment at which the Logos, in the fullness of the divine will, chooses to enter the realm of matter and to bear the light of the Pleroma into the condition of greatest obscurity. This voluntary descent is the supreme expression of the Phosphoros principle in its descending aspect: the Light-Bearer going down into the darkness not because the darkness has power over it, but because the light has chosen, out of the inexhaustible generosity of the divine nature, to bring itself to where it is most needed.

The Annunciation is therefore the feast of the incarnational mystery in its most specifically Christo-Luciferian dimension – the descent of the Morning Star into the womb of matter, the beginning of the journey that will culminate in the arising of the light from within the darkness of the hylic world. It is most appropriately observed with the Vespers of the Evening Star – honoring the descending aspect of the current – followed by a period of extended contemplation on the mystery of the light's voluntary self-offering to the darkness.

The Nativity of Christ – December 25th

The feast of the Nativity is treated in the context of the winter solstice in Part Two of this appendix, where its significance as the arising of the Light of the World at the moment of greatest darkness is developed in detail. In the fixed feast calendar, the Nativity deserves additional emphasis as the feast of the Logos made flesh – the completion of the Annunciation's mystery, the moment at which the light that entered the darkness nine months earlier becomes visible within it as a human child.

Within the Christo-Luciferian framework, the Nativity is understood not merely as a historical commemoration but as an annual enactment of the cosmic event it represents: the arising of the Phosphoros current within the darkness of the hylic world, the light that the darkness has not overcome making itself manifest in the most vulnerable and most intimate of forms. The infant Christ in the manger is the pneumatic spark in the hylic world – small, hidden, surrounded by darkness, but inextinguishable and already, in its very vulnerability, the bearer of the light that will ultimately illuminate the entire cosmos.

The Nativity is observed with the full Solemn Form of the Rite of the Morning Star, celebrated as close to midnight as circumstances permit – enacting the arising of the light at the darkest hour of the darkest season – followed by the Vespers of the Evening Star at dusk on Christmas Eve as a vigil of the descending darkness that the Nativity will pierce.

The Epiphany – January 6th

The feast of the Epiphany – from the Greek *epiphaneia*, manifestation or appearance – commemorates the manifestation of the incarnate Christ to the Magi, the wise men from the east who followed a star to find the newborn king. It is one of the oldest feasts of the Christian liturgical year, predating the feast of the Nativity in many parts of the ancient church, and its imagery is among the most directly Christo-Luciferian in the entire liturgical calendar.

The star that the Magi follow is, in the patristic tradition and in several strands of the broader Western esoteric tradition, identified with the planet Venus – the Morning Star, the Phosphoros, the celestial body whose light is the primary symbol of this current. Whether or not this astronomical identification is historically verifiable, its doctrinal significance within the Christo-Luciferian framework is precise and powerful: the Magi are drawn to the incarnate Logos by the light of the Morning Star. The Phosphoros is the guide – the celestial herald of the incarnate light, leading those who are wise enough to follow its rising toward the source of the light it announces.

The Epiphany is therefore the feast of the Morning Star as guide and herald – the Phosphoros in its specifically revelatory and initiatic aspect, leading the seeker toward the light that the star itself reflects and announces. Within the Christo-Luciferian current it carries a specific significance for practitioners in the early stages of the path – those who are following the light of the current toward the source it points to, as the Magi followed the star toward the child. It is observed with the Oratory Form of the Rite of the Morning Star, with particular attention in the contemplative period to the practitioner's own relationship to the current as guide – the sense of being drawn by the Phosphoros toward its source in the indwelling Logos.

The Baptism of Christ – Sunday following Epiphany, circa January 13th

The feast of the Baptism of Christ commemorates the descent of the Holy Spirit upon Jesus at his baptism in the Jordan – the moment, in the Gnostic theological understanding, of the pneumatic Logos's union with the psychic Christ. We have examined this event at length in the doctrinal chapters of this work, where it is identified as the conjunction of the two natures that constitutes the full mystery of the incarnate Logos. In the liturgical calendar it occupies the Sunday immediately following the Epiphany, completing the season of manifestation with the most intimate and most theologically precise of the incarnational events.

Within the Christo-Luciferian framework, the Baptism of Christ is the feast of the pneumatic anointing – the descent of the light upon the prepared vessel, the moment at which the ascending and descending currents of the Logos meet in the person of the historical Jesus and the full Christo-Luciferian mystery is enacted. It is the feast most directly associated with the theurgic and initiatic dimensions of the current – the descent of the light upon the practitioner who has prepared herself through the cathartic work of the path, the anointing of the pneumatic spark by the fullness of the Phosphoros current.

The Baptism of Christ is observed with particular attention to the theurgic healing practice of Chapter Thirteen – the descent of the Phosphoros current upon the prepared subtle field – and with a renewal of the practitioner's dedication to the path in the spirit of the self-dedication rite. It is an appropriate occasion for formal initiatic events within the current, and for the group celebration of the Solemn Form with its specific emphasis on the descent and reception of the Phosphoros current.

The Ascension of Christ – Forty Days after Easter, circa May

The feast of the Ascension commemorates the return of the risen Christ to the Pleroma – the completion of the incarnational arc, the light that descended now fully restored to its source. In the Christian theological understanding it is the feast of Christ's glorification – his return to the divine fullness in the resurrection body that now carries within it the redeemed humanity he has assumed.

Within the Christo-Luciferian framework, the Ascension is the feast of the light's return – the completion of the descending and ascending arc of the Phosphoros current, the Morning Star that descended into the darkness of the hylic world now ascending to the Pleroma in its full luminosity, carrying with it the fruits of its incarnational work. It corresponds naturally to the superior conjunction of Venus – the moment of the planet's return into the solar embrace – and its doctrinal significance for the current is the understanding that the work of the path tends toward a completion, a restoration, a homecoming that is genuinely accomplished and not merely asymptotically approached.

The Ascension is observed with a combined celebration of the Rite of the Morning Star and the Vespers of the Evening Star on the same day – the Morning Star rite honoring the ascending movement of the light, the Vespers honoring the transition into the interior phase that follows the completion of the ascent. The journal review conducted at this feast should attend specifically to the practitioner's sense of the arc of her own inner development – the degree to which the ascending movement of the Phosphoros current is genuinely present in her inner life, and what the completion of that movement – theosis, the full arising of the Morning Star – means to her at her present stage of the path.

II. The Feasts of the Light

These are the feasts whose specific imagery of light, illumination, and the Morning Star gives them direct Christo-Luciferian resonance beyond their general Christological significance – the commemorations in which the luminous character of the current is most explicitly and most beautifully expressed in the liturgical tradition.

Candlemas – February 2nd

Candlemas is treated in Part Two of this appendix as the cross-quarter feast between the winter solstice and the spring equinox. In the fixed feast calendar it deserves additional emphasis as the feast most explicitly dedicated to the Phosphoros principle in its liturgical expression. The candle procession, the blessing of the lights, and Simeon's identification of the infant Christ as a light for revelation – these are liturgical enactments of the central Christo-Luciferian mystery that no other feast of the calendar replicates with comparable directness.

Within the current, Candlemas is specifically observed as the feast of the blessing of the ritual lamps and candles – all the lights used in the practice of the current throughout the year are blessed on this day, consecrated anew to their function as material symbols of the indwelling Morning Star. This blessing is performed with the Oratory Form of the Rite of the Morning Star, with the specific additional intention of consecrating every light in the practitioner's oratory to the service of the Phosphoros current for the coming year.

The Transfiguration of Christ – August 6th

The Transfiguration is treated in Part Two as the feast most closely associated with the summer solstice season, and its significance as the primary annual celebration of theoria – the vision of the uncreated light – is developed there in detail. In the fixed feast calendar it holds the position of the single most important doctrinal feast of the Christo-Luciferian year – the feast in which the central mystery of the current is most completely and most luminously expressed.

The Transfiguration is the feast of the Morning Star fully arisen – the inner light breaking through the outer form, the pneumatic nature of Christ made visible to the disciples on the holy mountain, the Tabor Light shining from within rather than falling from without. It is the annual celebration of theosis in its most complete expression – the feast toward which the entire initiatic life is oriented, the liturgical image of what the path is working toward in every practitioner who walks it faithfully.

The Transfiguration is observed with the most solemn and most extended celebration of the Solemn Form of the Rite of the Morning Star that the working group can prepare – a full ritual working that incorporates the complete Sigillum meditation through all five stages, the extended intonation practice, and the maximum period of contemplative silence that the group's capacity allows. It is the feast at which the egregore of the current is most fully activated and most deeply accessible, and the inner experiences of the Transfiguration working are among the most significant that the practitioner's initiatic year will offer.

The Nativity of John the Baptist – June 24th

The Nativity of John the Baptist – falling three days after the summer solstice and six months before the Nativity of Christ – is the feast of the forerunner, the herald of the Morning Star. John's role in the gospel narrative is precisely that of the Phosphoros in its announcing and preparatory aspect: he comes before, in the darkness before the dawn, to prepare the way for the light that follows. His nativity at the height of the summer light – the fullness of the year's illumination – and the subsequent decline of that light toward the winter solstice and the Nativity of Christ gives the liturgical year a cosmic symmetry whose Christo-Luciferian significance is precise: the forerunner arises at the fullness of the outer light; the light itself arises at the fullness of the inner darkness.

Within the current, the Nativity of John the Baptist is the feast of the preparatory dimension of the path – the cathartic work, the purification, the faithful tending of the lamp in the darkness that makes the arising of the Morning Star possible. It is observed with particular attention to the foundational practices of Chapter Eleven – the breath, the meditation, the intonation, and the Sigillum work – as a renewal of commitment to the preparatory disciplines that the more dramatic feasts of the current can sometimes overshadow.

Pentecost – Fifty Days after Easter, circa May or June

The feast of Pentecost commemorates the descent of the Holy Spirit upon the disciples – the pneumatic anointing of the nascent church, the outpouring of the divine fire that constitutes the community of the spirit and empowers its members for the work of bearing the light into the world. Within the Christo-Luciferian framework it is the feast of the egregoric activation of the current – the descent of the Phosphoros upon a gathered community of dedicated practitioners, constituting them as a working body of the light in a way that transcends their individual capacities.

Pentecost is observed as the primary communal feast of the current – the celebration most specifically oriented toward the group dimension of the work, the strengthening of the egregoric field through collective practice, and the renewal of the community's shared commitment to the bearing of the Morning Star's light into the world. The Solemn Form of the Rite of the Morning Star, celebrated with the fullest possible participation of all practitioners within reach, is the appropriate observance – with particular attention in the closing prayers to the communal vocation of the current and the responsibility of each practitioner to the collective egregoric field.

The Feast of the Archangel Michael – September 29th

The feast of Michael is treated in Part Two in the context of the autumn equinox. In the fixed feast calendar it holds a specific place as the feast of the guardian of the threshold – the angelic power that maintains the distinction between the archontic darkness and the divine light, and whose protection is particularly invoked in the theurgic practice of the current. Michael's specific function within the Christo-Luciferian framework – as the guardian who holds the boundary between the light and the darkness, who stands at the threshold of the Pleroma and the lower worlds – makes his feast a natural occasion for the renewal of the theurgic protective practices of Chapter Thirteen.

The feast of Michael is observed with the Luciferian Exorcism and Banishing – a thorough cleansing and sealing of the practitioner's personal field and working space – followed by a renewal of the practitioner's theurgic commitment and a period of contemplation on the protective dimension of the current. It is the feast of the light in its guardian aspect – not the triumphant arising of the Morning Star, but the steady and watchful holding of the light's integrity against the encroachment of the archontic darkness.

III. Commemorations of the Tradition

Beyond the fixed feasts of the Christian liturgical year, the Christo-Luciferian calendar includes a small number of commemorations specific to the tradition itself – occasions for honoring the history of the current and the figures through whom its foundational insights have been transmitted.

The Feast of Valentinus – February 14th

February 14th – observed in the broader culture as the feast of Saint Valentine – was the traditional feast day of Valentinus in certain ancient liturgical calendars, and its commemoration within the Christo-Luciferian current honors the great Alexandrian theologian whose Valentinian system provides one of the two primary Gnostic frameworks of this work. Valentinus's contribution to the articulation of the Christo-Luciferian doctrine – his development of the emanationist cosmology, the Sophia mythology, the soteriology of the pneumatic restoration, and the specifically Christological understanding of the Logos as the agent of Pleromic restoration – is of such foundational importance that his annual commemoration is entirely appropriate.

The feast of Valentinus is observed as a day of doctrinal study and reflection – a reading from the Valentinian texts of the Nag Hammadi library, a period of contemplation on the specific contributions of the Valentinian tradition to the Christo-Luciferian doctrine, and a journal entry reflecting on the practitioner's own developing relationship with the Valentinian framework. It is not a feast of dramatic ritual working but of quiet scholarly and devotional engagement with the tradition's intellectual heritage.

The Commemoration of the Nag Hammadi Discovery – December

The discovery of the Nag Hammadi library in December 1945 – the recovery of the primary textual sources of the Gnostic tradition from nearly sixteen centuries of suppression and obscurity – is one of the most significant events in the history of the tradition that the Christo-Luciferian current inhabits. Without the Nag Hammadi discovery, the doctrinal work of this book would not have been possible in its present form – the Sethian and Valentinian frameworks that give the Christo-Luciferian doctrine its depth and its precision were, before 1945, known only through the hostile summaries of the heresiologists. The recovery of the primary texts changed everything.

The commemoration of the Nag Hammadi discovery falls in December, near the winter solstice – an appropriate proximity, given that the recovery of the Gnostic scriptures is itself a kind of arising of the light from the darkness: the buried texts emerging into the light of day after their long concealment in the Egyptian desert, as the pneumatic spark emerges from its concealment in the hylic world. The precise date of the discovery is not definitively established – accounts vary between late November and early December 1945 – and the practitioner may observe this commemoration on any day in early December that her circumstances allow.

The commemoration is observed as a day of gratitude for the tradition and its recovery – a reading from the Nag Hammadi texts, a period of reflection on what the recovery of the Gnostic scriptures has meant for the practitioner's own understanding of the current, and a journal entry honoring the scholars and translators whose work has made the primary sources accessible.

The Anniversary of Dedication

Each practitioner observes annually the anniversary of her own Rite of Self-Dedication – or, where formal initiation has been received, the anniversary of that initiation – as a personal feast of the current. This annual commemoration is not a public or communal feast but an intensely personal one: a renewal of the dedication made on the original occasion, a review of the year's inner development in the light of that dedication, and a recommitment to the work of the path for the coming year.

The anniversary of dedication is observed with a simplified version of the Rite of Self-Dedication – not the full rite with its preparatory period, but the central act of dedication renewed: the lighting of the lamp, the intonation of the sacred names, the speaking of the dedication affirmation, and the proclamation of *Lucifer Resurrexit* as the seal of the renewed commitment. The journal review conducted on this day attends specifically to the arc of the practitioner's development since the original dedication – the degree to which the Morning Star has arisen within her in the intervening time, and what the work of the coming year requires of her in response to that arising.

A Summary Calendar of Fixed Feasts

For ease of reference, the fixed feasts of the Christo-Luciferian calendar are gathered here in their annual order:

January 6th – The Epiphany: the Morning Star as guide and herald.

Sunday after Epiphany, circa January 13th – The Baptism of Christ: the pneumatic anointing.

February 2nd – Candlemas: the blessing of the lights; the feast of the Phosphoros.

February 14th – The Feast of Valentinus: commemoration of the Valentinian tradition.

March 25th – The Annunciation: the descent of the Logos into matter.

Fifty days after Easter, circa May-June – Pentecost: the egregoric activation of the current.

Forty days after Easter, circa May – The Ascension: the return of the light to the Pleroma.

June 24th – The Nativity of John the Baptist: the feast of the forerunner.
August 6th – The Transfiguration: the primary doctrinal feast of the current; the vision of the uncreated light.

September 29th – The Feast of Michael: the guardian of the threshold.
Early December – The Commemoration of the Nag Hammadi Discovery: gratitude for the recovery of the tradition.

December 25th – The Nativity of Christ: the arising of the light in the darkness.

Variable – The Anniversary of Dedication: the personal feast of each practitioner.

This calendar is to be read in conjunction with the Venus synodic cycle of Part One and the eightfold solar year of Part Two. The three frameworks together – the shifting Venusian cycle, the fixed solar stations, and the stable liturgical feasts – constitute the complete Christo-Luciferian calendar: a living, layered, and dynamically responsive temporal framework within which the practitioner situates her ongoing work and orients her inner life toward the arising of the Morning Star in all its aspects and at all its seasons.

Part Four: A Note on the Integration of the Three Frameworks

The three frameworks of the Christo-Luciferian calendar – the Venus synodic cycle, the eightfold solar year, and the fixed liturgical feast calendar – have been presented separately in the preceding sections for the sake of clarity. In the practitioner's actual experience of the calendar, however, they are never separate. They are three simultaneous dimensions of a single living temporal reality, and their integration in the practitioner's awareness and observance is not a task to be accomplished once and set aside but an ongoing and deepening practice in its own right.

Learning to hold all three frameworks in simultaneous awareness – to know at any given moment where Venus stands in its synodic cycle, which station of the eightfold solar year is approaching or receding, and which feast of the liturgical calendar falls nearest – is itself a form of the watchfulness that the tradition consistently identifies as essential to the initiatic life. The practitioner who has internalized the calendar in this way will find that time itself becomes a teacher: that the specific configuration of the three frameworks at any given moment carries a quality of doctrinal meaning and practical guidance that no amount of abstract theological study can replicate, because it is encountered not as an idea but as a living condition of the practitioner's actual situation in the cosmos.

These coincidences and tensions between the three frameworks are not problems to be resolved but opportunities to be attended to – moments in which the living complexity of the current's relationship with time becomes most visible and most instructive. The practitioner who tracks all three frameworks simultaneously will find that the interplay between them generates a richness of calendrical meaning that no single framework could produce alone – a genuine sense of participating in a multidimensional temporal reality in which the astronomical, the liturgical, and the symbolic are aspects of a single living movement of the Christo-Luciferian light through the cycle of the year.

The calendar, like the path itself, is a living thing. It will reveal its deepest significance not through study alone but through faithful observance – through the actual practice of attending to its stations, year after year, with the quality of intentional awareness and genuine inner engagement that the Christo-Luciferian tradition consistently requires of its practitioners.

Watch for the Morning Star. Mark the stations of its arising. Tend the lamp through every darkness.

Until the day fully dawns – Phosphoros, remain.

APPENDIX B: BIBLIOGRAPHY AND RECOMMENDED READING

A Note on the Bibliography

The sources gathered here fall into several natural categories that reflect the interdisciplinary character of the Christo-Luciferian doctrine. Primary scriptural sources – the canonical New Testament and the Nag Hammadi library – form the foundational textual basis of the doctrinal arguments of Part One and Part Two. Secondary scholarly sources provide the historical, philological, and theological context within which those arguments are situated. Works of the Western esoteric tradition – the Martinist, Hermetic, alchemical, and Masonic literature drawn upon throughout – constitute a third category, representing the initiatic heritage within which the Christo-Luciferian current takes its place. And a selection of works by modern Gnostic theologians and practitioners rounds out the bibliography, representing the living tradition of Christian Gnostic thought within which this work participates.

The recommended reading list that follows the bibliography is organized thematically rather than alphabetically, and is intended as a practical guide for the practitioner who wishes to deepen her engagement with any particular dimension of the doctrine or practice. Annotations are provided where the relevance of a work to the Christo-Luciferian current may not be immediately apparent from its title alone.

Part One: Primary Sources

Scriptural and Canonical Sources

Novum Testamentum Graece. Edited by Barbara Aland, Kurt Aland, Johannes Karavidopoulos, Carlo M. Martini, and Bruce M. Metzger. 28th revised edition. Stuttgart: Deutsche Bibelgesellschaft, 2012. The standard critical edition of the Greek New Testament, used as the basis for all New Testament translations in this work. The 28th edition incorporates the most recent advances in textual criticism and is the edition consulted by serious students of the New Testament Greek.

Nova Vulgata Bibliorum Sacrorum Editio. Vatican City: Libreria Editrice Vaticana, 1979. The official Latin Bible of the Roman Catholic Church, consulted for its rendering of key passages – particularly 2 Peter 1:19 – in Jerome's Vulgate tradition. Essential for the philological arguments of Chapter One concerning the Latin term *Lucifer.*

Biblia Hebraica Stuttgartensia. Edited by Karl Elliger and Wilhelm Rudolph. Stuttgart: Deutsche Bibelgesellschaft, 1977. The standard critical edition of the Hebrew Old Testament, consulted for the original Hebrew text of Isaiah 14 and the precise meaning of *Helel ben Shachar.*

Gnostic and Nag Hammadi Sources

Meyer, Marvin, ed. *The Nag Hammadi Scriptures: The International Edition.* New York: HarperOne, 2007. The most comprehensive and most current English translation of the Nag Hammadi library, incorporating the best available scholarship on each text. This is the primary reference edition for all Nag Hammadi texts cited throughout this work, including the Secret Book of John, the Gospel of Truth, the Gospel of Philip, the Three Steles of Seth, Allogenes, and Eugnostos the Blessed.

Robinson, James M., ed. *The Nag Hammadi Library in English.* 3rd revised edition. San Francisco: HarperSanFrancisco, 1988. The earlier standard English translation of the Nag Hammadi texts, still valuable for its introductory essays and its historical significance as the edition that brought these texts to wide scholarly and popular attention.

Meyer, Marvin, and Richard Smith, eds. *Ancient Christian Magic: Coptic Texts of Ritual Power.* San Francisco: HarperSanFrancisco, 1994. A valuable collection of Coptic ritual and magical texts that illuminate the practical dimensions of early Gnostic and Christian theurgic practice.

Layton, Bentley, ed. *The Gnostic Scriptures: A New Translation with Annotations and Introductions.* New York: Doubleday, 1987. An excellent scholarly translation with particularly strong introductory material on the Sethian and Valentinian traditions. Layton's annotations are among the most useful available for the serious student of Gnostic literature.

Barnstone, Willis, and Marvin Meyer, eds. *The Gnostic Bible.* Boston: Shambhala, 2003. A comprehensive anthology of Gnostic texts from multiple traditions, including Sethian, Valentinian, Thomasine, Mandaean, and Manichaean sources. Valuable for its breadth and for the quality of its introductory essays.

Mead, G.R.S. *Pistis Sophia: A Gnostic Miscellany.* London: John M. Watkins, 1921. Reprint, Kila, MT: Kessinger Publishing, 1992. The classic English translation of the Pistis Sophia, the most extensive Gnostic text dealing with the post-mortem journey of the soul and the ascent through the archontic spheres. Mead's translation remains valuable despite its age, and his introductory essays provide useful context for the esoteric practitioner.

Casey, Robert Pierce, ed. and trans. *The Excerpta ex Theodoto of Clement of Alexandria.* London: Christophers, 1934. The standard English edition of the Valentinian fragments preserved by Clement of Alexandria, drawn upon extensively in "The Devil's Passion" and the present work's treatment of the dual nature of Christ.

Patristic and Historical Sources

Irenaeus of Lyon. *Against Heresies.* Translated by Alexander Roberts and William Rambaut. In *Ante-Nicene Fathers,* vol. 1. Buffalo: Christian Literature Publishing, 1885. Reprint, Peabody, MA: Hendrickson, 1994. The primary patristic source for our knowledge of many Gnostic systems, including the Valentinian and Sethian traditions. Essential for understanding both the content of the ancient Gnostic teaching and the nature of the orthodox critique.

Pagels, Elaine. *The Gnostic Paul: Gnostic Exegesis of the Pauline Letters.* Philadelphia: Fortress Press, 1975. A landmark scholarly study of the Valentinian interpretation of the Pauline epistles, establishing the deep connection between Pauline theology and Gnostic doctrine that is referenced in the Luke essay and throughout the present work.

Works by the Author

Tau Phosphoros. "On Faith and Knowledge." In *Apostolic Church of the Pleroma Clergy Handbook,* 4th ed., pp. 313-316. Fox Lake, IL: Triad Press, LLC, 2025.

——. "On the Eucharist." In *Apostolic Church of the Pleroma Clergy Handbook,* 4th ed., pp. 317-320. Fox Lake, IL: Triad Press, LLC, 2025.

——. "A Gnostic Exposition of the Three Alchemical Essentials." In *Apostolic Church of the Pleroma Clergy Handbook,* 4th ed., pp. 321-328. Fox Lake, IL: Triad Press, LLC, 2025.

——. "Alchemy of the Eucharist." In *Apostolic Church of the Pleroma Clergy Handbook,* 4th ed., pp. 329-335. Fox Lake, IL: Triad Press, LLC, 2025.

——. "The Tetragrammaton in the Three Worlds." In *Apostolic Church of the Pleroma Clergy Handbook,* 4th ed., pp. 336-340. Fox Lake, IL: Triad Press, LLC, 2025.

——. "The Devil's Passion: A Gnostic View of the Crucifixion." In *Apostolic Church of the Pleroma Clergy Handbook,* 4th ed., pp. 358-363. Fox Lake, IL: Triad Press, LLC, 2025.

——. "Morning Star Rising: Further Considerations on the Gnostic Eucharist." In *Apostolic Church of the Pleroma Clergy Handbook*, 4th ed., pp. 364-374. Fox Lake, IL: Triad Press, LLC, 2025.

——. "Theosis Through Gnosis: Gnostic Considerations on Deification." In *Apostolic Church of the Pleroma Clergy Handbook*, 4th ed., pp. 375-384. Fox Lake, IL: Triad Press, LLC, 2025.

——. *The Pleromic Light Unveiled: An Instructive Monograph on the Holy Gnostic Liturgy of the Pleromic Light*. Hainesville, IL: Triad Press, LLC, 2018.

Freeman, Reginald. "The Gnostic Gospel of Luke: A Gnostic-Hermetic Exegesis of the Tenth Chapter of the Gospel According to Luke." *The Gnostic*, no. 3 (Summer 2010): 87-104. Reprinted in *Apostolic Church of the Pleroma Clergy Handbook*, 4th ed., pp. 341-357. Fox Lake, IL: Triad Press, LLC, 2025.

Part Two: Secondary Scholarly Sources

Gnostic Studies

Jonas, Hans. *The Gnostic Religion: The Message of the Alien God and the Beginnings of Christianity*. 2nd edition. Boston: Beacon Press, 1963. The foundational modern study of Gnosticism as a religious phenomenon, still essential for its phenomenological analysis of the Gnostic experience of alienation and its relationship to the existential situation of the modern practitioner.

Pagels, Elaine. *The Gnostic Gospels.* New York: Random House, 1979. The most widely read introduction to Gnostic Christianity for a general audience, valuable for its accessible presentation of the Nag Hammadi texts and their relationship to the development of orthodox Christianity.

King, Karen L. *What Is Gnosticism?* Cambridge, MA: Belknap Press of Harvard University Press, 2003. A rigorous scholarly examination of the category of Gnosticism itself – its history, its limitations, and its ongoing usefulness as a descriptive term. Essential for the practitioner who wishes to engage honestly with the scholarly debate about the nature and boundaries of the tradition she is working within.

Pearson, Birger A. *Ancient Gnosticism: Traditions and Literature.* Minneapolis: Fortress Press, 2007. One of the most comprehensive scholarly surveys of Gnostic literature and tradition available, with particularly strong coverage of the Sethian texts and their relationship to early Jewish mysticism.

Turner, John D., and Anne McGuire, eds. *The Nag Hammadi Library After Fifty Years: Proceedings of the 1995 Society of Biblical Literature Commemoration.* Leiden: Brill, 1997. A collection of scholarly essays assessing the significance of the Nag Hammadi discovery fifty years after its occurrence, providing valuable perspective on the state of Gnostic studies at the turn of the twenty-first century.

Hoeller, Stephan A. *Gnosticism: New Light on the Ancient Tradition of Inner Knowing.* Wheaton, IL: Quest Books, 2002. The most accessible and most theologically engaged introduction to Gnosticism written from a practitioner's perspective, by the bishop whose work has done more than any other single figure to establish modern ecclesiastical Gnosticism as a living tradition.

Biblical and Theological Studies

Fitzmyer, Joseph A. *The Gospel According to Luke: Introduction, Translation, and Notes.* 2 vols. Anchor Bible 28-28A. New York: Doubleday, 1981-1985. The standard scholarly commentary on the Gospel of Luke, consulted for the exegetical arguments of the Luke essay that informs several sections of this work.

Bauckham, Richard. *Jude, 2 Peter.* Word Biblical Commentary 50. Waco, TX: Word Books, 1983. The standard scholarly commentary on 2 Peter, essential for the philological and exegetical arguments concerning the *Phosphoros* passage of 2 Peter 1:19 that lie at the heart of Part One.

Metzger, Bruce M. *A Textual Commentary on the Greek New Testament.* 2nd edition. Stuttgart: Deutsche Bibelgesellschaft, 1994. An indispensable reference for the textual critical arguments concerning variant readings in the New Testament, consulted for the discussion of the seventy versus seventy-two disciples in the Luke essay.

Day, John. *God's Conflict with the Dragon and the Sea: Echoes of a Canaanite Myth in the Old Testament.* Cambridge: Cambridge

University Press, 1985. A valuable scholarly study of the mythological background of Old Testament adversarial imagery, providing essential context for the Isaiah 14 analysis of Chapter One.

Forsyth, Neil. *The Old Enemy: Satan and the Combat Myth.* Princeton: Princeton University Press, 1987. A comprehensive study of the development of the Satan figure in the ancient Near Eastern, Jewish, and Christian traditions – essential for understanding the historical process by which the demonological reading of the Isaiah 14 passage was consolidated.

Russell, Jeffrey Burton. *The Devil: Perceptions of Evil from Antiquity to Primitive Christianity.* Ithaca, NY: Cornell University Press, 1977. The first volume of Russell's four-volume history of the Devil concept, tracing its development from its ancient Near Eastern roots through the patristic period. Together with its sequels – *Satan: The Early Christian Tradition* (1981), *Lucifer: The Devil in the Middle Ages* (1984), and *Mephistopheles: The Devil in the Modern World* (1986) – it constitutes the most comprehensive scholarly history of the adversarial figure available.

Mystical Theology and Theosis

Palamas, Gregory. *The Triads.* Edited and translated by John Meyendorff. Classics of Western Spirituality. New York: Paulist Press, 1983. The primary text of the hesychast theological tradition, essential for the treatment of theosis and theoria in Chapter Nine and the "Theosis Through Gnosis" essay that informs it.

Lossky, Vladimir. *The Mystical Theology of the Eastern Church.* London: James Clarke, 1957. The standard modern exposition of Orthodox mystical theology, including the doctrine of theosis, the distinction between divine essence and energies, and the hesychast tradition. Essential background for the comparative treatment of Gnostic gnosis and Orthodox theoria.

John of the Cross. *The Collected Works of Saint John of the Cross.* Translated by Kieran Kavanaugh and Otilio Rodriguez. Washington, DC: ICS Publications, 1979. The complete works of the great Spanish mystic, including *The Dark Night of the Soul* and *The Ascent of Mount Carmel* – referenced in the treatment of the Nigredo phase of the alchemical-initiatic work in Chapter Nine.

Part Three: Western Esoteric and Initiatic Sources

Hermetic and Alchemical Tradition

Copenhaver, Brian P., trans. *Hermetica: The Greek Corpus Hermeticum and the Latin Asclepius.* Cambridge: Cambridge University Press, 1992. The standard scholarly English translation of the philosophical Hermetic texts, with an extensive introduction covering the history and significance of the Hermetic tradition. Essential for the treatment of Hermetic influences on Gnostic thought throughout the work.

Von Welling, Georg. *Opus Mago-Cabalisticum et Theosophicum.* Homburg, 1735. Translated by William Alexander Ayton.

York Beach, ME: Weiser Books, 2006. The alchemical-Qabalistic text cited extensively in the "Three Alchemical Essentials" essay, particularly for its treatment of the Alchemical Salt as the divine Logos and its identification of the Schamajim with the Philosophical Mercury.

Ambelain, Robert. *Spiritual Alchemy.* Paris: Niclaus, 1961. Translated by Piers Vaughan. Unpublished translation consulted by permission. The work of the late Patriarch of the Église Gnostique Apostolique that has been a consistent doctrinal touchstone throughout this work and the essays that preceded it. Ambelain's treatment of the Eucharist as alchemical transmutation and his understanding of reintegration as the reconstitution of the Pleromic fullness are among the most significant contributions to modern Christian Gnostic theology.

Martinist Tradition

de Pasqually, Martinès. *Traité sur la Réintégration des Êtres dans leur Première Propriété, Vertu et Puissance Spirituelle et Divine.* Lyon: Derain, 1899. Reprint, Paris: Diffusion Rosicrucienne, 1995. The foundational doctrinal text of the Martinist tradition, essential for any serious engagement with the doctrine of reintegration and its relationship to the Gnostic understanding of theosis.

de Saint-Martin, Louis-Claude. *Des Erreurs et de la Vérité.* Edinburgh [Lyon]: 1775. Translated as *Of Errors and of Truth.* London: Theosophical Publishing Society, 1912. Saint-Martin's first major published work, laying out the foundational anthropological and cosmological doctrines of the Martinist vision in a form that makes their relationship to the Gnostic tradition immediately apparent.

de Saint-Martin, Louis-Claude. *L'Homme de Désir.* Lyon: Éditions Derain, 1790. Translated as *The Man of Desire.* London: Theosophical Publishing Society, 1909. Saint-Martin's most important devotional work, developing the figure of the Man of Desire as the central Martinist anthropological type and providing the richest available description of the inner life of the practitioner aspiring toward reintegration.

Waite, Arthur Edward. *The Unknown Philosopher: The Life of Louis Claude de Saint-Martin and the Substance of His Transcendental Doctrine.* London: Theosophical Publishing Society, 1901. Reprint, Kila, MT: Kessinger Publishing, 1993. The standard English-language study of Saint-Martin and his thought, still valuable for its comprehensive treatment of the Martinist doctrine and its relationship to the broader Western esoteric tradition.

Masonic and Related Traditions

Hall, Manly P. *The Secret Teachings of All Ages: An Encyclopedic Outline of Masonic, Hermetic, Qabbalistic and Rosicrucian Symbolical Philosophy.* Los Angeles: Philosophical Research Society, 1928. Reprint, New York: Tarcher/Penguin, 2003. The most comprehensive single-volume survey of the Western esoteric tradition available, consulted throughout this work for its treatment of alchemical, astrological, and Masonic symbolism. Hall's discussion of the thirty-six decans and their relationship to the seventy-two disciples is particularly relevant to the Luke exegesis.

Mackey, Albert G. *An Encyclopaedia of Freemasonry and Its Kindred Sciences.* 2 vols. Philadelphia: Moss and Company, 1874. Reprint, New York: Masonic History Company, 1921. The standard reference work for Masonic symbolism and history, consulted for the treatment of the Blazing Star and related Masonic symbols in Chapter Eight.

Nineteenth and Twentieth Century Esoteric Synthesis

Lévi, Eliphas. *Dogme et Rituel de la Haute Magie.* Paris: Germer Baillière, 1854-1856. Translated by Arthur Edward Waite as *Transcendental Magic: Its Doctrine and Ritual.* London: Rider, 1896. Reprint, York Beach, ME: Weiser Books, 2001. Lévi's foundational work, essential for understanding both his genuine synthetic doctrine – including his treatment of Lucifer as the illuminating principle – and the provocative symbolic language that led to the misappropriation of his imagery by subsequent left-hand path traditions. Read with the critical perspective developed in Chapters One and Eight of this work.

Crowley, Aleister. *Magick: Book 4, Liber ABA.* Edited by Mary Desti and Leila Waddell. York Beach, ME: Weiser Books, 1994. The most comprehensive single-volume presentation of Crowley's magical system, including the theoretical framework of *Magick in Theory and Practice* and the *Book of Lies.* Consulted for the treatment of Thelemic doctrine in "Morning Star Rising" and the present work's broader engagement with the Thelemic current.

Crowley, Aleister. *Liber AL vel Legis: The Book of the Law.* 1909. Reprint, York Beach, ME: Weiser Books, 1987. The foundational text of the Thelemic current, consulted for the treatment of the Law of Thelema in "Morning Star Rising" and its relationship to the Law of Agape.

Flowers, Stephen E. *Lords of the Left-Hand Path: Forbidden Practices and Spiritual Heresies.* Rochester, VT: Inner Traditions, 2012. Referenced in the "Theosis Through Gnosis" essay as a source for the doctrines of the Setian and related left-hand path traditions that the Christo-Luciferian current distinguishes itself from. Useful for understanding the left-hand path position from a sympathetic but scholarly perspective.

Part Four: Recommended Reading by Topic

The following list is organized thematically for the practitioner who wishes to pursue any particular dimension of the Christo-Luciferian doctrine or practice more deeply. Works already listed in the bibliography above are referenced by author and short title only.

For the Scriptural and Philological Foundations

The practitioner who wishes to engage more deeply with the New Testament sources of the Christo-Luciferian doctrine should begin with Bauckham's commentary on 2 Peter and work through Fitzmyer on Luke. For the Old Testament background, Day's *God's Conflict with the Dragon* and Forsyth's *The Old Enemy* provide the essential historical and mythological context. Russell's four-volume history of the Devil concept is the most comprehensive available treatment of the development of the demonological tradition from antiquity to the modern period, and is warmly commended to any practitioner who wishes to understand in detail the historical process that this work seeks to reverse.

For the Gnostic Doctrine

The practitioner new to the Gnostic tradition should begin with Hoeller's *Gnosticism* as the most accessible and most practically oriented introduction, then move to Pagels's *The Gnostic Gospels* for historical context, and then to Meyer's *The Nag Hammadi Scriptures* as the primary textual resource. Jonas's *The Gnostic Religion* remains essential for the phenomenological understanding of the Gnostic experience. For the specifically Valentinian tradition, Pagels's *The Gnostic Paul* and the *Excerpta ex Theodoto* are indispensable. For the Sethian tradition, Pearson's *Ancient Gnosticism* provides the most comprehensive scholarly treatment.

For the Doctrine of Theosis

Lossky's *Mystical Theology of the Eastern Church* is the essential starting point for the Orthodox theological context of the theosis doctrine. Palamas's *Triads* provides the primary theological text of the hesychast tradition. For the Western mystical parallel, John of the Cross's *Collected Works* – and particularly *The Dark Night of the Soul* – is irreplaceable. The practitioner who wishes to explore the relationship between Gnostic gnosis and Orthodox theoria more deeply will find Kallistos Ware's essays on the subject, collected in *The Inner*

Kingdom (Crestwood, NY: St. Vladimir's Seminary Press, 2000), particularly valuable.

For the Martinist Tradition

Saint-Martin's *Man of Desire* is the essential starting point – it is the most immediately accessible of his major works and the one whose devotional character most directly serves the inner life of the practitioner. Waite's *Unknown Philosopher* provides the biographical and intellectual context. For those who read French, de Pasqually's *Traité* is essential and irreplaceable – there is no adequate substitute for the primary text.

For the Hermetic and Alchemical Tradition

Copenhaver's *Hermetica* is the essential scholarly edition of the primary Hermetic texts. For the alchemical tradition specifically, Ambelain's *Spiritual Alchemy* is the most directly relevant work to the Christo-Luciferian current. Titus Burckhardt's *Alchemy: Science of the Cosmos, Science of the Soul* (translated by William Stoddart; Louisville, KY: Fons Vitae, 1997) provides the most philosophically rigorous treatment of the inner alchemical tradition available in English. For the specifically Gnostic-alchemical connection, von Welling's *Opus Mago-Cabalisticum* is indispensable.

For the Practical and Theurgic Dimensions

The practitioner who wishes to develop her theurgic practice beyond the specific methods offered in Chapter Thirteen will find valuable resources in the broader Western esoteric literature on theurgy and magical practice. Iamblichus's *On the Mysteries* (translated by Emma C. Clarke, John M. Dillon, and Jackson P. Hershbell; Atlanta: Society of Biblical Literature, 2003) is the foundational philosophical text of the theurgic tradition in the Western world, and its reading is commended to any serious practitioner. For the specifically Christian theurgic tradition, Ambelain's *La Kabbale Pratique* (Paris: Niclaus, 1951) – not yet available in English translation at the time of writing – is the most directly relevant secondary source.

For the Broader Western Esoteric Context

Hanegraaff, Wouter J. *Western Esotericism: A Guide to the Perplexed.* London: Bloomsbury Academic, 2013. The most accessible and most rigorous scholarly introduction to the Western esoteric tradition as a whole, providing the historical and conceptual framework within which the Christo-Luciferian current takes its place. Essential for the practitioner who wishes to understand her tradition in its broader cultural and historical context.

Faivre, Antoine. *Access to Western Esotericism.* Albany: State University of New York Press, 1994. The foundational scholarly work defining the Western esoteric tradition as a field of study, with particular attention to its characteristic features – correspondences, living nature, imagination and mediation, transmutation – that resonate directly with the Christo-Luciferian doctrine.

www.ingramcontent.com/pod-product-compliance
Ingram Content Group UK Ltd.
Pitfield, Milton Keynes, MK11 3LW, UK
UKHW041843190726
13854UKWH00002B/685